Interreligious Dialogue and Cultural Change

Interreligious Dialogue Series

Catherine Cornille, Series Editor

Interreligious Dialogue and Cultural Change

edited by
CATHERINE CORNILLE &
STEPHANIE CORIGLIANO

CASCADE *Books* · Eugene, Oregon

INTERRELIGIOUS DIALOGUE AND CULTURAL CHANGE
Interreligious Dialogue Series 4

Cascade Books
An Imprint of Wipf and Stock Publishers
199 W. 8th Ave., Suite 3
Eugene, OR 97401

www.wipfandstock.com

ISBN 13: 978-1-62032-263-5

Cataloging-in-Publication data:

Interreligious dialogue and cultural change / edited by Catherine Cornille and Stephanie Corigliano.

Interreligious Dialogue Series 4

vi + 270 p. ; 23 cm.

ISBN 13: 978-1-62032-263-5

1. Multiculturalism—Religious aspects. 2. Multiculturalism—United States. 3. Religion—Relations. 4. Religious pluralism—United States. 5. Dialogue—Religious aspects. I. Cornille, C. (Catherine). II. Corigliano, Stephanie. III. Title. IV. Series.

BL2525 I57 2012

Manufactured in the U.S.A.

Contents

Contents

Introduction

On Interreligious Dialogue and Cultural Change

Catherine Cornille

Whereas the idea of dialogue between religions may at times appear somewhat contrived, one context in which it occurs almost naturally, if not always consciously, is that of cultural change. In so far as religions are shaped by particular cultures, and cultures by particular religions, changes of or within cultures tend to challenge religions and open them up to one another. This is very obviously the case in the process of acculturation, when religions move from one cultural context to another and need to adjust to the particularity of the new culture. Such adaptation inevitably involves some level of engagement with the religion that has traditionally shaped that culture. But changes within the culture itself also tend to destabilize the religions embedded in that culture, prompting them to enter into dialogue with one another. Thus, interreligious dialogue may be seen to evolve spontaneously from the dynamic interplay between religions and cultures.

The category of interreligious dialogue is here understood as the engagement between different religious traditions oriented toward mutual understanding and growth. In the context of cultural change, understanding takes the form of gaining insight into the traditional worldview and the religious mores of a people, and into the ways other religions may have coped with or creatively responded to shifts in a particular culture. And growth involves the appropriation of new religious ideas and practices that may come to enrich the tradition. Such growth may take place inadvertently, as categories and ritual elements from other religions are spontaneously incorporated in the process of acculturation, often without acknowledging their source. But it may also occur through deliberate, methodical and systematic engagement with the teachings and practices of another religion. As in all cases of dialogue, it involves both a critical and constructive engagement with the religious elements that have shaped or that have come to reshape a particular culture.

The meaning of the terms *religion* and *culture* and their relationship to one another constitute some of the most debated issues in the humanities. Whereas the categories of religion and culture were at one time considered fairly stable and defined, postmodern and postcolonial theories have come to expose the fragility and porousness, not only of particular cultural and religious identities, but of the very categories of religion and culture. In the opening essay of this volume, Peter Phan traces this development in some detail, together with different approaches to the relationship between religion and culture. Focusing primarily on the Roman Catholic tradition, he argues that while the model of "Christianity transforming culture" continues to dominate the official Church discourse, Christianity has been itself profoundly shaped by culture, not only in the areas of arts and architecture, but also in its core teachings, ritual practices, and institutional structures. As such, the new cultural reality and awareness of religious plurality challenges Christianity as well as other religions to a new way of being religious and spiritual. Putting it succinctly, Phan states that "interreligious dialogue is unavoidably intercultural dialogue and vise versa." While there are good reasons for preserving the distinction between religion and culture and between interreligious and intercultural dialogue, it is indeed in the interplay between religions and cultures that both the particularities of particular cultures and the degree of cultural determination of particular religions come to the fore.

The term *acculturation* is used in general to refer to the processes by which individuals or groups adopt the cultural traits and the social patterns of another culture. In the study of religion, it refers to the changes that take place when a religion shaped in one cultural context adapts to the particularities of another. This process of acculturation may take various forms, from the simple translation of traditional religious

language and categories, to the integration of new symbols, categories
and rituals and the reinterpretation of the religion in terms of the new
culture and tradition. Different religions may use specific terminologies
for the various types of acculturation. Often, terms such as *translation*
and *adaptation* are used to refer to the processes of appropriation of
categories of a local culture to explain one tradition or to render it more
intelligible to another culture. The terms *inculturation, contextualiza-*
tion, and *transculturation,* on the other hand, have been used to denote
a greater appreciation for the alterity and the intrinsic value of the traditional culture and religion, and the engagement of that culture in a spirit
of reciprocity.[1] Though all forms of acculturation involve some degree
of dialogue, it is of course the latter attitude toward the local culture and
religion which most likely to involve genuine interreligious dialogue.

The history of religions is replete with examples of interreligious
borrowing, of conscious or unconscious appropriation of elements from
other religions in the process of territorial expansion. While this cannot
be regarded as interreligious dialogue in the mutual or reciprocal sense
of the word, it does point to the natural tendency of religions to engage
alternate religious systems and to integrate them where possible. To be
sure, such integration is or was often informed by a sense of cultural
and religious superiority and entitlement, and borrowed categories,
symbols and ritual elements were readily reinterpreted to fit the new religious framework. But original semantic fragments often lingered and
produced distinctive variations of the expanding religion. This is clearly
illustrated in Robert Schreiter's article "Forests, Food and Fighting: the
Vagaries of Christianity and Cultures," which discusses three historical examples of encounter between Christianity and different cultures.
While the intent of Christianity in the course of history may have been
to transmit the Christian message in its entirety and in its original purity by using indigenous symbols and signs, Schreiter points out that
this process of translation often led to unpredictable semantic shifts as
the codes from different cultures came to mix. Particular aspects of the
message are emphasized at the expense of others (as in the example of
the Lithuanian Christ in the tree) and radically new meanings accrued
(as in the case of the Aztec understanding of the Eucharist as sacrifice,

1. Though these categories have been developed largely in Christian discourse of
acculturation, they are also increasingly found, and are perfectly applicable to any religion's processes of engagement with new and different cultures.

or the notion of Spiritual Warfare in African Pentecostalism). While these renderings of the Christian message became subject to critical rectification within the tradition, they point to the fact that some form of implicit dialogue is much older than any conscious or systematic attempt at it, and that it has always been part of the process of acculturation. Operating from a more literal understanding of interreligious dialogue, Schreiter suggests that "interreligious dialogue begins where cultural adaptability ends." It is indeed only when a tradition resists the other's attempts at domestication that a mature and critical dialogue may ensue.

While the phenomenon of religious acculturation has generally been approached from the perspective of Western religions, especially Christianity, engaging non-Western cultures, this volume focuses predominantly on the reverse type of acculturation, i.e. of non-Christian religions engaging Western and more particularly North American culture. In the course of the twentieth century, the United States has become "the World's Most Religiously Diverse Nation" as Diana Eck states in the subtitle of her book *A New Religious America* (2002). Since the US Immigration Act of 1965, a steady influx of immigrants from Asia and other parts of the world has changed the American religious landscape from a predominantly Christian to a thoroughly diversified one. Not only are all of the major traditional religions of the world represented in significant numbers, but many new religions have branches in America, and some have also emerged from its own soil. Immigrants from different cultural and religious origins continue to practice their faith, while Americans are themselves also converting in significant numbers to religions barely known a century ago. The American religious architecture includes not only churches and synagogues but also mosques, shrines, temples, zendos, dojos, and gurdwaras, all with their own types of religious leadership and institutional organization. This reality of religious diversity within the United States provides various avenues for interreligious dialogue. The very proximity of other religions offers ready opportunity for encounter and exchange. But the actual pursuit of dialogue tends to require a pressing need or religious incentive. The challenges of acculturation within the American context may represent one such pressing challenge or incentive for dialogue, not only with the religions that have originally shaped American culture, but also with other religions dealing with the same challenges.

It is of course impossible to capture the essence of the American culture. While it is undeniably the case that this it has been shaped by Christian values and ideas, the contemporary context is as much informed by "post-Christian" or secular views and values, and by the very fact of religious diversity. Some characteristics of American culture come to light in the very process of acculturation. Several of the papers in this volume discuss democracy, individual freedom, transparency, gender equality, scientific rationality and consumerism as elements which particular religions have felt compelled to come to terms with in the process of acculturation. But American culture is itself continuously changing and these changes may become themselves the occasion for dialogue between religions affected by that change. The papers in this volume indeed deal with various ways in which cultural change may lead to interreligious dialogue: dialogue with the original or dominant religion of a particular culture, dialogue among religions about a particular culture, and dialogue as a means of affirming or discovering one's distinct religious identity within a foreign culture.

Acculturation and Dialogue with the Original or Dominant Religion

Even though the United States has become religiously and culturally diverse, the culture continues to be colored predominantly by the Christian tradition, which was and still is the religion of most of the immigrants. Every attempt at acculturation thus directly or indirectly involves some form of implicit or explicit dialogue with Christianity. The term *dialogue* is here used in the broadest possible way as engaging the traditional religion, often for purely practical reasons. It may involve consciously or unconsciously borrowing terms, symbols, and ritual or educational elements from the traditional religion in order to make oneself understood and to simply fit into the local culture. But it may also entail rejecting elements of the traditional religion and asserting one's distinctiveness or superiority. Most forms of acculturation in fact proceed through a complex mix of accepting and rejecting ingrained religious and cultural elements leading to some degree of transformation and change, not only of the immigrating religion, but also of the traditional religion and culture.

In his article on Jewish Sunday-School education in America in the nineteenth century, Jonathan Sarna discusses the various ways in which Jewish textbooks copied both the style and the contents of Christian catechisms, pasting over teachings unacceptable for Jewish children. In contrast to traditional Jewish learning, which was based on study of the Torah, American Jewish children were taught rote memorization of articles of Jewish faith. This process of borrowing, however, was interspersed with elements of clear resistance to Christian cultural and religious expressions and with a desire to assert the distinctiveness of the Jewish tradition. With the eventual publication of Jewish textbooks, emphasis was placed on distinctly Jewish prayers, such as the *Shema*, which became, as Sarna puts it, the "watchword" of Jewish faith. As Judaism became a more integral part of American culture, traditional forms of Jewish learning returned, though not without being affected by its new cultural context.

While some forms of engagement with the traditional religion of a culture occur reflectively and methodically, others take place spontaneously or under significant cultural pressure. In his article focusing on the acculturation of Hindus in the United States, Deepak Sarma discusses the ways in which the celebration of Christmas has affected Hindu faith and practice. He sketches various types of acculturation, from the appropriation of Christmas as a purely cultural custom with few religious overtones to the conflation of Christmas and Divali rituals in which the mythology of the latter comes to be reinterpreted to fit the more Christian imagery of the victory of light over darkness and good over evil. Besides the tendency to superimpose Hindu upon Christian imagery, and the reinterpretation of Christmas in Hindu terms, some Hindus attempt to offset the threat of assimilation by reinforcing distinctive Hindu symbols and rituals, such as those surrounding the god Ganesha. The possibilities of virtual participation in Hindu rituals in India through the Internet, combined with the more numerous community of Hindus in the United States seems to lessen the pressure to conform and to engage in ritual acculturation and dialogue with Christianity.

While acculturation and the implicit dialogue that takes place is often seen to be initiated and engineered by religious leaders or official institutional bodies, James Heisig reminds us of the immediacy of dialogue and inculturation. Focusing on Japan, he points out that the formal dialogue between Christianity and Buddhism has largely come to a halt, due in part to the fact that the initiative almost always came from the Christian side and that Buddhists do not seem to share the interest in dialogue. Rather than forcing the issue, or engaging in theoretical discussion about dialogue, Heisig suggests returning to the immediacy of dialogue and inculturation as it presents itself to individuals who live in particular cultures and who attempt to integrate their religious and cultural experiences in the periphery of cultural and religious institutions. He argues that it is in the immediacy of lived encounter with the other that genuine dialogue takes place as a completely purposeless or gratuitous act, free from predetermined goals or boundaries.

Focusing similarly on dialogue as an event that takes place within and between individuals rather than entire traditions, Thomas Kasulis traces the ways in which Zen Buddhism, in particular the figure of D. T. Suzuki, has been received in the United States. While many Christians originally embraced Buddhist teachings and practices as a welcome complement or alternative to Christian dogmatism, greater familiarity with the ambivalent history of Zen Buddhism in Japan has led to a more critical and nuanced engagement with the tradition. Arguing that all forms of acculturation and dialogue involve not so much the creation of something new, but rather the rediscovery and development of something already there, Kasulis points to ways in which the acculturation of Buddhism in the United States and the dialogue with Christianity have affected both traditions, from a Christian rediscovery of its mystical tradition to a Buddhist development of its ethical tradition.

Culture and Cultural Change as Topics of Interreligious Dialogue

In addition to implicit and explicit dialogue with the original or majority religion of a particular culture, acculturation may also itself become the topic of dialogue, not only with the traditional religion, but also with other religions that have more recently entered a particular culture. The very presence of other newly arrived religions within a particular culture offers an opportunity to learn from the ways in which other religions may have negotiated the particularities of that culture. As James Morris points out, Muslims have learned from the ways in which Jews have adapted to American culture through a process of borrowing and resistance, while all religions undoubtedly learn, whether through explicit dialogue or not, from the successes and failures of other religions' engagement with American culture. Moreover, since cultures are never static, religions in any particular culture tend to all be similarly confronted with the same cultural changes and challenges. And this, in turn, may become the occasion for fruitful dialogue.

In discussing the acculturation of Buddhism in the United States, David McMahan deals less with Christianity than with secularism as the dominant cultural factor that has led to significant changes in Buddhist teachings and practices. In response to secularism, Buddhism in the West has come to shed most of the metaphysical, ritual, ethical, and institutional framework in which it was originally framed and to focus almost exclusively on the practice of meditation. Even though not all Buddhists approve of the changes that have taken place in secularized Buddhism, it has resonated with American audiences and has left its own mark on American culture. Categories such as karma or nirvana have become part of the common vocabulary of many Americans, and neuroscientific research has taken Buddhist meditation practices as an object of study. While this form of acculturation does not entail direct engagement with other religions, the challenges of secularism may become an indirect point of discussion or an "interface" for dialogue between religions in the West. In so far as there is a perceived relationship between Christianity and secularism, or in so far as secularism is regarded as more entrenched in Western cultures, there is some interest on the part of other religions in the ways in which Christianity has come to deal with its challenges. And Buddhism's success in appealing to Western secularized audiences, in turn, may become a source of inspiration for other religions appealing to the same population.

Challenges and changes within a religion in a new cultural context may also translate back to the original culture. Kasulis points out that a more scientific study of Zen Buddhism and of the physiological effects of meditation is now also undertaken in China and in Japan. In the context of contemporary globalization, the origin and direction of cultural influences and religious changes are no longer always clear and evident, and religious changes taking place in one culture tend to reverberate in other cultures.

Like Buddhism, the acculturation of Hinduism in the United States has proceeded largely through an engagement with Western secularism and scientific thought. Swami Tyagananda states that in America,

Hinduism is taught free or bereft of most mythological elements so as to render it more palatable to Western modes of thinking. Whereas Hinduism largely developed in India as an ethnic religion, acculturation in the United States has led to an emphasis on the universality of its teachings and on its truth as transcending any particular religion. An issue that has become somewhat neuralgic among American Hindus is the question of preservation and transmission of knowledge about the tradition. Teaching and research about Hinduism at American universities tends to be done by non-Hindus. Together with the building of Hindu temples and the offering of Hindu rituals, Hindus are gradually pressing for a greater role in the production and transmission of knowledge about the tradition. Rather than being only guests in a predominantly Christian context, Hindus in America are now also increasingly becoming hosts, receiving visitors into their temples and engaging in dialogue and sharing about their own tradition with non-Hindus.

As is often the case, the occasion for dialogue between religions often presents itself in the form of confrontation with a common external adversity or enemy. Some of the cultural challenges that confront all religions in the context of the United States are materialism, consumerism, individualism, religious relativism, and ecological degradation. Many of these challenges are of course not unique to the United States, but they have come to form a powerful combination of forces that threaten religious identity and cohesion. Various organizations have gathered leaders and scholars from different religious traditions to reflect together on such critical issues as ecology, poverty and peace.[2] Any of these common challenges may become the occasion for sustained and constructive dialogue in which religions may learn from the insight and wisdom of other religions on a particular topic.

Cultural Hybridity, Religious Identity, and Interreligious Dialogue

One characteristic of contemporary culture is its own hybrid nature. Though cultures may still maintain certain dominant traits, traces of any number of other cultural influences have become evident in music, food, clothing, architecture, film, etc. This cultural hybridity is

2. The Millenium World Peace Summit in 2000, organized by the United Nations, is but one example of this.

particularly evident among immigrants who attempt to function in American society while maintaining some of their original and deep-seated cultural habits, and in converts who attempt to negotiate both the religious and the cultural elements of the new religion while remaining rooted in American culture. In both cases it increasingly forms part of the dominant cultural matrix that affects everyone's life. This cultural hybridity forms both a challenge and an opportunity for interreligious dialogue.

Marcia Hermansen's contribution focuses on ways in which converts may function as culture brokers in the process of acculturation. Dealing primarily with converts from Christianity and Judaism to Islam, she discusses various forms of negotiation of religious and cultural identities among American Muslims. A good number of converts in the United States have been drawn to the Sufi tradition of Islam, which has a long history of acculturation or of engaging other cultures and religions. Prominent American Sufis such as Fritzjov Schuon or Seyyed Hossein Nasr advocate the perennialist belief that all religions derive from and/or lead to the same ultimate religious experience, and became deeply involved in interreligious dialogue. Progressive Muslim converts also remain rooted in American culture but tend to engage in dialogue with other religions mainly on issues of social justice. For women converts to Islam, this takes the form of dialogue with women from other religions on specific feminist issues. While many converts thus continue to engage their culture and traditional religion, some turn to Islam in reaction to American culture. These individuals and groups (such as the Islam First movement) are more inclined to emphasize the identity of Islam over against culture and other religious traditions and to reject dialogue.

A group of Muslims that epitomizes religious and cultural hybridity are African American Muslims. Their religiosity combines elements from African, American, and Arabic cultures with one or the other dominating at different times, depending on the social and political context. James Morris traces some of the developments that occurred as African American Islam moved from a largely reactionary movement to becoming increasingly more part of the Muslim mainstream in the United States. He notes a shift from involvement with racist and Marxist causes to a greater interest among young contemporary Muslims in ecological and feminist issues, and a greater awareness of the need for collaboration with other religions in addressing these issues. One of the main concerns uniting different Muslim groups in the United States is how to transmit a Muslim religiocultural identity in a minority religious and cultural context. This concern with religious identity and adaptation tends to foster dialogue and collaboration between Muslim communities in the United States rather than with other religious traditions. But the presence of and dialogue with other religious traditions forms the horizon within which such intrareligious dialogue takes place.

A special case of the acculturation of Islam in the West may be found in the Bawa Muhaiyaddeen Fellowship, founded by Guru Bawa in the second half of the twentieth century. In his discussion of the movement's history in the United States, Frank Korom describes the process by which it developed from a fairly undefined or eclectic spiritual group to an explicitly and confessedly Islamic movement. While originally espousing a perennial religious message and using Christian language and symbols to express his teachings, Bawa became increasingly insistent on emphasizing the Islamic teachings and identity of the movement. This was done in an attempt partly to distinguish himself from the many other Indian gurus who came to America, and partly in an attempt to provide his followers with a clear set of teachings and practices and a defined religious identity. It also provided Bawa and his followers with a larger and more established platform from which to engage in interreligious dialogue.

Though the agents of acculturation and dialogue are generally members of the particular religion or converts, in some cases scholars may create a bridge between the original and the new cultural context. This is evident in John Berthrong's paper, which focuses on the transmission of Confucianism in the United States. Because of the checkered recent history of Confucianism in China, many Chinese immigrants have little reflective or systematic knowledge of Confucian history and principles. It is then through the teaching of Western experts that Chinese immigrants come to learn about and appropriate their own tradition. In the process of transmission, Western scholars may develop their own emphases, shaped by the way Western recipients, both from a Chinese background and from others, respond to the teachings. Therefore, Boston Confucianists such as Neville and Berthrong tend to emphasize the ethical teachings of Confucianism as a form of virtue ethics or role ethics, and the more metaphysical teachings as a form of immanent transcendence or transcendent immanence. Besides Western and Christian interpreters, some Chinese scholars have also been involved in the teaching and inculturation of both traditional and so-called New Confucianism in the West. Since the latter represents a relatively new phenomenon, Berthrong is hesitant to elaborate on the ways in which it might further develop, both in China and in the West.

The encounter between religions that emerges from the process of religious acculturation may lead to various forms of change and growth. It may result in a sharpening of one's religious identity and boundaries or in a new religious self-understanding, expanded and enriched with new religious meanings derived from the encounter with new cultures and religions. It may broker some form of a rapprochement between different schools or sects within a particular religion or precisely a greater schism and alienation. Acculturation and interreligious dialogue may also bring about a new awareness of the limits of religious adaptability and change. The difficulty of mutual understanding and learning across religions may be often as much a matter of cultural as of religious barriers. But in so far as both cultures and religions are continuously changing, partly through interaction, it is impossible to a priori determine an essential and unchanging core or to delimit the possibilities of change and growth through the process of acculturation and dialogue.

1

The Mutual Shaping of Cultures and Religions through Interreligious Dialogue

Peter C. Phan

The theme of my essay is the process in which culture and religion shape each other and the role, if any, of interreligious dialogue within it. The topic, while fascinating, is undoubtedly vast and complex. In postmodernity, all the three realities under inquiry, namely, culture, religion, and interreligious dialogue, are vigorously contested, which makes considerations of their mutual relationships even more intricate and controversial. Yet it is urgent to broach these relationships, as religions, contrary to their vastly premature and much-trumpeted obituaries, have not only endured but also flourished, and in places least expected. There is widespread talk of the "return of religion," especially to the public sphere. Furthermore, globalization and migration, to mention just two important contemporary movements, have rendered the encounter among the followers of different religions not only a daily necessity but also opportunities for either peace building or a "clash of civilizations."

In general, the connotation of *culture* is larger than *religion*, insofar as there can be no religion except as inculturated in a particular culture, whereas there may be a culture that has no religion as one of its intrinsic and institutional constituents. Similarly, *religion* is connotatively larger than *interreligious dialogue*, since there can be no interreligious dialogue without at least two religions, whereas there may be a religion that regards interreligious dialogue as theologically impermissible or even impossible. Theoretically, then, it is not inconceivable that culture and religion can exist apart from each other as two hermetically sealed circles, without any interaction, either one-way or two-way, between them, just as it is possible that a particular religion can shut itself off from interreligious dialogue.

From a historical point of view, however, it is indisputable that culture and religion, as traditionally defined, have interacted with each other, mutually shaping and reshaping their identities and their spheres of influence through the course of their developments, so much so that often it is not easy to tell where culture ends and where religion begins. The issue then is not *whether* there has been a reciprocal interaction between culture and religion—the answer is embarrassingly obvious— but rather *how* this process of mutual fertilization has taken place. In surveying this process, which may be called the "inculturation" of religion, or better still, the "interculturation" between culture and religion, it may be asked whether there are new factors in our time that impact, positively and negatively, on this process. Among these factors no doubt interreligious dialogue obtains pride of place. The central issue for our reflections may then be formulated thus: How does interreligious dialogue affect the process of mutual shaping between culture and religion?

Even with this narrowed scope, the theme is still too vast and remains at a boringly abstract level. To avoid bland and banal generalities about the relationship between culture and religion, I propose to examine the mutual shaping of culture and religion, and the role of interreligious dialogue within it, with historical references to Christianity, though it is hoped that my reflections will also prove helpful in understanding the relationship between other religions and their cultures, in particular Judaism and Islam, the other two Abrahamic faiths or "Religions of the Book." As to the time frame for our inquiry, it is limited, for all intents and purposes, to the last fifty years—for the Roman Catholic Church, to the post-Vatican II era—since interreligious dialogue as a genuinely dialogical activity between Christianity and other religions was undertaken officially only since the end of the Second Vatican Council in 1965. I begin with brief considerations of contemporary understandings of culture and religion. I then move to inquire into how they mutually shape each other. Finally, I explore the role of interreligious dialogue in the dynamics of the interaction between culture and religion for our time. To describe the mutual shaping between culture and religion it may be helpful to give here a brief outline of the postmodern understanding of these two realities.

Culture: From Integration to Contest of Relations

Since our theme is the mutual shaping between culture and religion, and more specifically between culture and Christ/Christianity, H. Richard Niebuhr's classic *Christ and Culture*, though published sixty years ago, can still serve as a helpful launching pad for our discussion of culture in the modern and postmodern usages of the term, and later, of the relationship between culture and religion/Christianity.[1] Niebuhr argues that culture should not be taken simply as secular (godless), or idolatrous (anti-God), or particular (e.g., Greco-Roman), or referring to a particular human activity (e.g., economics and politics). Rather, culture (or civilization) is "that total process of human activity and that total result of such activity."[2] In this sense, Niebuhr notes, culture is characterized by seven features: (1) it is always a social and communal activity; (2) it is an achievement of human creativity (as opposed to nature); (3) it is a design guided by a world of values; (4) it is geared toward serving the human good; (5) it aims at realizing this human good in temporal and material terms; (6) it concerns with both creating and conserving values; and (7) it is pluralistic, in the sense that the values that it seeks to realize in any time or place are many in number.[3]

Niebuhr's notion of culture as outlined above faithfully reflects the modern anthropological understanding of culture, one to which American readers of the second half of the twentieth century could readily relate. It is this concept of culture, much in ascendancy during Niebuhr's time, that accounts for the enormous success of *Christ and Culture* in the United States in addition to its illuminating typology of the relation between Christ and culture. It was operative in modern anthropology, whether functionalist, structuralist, or symbolic, in which culture is

---

1. H. Richard Niebuhr, *Christ and Culture* (New York: Harper & Row, 1951). The 2001 edition of the work contains an insightful foreword by Martin F. Marty and a preface by James M. Gustafson.

2. Ibid., 32.

3. Ibid., 32–38.

commonly taken to mean a human construction or convention, universally present but diversified according to social groups. It is composed of various elements such as language and patterns of communication, beliefs and values, social mores and institutions, rituals and symbols, and sundry artifacts into which the members of the group are socialized and according to which they pattern their way of life.

This anthropological usage of culture, which emerged in the 1920s and predominated in Britain and the United States, highlights its socially constructed nature, its group-differentiating function, its holistic character, and its context-dependent development. As opposed to what is found in "nature" and made by "animals," culture is the product of human creativity and the defining hallmark of being human. At the same time, culture, itself a human convention, forms and shapes the way its creators live and interact with each other and constitutes them into separate social groups, each with its own distinct culture. Thus, culture sets up identity-marking ways of life for the group, characterizing observant members as good citizens and transgressors as deviants. Culture in this sense, as distinct from the social behaviors, is conceived as an integrated and integrating whole. The constituent elements of this whole are seen as functionally interrelated to one another because they are perceived to express an overarching meaning system, to be mutually consistent, to operate according to certain common laws or structures, or to maintain and promote the stability of the social order. Lastly, because culture is a human product, it evolves and changes, but always in dependence on the context of the group. To understand a particular cultural practice, then, one must place it in relation with the other elements of culture, even cross-culturally, and analyze all the relevant elements in a synchronic manner.

An important feature of the anthropological approach to culture is its nonevaluative posture. Unlike the proponents of the elitist notion of *civilization* with its uniform and universally binding ideal, or of *Kultur* with its claim to intellectual, artistic, and spiritual nobility, or of *high culture* as the principle of social reform and the standard for individual self-discipline, cultural anthropologists look upon cultures (note the plural!)—including local and popular customs—as self-contained, clearly bounded, internally consistent, and fully functioning systems. Consequently, they successfully eschew ethnocentrism, concentrating on an accurate description of a particular culture, rather than judging it according to some presumed norms of truth, goodness, and beauty.[4]

The modern anthropological concept of culture has its own advantages. As Robert Schreiter has noted, the concept of culture as an integrated system of beliefs, values, and behavioral norms has much to commend it. Among other things, it promotes holism and a sense of coherence and communion in opposition to the fragmentation of mass society, is congenial to the harmonizing, both/and way of thinking prevalent in oral cultures, and serves as an antidote to the corrosive effects of modernity and capitalism.[5]

In recent years, however, this modern anthropological concept of culture has been subjected to a searing critique by self-styled postmodern thinkers. The view of culture as a self-contained and clearly bounded whole, as an internally consistent and integrated system of beliefs, values, and behavioral norms that functions as the ordering principle of a social group and into which its members are socialized, has been shown to be based on unjustified assumptions.[6]

Rather than being viewed as a sharply demarcated, self-contained, homogeneous, and integrated and integrating whole, culture today is seen as "a ground of contest in relations"[7] and as a historically evolving, fragmented, inconsistent, conflicted, constructed, ever-shifting, and porous social reality. In this contest of relations the role of power in the shaping of cultural identity is of paramount importance, a factor that the modern concept of culture largely ignores. In the past, anthropologists tended to regard culture as an innocent set of conventions rather than a conflicted reality in which the colonizers, the powerful, the wealthy, the victors, the dominant can obliterate the beliefs and values of the colonized, the weak, the poor, the vanquished, the subjugated. This role of power is, as Michel Foucault and other masters of suspicion

---

4. For a development of this concept of culture, see Kathryn Tanner, *Theories of Culture: A New Agenda for Theology*, Guides to Theological Inquiry (Minneapolis: Fortress, 1997) 25–37. The anthropologist Gerald A. Arbuckle gives a highly accessible account of the modern and postmodern notions of culture in his *Culture, Inculturation, and Theologians: A Postmodern Critique* (Collegeville, MN: Liturgical, 2010) 1–18.

5. See Robert J. Schreiter, *The New Catholicity: Theology between the Global and the Local*, Faith and Cultures Series (Maryknoll, NY: Orbis, 1997) 49–50.

6. For a detailed articulations of these six objections against the anthropological concept of culture, see Kathryn Tanner, *Theories of Culture*, 40–56.

7. The phrase is from Schreiter, *The New Catholicity*, 54.

have argued, central in the formation of knowledge in general. In the formation of cultural identity the role of power is even more extensive, since it is constituted by groups of people with conflicting interests, and the winners can dictate their cultural terms to the losers.

This predicament of culture is exacerbated by the process of globalization in which the ideals of modernity and technological reason are extended throughout the world (globalization as *extension*), aided and abetted by a single economic system (i.e., neoliberal capitalism) and new communication technologies. In globalization, geographical boundaries, which at one time helped define cultural identity, have now collapsed. Even our sense of time is largely compressed, with the present predominating and the dividing line between past and future becoming ever more blurred (globalization as *compression*). In this process of globalization, a homogenized culture is created, consolidated by a "hyperculture" based on consumption.

Like the anthropological concept of culture as a unified whole, the globalized concept of culture as a ground of contest in relations has its own strengths and weaknesses. On the positive side, it takes into account features of culture that are left in the shadow by its predecessor. While recognizing that harmony and wholeness remain ideals, it views culture in its lived reality of fragmentation, conflict, and ephemerality. Cultural meanings are not simply discovered ready-made but are constructed and produced in the violent cauldron of asymmetrical power relations. It recognizes the important role of power in the formation of cultural identity. Furthermore, it sees culture as a historical process, intrinsically mutable, but without an a priori, clearly defined *telos* and a controllable and predictable synthesis. On the debit side, this postmodern concept of culture runs the risk of fomenting fundamentalistic tendencies, cultural and social ghettoization, and romantic retreat to an idealized past.

Religion and Religions: The Postcolonial Context

No less contested is the notion of 'religion.' Today, like 'culture,' 'religion' is preferably used in the plural, just as the plural 'Christianities' is preferred to the singular 'Christianity,' to highlight the historical particularities of and diversities among different religions. There is a plethora of detailed historical studies of how the term *religion* (Greek: *thrēskeia*, Latin: *religio*) has been used in the West with a view to determine its various meanings.[8] In his survey of the concept of religion from Cicero to Schleiermacher, Peter Henrici discerns four stages in the usage of the term *religion*. First, it refers to the Roman cult and is associated with the virtue of justice (Cicero); secondly, to Judaism, Christianity, and Islam (Nicholas of Cusa); thirdly, to reason-based, nonrevealed, natural religion (Jean Bodin and the Deists); and fourthly, to historical religious traditions, with Christianity as the absolute and final religion (Rousseau, Kant, Hegel, and Schleiermacher).[9]

As to definitions of religion, there are perhaps as many of them as there are religious people, and they vary widely, depending on the disciplinary perspectives and, not rarely, the biases of those making the defining. Modernity has produced a plethora of theories of religion. Daniel L. Pals provides a helpful summary of eight modern theories of religion.[10] Defining religion seems to be a distinctly Western concern, especially since the eighteenth century. Partly with a view to neutralize the influence of Christianity on public life and to confine it to the private sphere, partly as the result of the newly acquired knowledge of "Oriental" religions, attempts were made to reduce religion to what can be established by reason (*naturalis religio*, which is essentially an ethical system), as in the case of British Deists, or to reify it into a generic reality comprising all historical religions, granting no special status to anyone of them. There is thus a movement from "exclusivism," wherein Christianity is asserted to be the only true religion, to "pluralism," which holds that there are many and diverse "religions," more or less true and good, belonging to the genus of "religion."

However, even among those who propose a *naturalis religio*, there are some who on account of their Christian background still hold that Christianity is the superior religion or the ultimate goal of humanity's religious development. Thus, Kant sets out to limit the scope of the *reine Vernunft* to make room for (Christian) faith, attempts to establish

---

8. The most detailed study is the four-volume by Ernst Feil, *Religio*, Forschungen zur Kirchen- und Dogmengeschichte 36, 70, 79, 91 (Göttingen: Vandenhoeck & Ruprecht, 1986–2004).

9. See Peter Henrici, "The Concept of Religion from Cicero to Schleiermacher: Origins, History, and Problems with the Term," in Karl J. Becker and Ilaria Morali, eds., *Catholic Engagement with World Religions*, Faith Meets Faith Series (Maryknoll, NY: Orbis, 2010) 1–20.

10. See Daniel L. Pals, *Eight Theories of Religion* (New York: Oxford University Press, 2006).

religion within the limits of mere (*blossen*, as opposed to "pure") reason, admits the usefulness of the *idea Christi* as the personified good
principle, and argues for the existence of an ethical community called
church. G. W. F. Hegel maintains that Christianity represents the "Absolute Religion," not in the sense that it contains the Absolute Truth—
which is impossible insofar as it is a religion—but in the sense that in the
process of historical evolution, of all religions Christianity comes closest
to express God, the Absolute Idea. To be more precise, Hegel believes
that Christianity with its doctrine of the Trinity best exemplifies his own
"speculative philosophy" of the Absolute Spirit. For Schleiermacher, the
"feeling of utter dependence," which for him constitutes the essence of
religion, is best realized in Christianity, the "religion of all religions."
These thinkers may be said to be the pioneers of the "inclusivist" theology of religions (in contrast to the exclusivist and pluralist paradigms
mentioned above), insofar as they recognize the validity of other religions while maintaining the superiority of Christianity.

Like the modern notion of culture, this modern understanding
of religion has been subjected to severe criticisms, this time from the
perspective of postcolonial and subaltern studies. It has been argued
that the modern notion of religion as expounded above is the legacy of
the European Enlightenment and its attempt to negotiate the relationship between Christianity and the emerging nation-states (the issue of
church-state relation) and the status of Christianity vis-à-vis newly discovered Asian religions (the concomitant rise of comparative religion
and religious studies as opposed to allegedly sectarian theology).

First, it has been pointed out that the universal reason on which
the *naturalis religio* is based is not at all universal as it claims to be but
a highly particular form of Enlightenment antireligious, and even anti-
woman, rationality arrogating for itself universal and exclusive validity.

Second, this conception of religion assumes, even in the Deist version, that monotheism represents the highest stage of humanity's religious evolution, starting from polytheism, moving through henotheism,
and culminating in monotheism. Such a historical trajectory not only is
historically unverifiable but also fails to duly acknowledge the religious
status of polytheistic and nontheistic religions such as Hinduism and
Buddhism respectively.

Third, this modern notion of religion, despite its explicitly anti-
Christian bias, is parasitic upon (mostly Protestant) Christianity,

especially in its theologies of the deity, historical revelation, and the Trinity, which are employed as criteria for evaluating non-Christian religions and excluding certain beliefs and practices from the category of 'religion.'

Finally, the modern understanding of religion suffers from an unawareness of the relation between the production of knowledge and its diverse contexts and grounds. More specifically, it disconnects the claim to absolute and universal truth from the exercise of power in all its forms, especially political and religious. As Edward Said has argued in literary criticism,[11] Talal Asad in the study of religions,[12] and Ranajit Guha[13] in subaltern studies, "Orientalism" has functioned as a lens through which the Middle East and Asia were projected as the irrational, weak, feminized "Other" to be dominated by the rational, strong, masculine West. Politically, the Orientalist discourse is claimed to have aided and abetted Western imperialist and colonialist enterprises.[14]

While the first three critiques have garnered widespread agreement, postcolonialist theories, in particular Said's, while influential in many academic disciplines, have been faulted for historical omissions and overgeneralizations. In particular, Said has been charged with having committed the same sin that he accused Western scholars of, namely, creating a fictional West as the "Other" of the East ("Occidentalism"). It is not my intention to arbitrate this postmodern debate on religion. Rather, it is to point out how the modern understanding of religion as an anthropological constant found among all peoples, dominant though it was until the middle of the twentieth century, is, as Ernst Feil has noted, now dead.[15] Along with Feil, other scholars are suspicious of even the category of 'religion' and propose to replace it with terms such as *faith* (W. C. Smith) and *worldview* (Ninian Smart). Most scholars are

11. See Edward Said, *Orientalism* (New York: Vintage,1978); and Said, *Culture and Imperialism* (New York: Vintage, 1994).

12. See Talal Asad, *Genealogies of Religion: Discipline and Reasons of Power in Christianity and Islam* (Baltimore: Johns Hopkins University Press, 1993).

13. See Ranajit Guha, *Elementary Aspects of Peasant Insurgency in Colonial India* (Durham: Duke University Press, 1999); and Guha, *Selected Subaltern Studies: Essays from the Five Volumes and a Glossary* (New York: Oxford University Press, 1988).

14. For an extensive critique of the Orientalist ideology in the understanding of Asian religions, see Tomoko Masuzawa, *The Invention of World Religions* (Chicago: University of Chicago Press, 2005).

15. See Ernst Feil, ed., *On the Concept of Religion*, trans. Brian McNeil (Binghampton, NY: Global Publications, 2000) 1–35.

skeptical of the possibility of formulating a generic concept of religion and prefer to speak of specific religious traditions, even though they do not think that the concept of religion needs to be jettisoned altogether. Needless to say, this predicament vastly complicates the issue of the encounter between cultures on the one hand and religions, especially Christianity on the other.

Culture and Religion: How Do the Twain Mutually Shape Each Other?

It has been mentioned above that historically, there have always been interactions between culture and Christianity, particularly in the West, resulting in their mutual shaping and reshaping. The real question then is not *whether* but *how* this process has taken place and how it will be affected by the changing understandings of both culture and religion as outlined above. From the theological perspective, the issues to be considered are twofold: first, how does Christianity shape culture, and second, how does culture shape Christianity? So far, the hierarchical magisterium, church historians, and theologians have given much attention to the first issue, that is, how Christianity has shaped and, above all, should shape culture so as to impart to it a Christian character. In contrast, much less reflection has been done on the second issue, namely, how culture has shaped and will shape Christianity.

The reasons for this dearth of considerations of the *mutual* shaping between Christianity and culture are not far to seek. Christian mission lends itself easily to a discourse on how to Christianize culture; consequently it is natural to highlight the positive contributions made by Christianity to culture. Furthermore, where Christianity has lost its age-old influence on society, as is the case in Europe for instance, strategies are being formulated and new structures established to restore its Christian heritage through a "new evangelization." Thus, the predominant theological and missiological discourse has been about how Christianity can shape culture in a positive way. In contrast, though there is an occasional nod to how culture has shaped Christianity—an unavoidable gesture, of course—fear of syncretism, anxiety about the dilution or loss of Christian identity, and the concern to preserve uniformity and ecclesiastical control have forestalled a full-fledged reflection on how culture has molded Christianity positively and in diverse and multiple ways, resulting in different types of *Christianities* rather than a homogeneous Christianity. As a result, an unfortunate impression has been created, at least in conservative circles, both Catholic and Protestant, that the relationship between Christianity and culture is a one-way traffic in which Christianity has everything to give to culture and little if not nothing to receive from it, especially if culture is viewed, in the Augustinian tradition, as *massa damnata* to be Christianized and redeemed. In what follows I will consider the shaping of cultures by Christianity and the shaping of Christianity by cultures successively, giving greater attention to the latter.

Christianity Shaping Cultures

Among theological accounts of how religion, and more specifically, Christianity relates to and shapes culture, arguably the best known is H. Richard Niebuhr's *Christ and Culture*, already alluded to above. There is no need to rehearse here Niebuhr's five typologies represented by the shorthands of Christ *against, of, above, in paradox with*, and *transforming* culture, nor is it necessary to mention the various assessments of the theological validity of Niebuhr's typologies as well as the historical accuracy of his categorizations of past theologians under these typologies.[16]

For our purposes suffice it to note that Niebuhr unsurprisingly was working with the modern notion of culture when he attempted to delineate the five typical ways in which the relationships between Christ—and by extension, Christianity—and culture have been understood. The question that needs to be raised now is whether within the postmodern notion of culture as "a ground of contest in relations" and of religions as particular and conflictive sites of human spiritual self-transcendence, other typologies of the ways in which religion in general and Christianity in particular can shape culture may and should be devised. We will come back to this point below when discussing the limits of Niebuhr's typologies.

Furthermore, though Niebuhr ostensibly discusses the relationship between *Christ* and culture, as the title of his book implies, what is in fact at stake is not so much Christ as *Christianity* as a social institution or, more narrowly, the Christian church vis-à-vis culture. It is not

---

16. For a critique of Niebuhr's theology of culture from an evangelical perspective, see D. A. Carson, *Christ and Culture Revisited* (Grand Rapids: Eerdmans, 2008).

the theological issue of Christology as such but the practical question of how Christianity should relate to culture. In this connection it is of great interest to note that for Niebuhr it is still Christianity in the singular (and not Christianities in the plural) that exercises an impact on culture (incidentally, culture is also in the singular), though of course Niebuhr was much aware of denominational differences and divisions—during his preecumenical days, quite pronounced—in Christianity. In Niebuhr's framework, Christianity (or, more concretely, Christians) can either refuse to shape culture by totally rejecting it or by being fully absorbed into it. Or they can attempt to shape culture in one of the following three ways: working out a synthesis with it; or subjecting its sinfulness to the wrath and mercy, the law and grace of God; or laboring toward transforming and converting the corrupted culture and contributing positively to the creation of a truly Christian culture.

It is to be noted that Niebuhr's five typologies, though sharply delineated and contrasted with each other, should not be viewed as mutually exclusive options from the historical standpoint. They are no more than heuristic devices, or to use Niebuhr's terms, "typical answers" or "motifs," to discern patterns of theological thought about Christ and culture. In fact, great theologians such as Tertullian, Clement of Alexandria, Thomas, Luther, and Augustine, whom Niebuhr takes to be representatives of each of the five typologies, can be said to embody more than one of the typologies. Though Niebuhr's own preference seemingly leans toward the last typology that is, Christ transforming culture, this conversionist typology, historically speaking, is quite mixed. It has included, to various degrees of course, elements of the Christ *against, of, above*, and *in paradox with* culture typologies. A mixture of Niebuhr's typologies occurs especially in theologies that employ, to use David Tracy's expression, the "analogical imagination" of both/and rather than the dialectical either/or approach in theological method. Furthermore, a combined use of different typologies is most appropriate particularly when dealing with cultures in the plural and in their historical particularities, as in postmodernity.

This Christ-transforming-culture typology but with a distinctive both/and approach is prevalent in the Catholic Church's stance toward culture. The most authoritative text on it is no doubt Vatican II's Pastoral Constitution on the Church in the Modern World (*Gaudium et*

Spes).[17] In its second part devoted to "Some More Urgent Problems," the conciliar document treats of the "Proper Development of Culture" (nos. 33–62). The council asserts that "the church has been sent to all ages and nations, and, therefore, is not tied exclusively and indissolubly to any race or nation, to any particular way of life, or to any set of customs, ancient or modern." Yet, due to its universal mission, the church can also "enter into communion with different forms of culture, thereby enriching both itself and the cultures themselves" (no. 58).

In spite of the altogether brief acknowledgment of the possibility of the church being "enriched" by the cultures, Vatican II's overriding interest is in how the church can shape and enrich cultures, as is clear from the following paragraph:

> The good news of Christ continually renews the life and culture of fallen humanity; it combats and removes the error and evil which flow from the ever-present attraction of sin. It never ceases to purify and elevate the morality of peoples. It takes the spiritual qualities and endowments of every age and nation and enriches them with heavenly resources, causes them to bear fruit, as it were, from within; it fortifies, completes and restores them in Christ. In this way the church carries out its mission and in this act it stimulates and advances human and civil culture, as well as contributing by its activity, including liturgical activity, to humanity's interior freedom. (no. 58)

While the truth of these affirmations as a whole cannot be gainsaid, they sound, half a century later, rather patronizing, tendentious, and even disingenuous, especially since the council has made only a cursory acknowledgment of how culture has shaped Christianity and has not elaborated at any length on the dynamics of this process. Equally significant, especially in light of the postmodern understanding of culture, is the fact that Vatican II seemingly views the "good news of Christ" or the "gospel" as something in itself acultural that can be implanted into other cultures without serious conflicts and power struggles. It fails to acknowledge that the "gospel" has already been embodied in several different cultural layers—Jewish, Greek, Latin, and Western languages, modes of thoughts, sociopolitical structures, cultural customs, and religious practices—and that indeed, it is the at times unconscious, at times

17. For an English translation, see Austin Flannery, ed., *Vatican II: Constitutions, Decrees, Declarations* (Northport, NY: Costello, 2007) 163–282.

deliberate identification of the gospel with Western cultures, aided and abetted by colonial powers, that brought about the wholesale destruction of the cultures of the peoples to be evangelized, especially in Latin America.

In light of the inevitable cultural embeddedness of religion/Christianity, Niebuhr's five typologies of the relation between Christ/Christianity and culture are of little use in elaborating on the ways Christianity can shape culture, and especially vice versa. In fact, implicit in Niebuhr's typologies is the notion that Christ/Christianity is in himself/itself acultural and can from this acultural position relate to culture in different ways. Furthermore, Niebuhr envisages the relation between Christ and culture only unidirectionally, from Christianity to culture, in the sense that Christians can opt to totally reject, or totally accept culture, or achieve some kind of positive impact on it, but always from the superior and normative position of Christianity.

There is no doubt that, as has been mentioned above, Christianity has shaped various cultures in different ways. Graydon F. Snyder has shown how the Jesus tradition has transformed both the Jewish and Roman cultures during its early years in symbols (e.g., the shepherd, the fish, bread and wine, the boat), art (e.g., illustrations of biblical stories), architecture (e.g., shift of places of worship from family-oriented square buildings to hierarchically structured, longitudinal churches with apses, domes, and cruciform wings), meals (e.g., abolition of class distinctions and dietary laws), calendar (e.g., the "first day of the week" to mark time and schedule festivals), gender (a more egalitarian treatment of women), and institutions to care for the poor, widows, orphans, and the sick.[18] These contributions of Christianity to culture are undoubtedly significant and would acquire monumental proportions during its Constantinian era and, later down the centuries, throughout the globe, thanks to the worldwide Christian missionary enterprise.

Cultures Shaping Christianities

As important and long-lasting as these contributions of Christianity to culture have been, historical influences are rarely, if ever, unidirectional, especially in the case of a religion as incarnational as Christianity. To

18. Graydon F. Snyder, *Inculturation of the Jesus Tradition: The Impact of Jesus on Jewish and Roman Cultures* (Harrisburg, PA: Trinity, 1999).

understand how Christianity has shaped cultures, it is necessary to study in reverse the process whereby cultures have shaped Christianity. Again, there is little doubt that throughout history, cultures have molded and remolded Christianity, producing a variety of Christianities. The mention of the "Constantinian era" above alerts us to the length and depth of the centuries-long impact, for good or for ill, of culture on Christianity, or better still, Christendom. In turn, it was new developments in European culture, especially modernity and secularization, that brought a form of Christianity, namely Christendom, to an end.

One of the effects of the impact of culture on Christianity is diversity and pluralism within the Christian churches. This phenomenon is taking place even in the Catholic Church whose centripetal force is beyond doubt. In spite of its powerful centralizing strategies and structures (e.g., through canon law and the Roman Curia's control), and in recent decades, counter to the restorationist agenda of the "reform of the reform" (especially under the impetus of the then Cardinal Ratzinger and now Pope Benedict XVI) the Roman Catholic Church is becoming less and less Roman and more and more catholic—with the small c—that is, culturally polycentric and multiform.

Within the Catholic Church, awareness of the contributions of culture to the formation of Christianity, and consequently of the diversity within Christianity itself, came to a head at the Second Vatican Council, which, in Karl Rahner's memorable interpretation, marked the end of the Eurocentric church of the Constantinian era and the emergence of the "world church."[19] Of course, this does not mean that it is only since Vatican II that cultures began to shape the church. On the contrary, culture shaped Christianity since its very beginnings, and the Constantinian era itself is a, if not *the*, eloquent witness to the power of culture to mold the church in all aspects of its life. In fact, the shaping of Christianity by culture during the Constantinian era was so pervasive and thorough that in spite of repeated protests against it by monastic and religious orders and prophetic renewal movements such as the Reformation, the lines of demarcation between culture and Christianity were most often blurred. Like fish in water, Christians in Christendom were not aware that they were swimming—and perhaps drowning—in culture.

---

19. See Karl Rahner, "Towards a Fundamental Theological Interpretation of Vatican II," *Theological Studies* 40 (1979) 716–27.

What is new with Vatican II, however, is the lively *consciousness* of the cultural matrix of religion, and, hence, of Christianity and of cultural diversity. Clearly, for Vatican II, Christianity is not, to use Niebuhr's typologies, *against* culture; *Gaudium et Spes* is an incontrovertible evidence for that. Indeed, as a sign of a growing appreciation of the role of culture in evangelization, a new dicastery in the Roman Curia, the Pontifical Council for Culture, was founded in 1982 by Pope John Paul II. But Vatican II does not propose the Christ *of* culture model, either, as its restorationist critics have charged. Of course, in faithfulness to the gospel, the council cannot but incorporate certain elements of both the Christ *against* and *of* culture typologies, insofar as Christians must be *in* but not *of* the world. But clearly Vatican II does not endorse the Christ *against* or *of* culture models. Nor does Vatican II subscribe fully to the models of Christ *above* or *in paradox with* culture models.

The model that comes closest to Vatican II is the last, that is, the Christ *transforming* culture model. As the text of *Gaudium et Spes* (no. 58) cited above makes clear, Vatican II asserts that Christianity's task vis-à-vis culture is to "purify," "elevate," "fortify," "complete," and "restore" it. At first blush, these terms seem to advocate Niebuhr's Christ *transforming* culture model and evoke his very words in describing Augustine's theology of culture: "Christ is the transformer of culture for Augustine in the sense that he redirects, reinvigorates and regenerates that life of man, expressed in all human works, which present actuality is the perverted and corrupted exercise of a fundamentally good nature."[20] At closer inspection, however, it is undeniable that the council does not adopt Augustine's overall pessimistic outlook on human culture, even acknowledging, albeit rather cursorily, the potential contributions of culture to Christianity, and hence the possibility of culture shaping Christianity.

In which ways can culture be said to have shaped Christianity? In the post–Vatican II era, the Catholic magisterium (in particular Pope John Paul II) and theologians have discussed at great length what is referred to in Catholic circles as "inculturation" and in Protestant ones as "contextualization."[21] The Federation of Asian Bishops' Conferences

20. Niebuhr, *Christ and Culture*, 209.

21. For a helpful historical overview, see Robert A. Hunt, *The Gospel among the Nations: A Documentary History of Inculturation*, American Society of Missiology Series 46 (Maryknoll, NY: Orbis, 2010).

promotes inculturation, along with liberation and interreligious dialogue, as three fundamental tasks of the church's mission. Implicit in this project of inculturation is the acknowledgment that culture has something to contribute to Christianity, and more precisely, in making the Christian faith understandable and practicable to peoples who do not share the cultures in which Christianity has been embedded.

In the revised and expanded edition of his well-received book *Models of Contextual Theology*, Stephen Bevans, with a preference for "context" rather than "culture," discusses six models of contextual theology: translation, anthropological, praxis, synthetic, transcendental, and countercultural.[22] Here is not the place to give an overview of Bevans's models nor to assess their validity nor to correlate them with Niebuhr's five typologies, with which they obviously bear great similarities. The issue at hand is not *whether* but *how* or which are the conditions of possibility for culture to shape religion/Christianity.

Before broaching this issue, it would be helpful to highlight six areas in which cultures have contributed to religion in general and to Christianity in particular. In addition to the four *c*'s of religion, namely, creed (doctrines), code (ethics), cult (worship), and community (organization), there are spirituality (mysticism) and the arts (architecture, sculpture, painting, music, dance, literature, etc.). In each of these six areas different cultures in all parts of the globe—and not only in the West—have made immense and enduring contributions to religion/Christianity. It is of course impossible to even list representative samples in each of these areas. Allow me to mention only one example for each category. In doctrines, developments of Christian theology would be unthinkable without the contributions of various philosophies: Greek (e.g., Neoplatonism and Aristotelianism), Indian (e.g., Samkara's Advaita Vedānta), Chinese (Confucianism and Daoism), modern European (e.g., Descartes, Kant, and Hegel), and contemporary (e.g., Marxism, existentialism, Heidegger, and Wittgenstein). In Christian ethics, Stoicism, and in recent times the human rights theory have played a pivotal role. In worship and liturgy, popular and indigenous religiosity has left an indelible mark. In organization, the legal structures of the Catholic Church bear the heavy imprint of the centralized, absolutist model of government of the Roman empire. In spirituality and mysticism, the

22. Stephen Bevans, *Models of Contextual Theology* (Maryknoll, NY: Orbis, 1st ed., 1992; rev. ed., 2002).

impact of Neoplatonism through Pseudo-Dionysius the Areopagite is profound. As for architecture and the arts, it is enough to visit major church buildings, browse art galleries and museums, and attend concerts to appreciate the extent to which architecture and the arts have shaped Christianity when they serve as expressions of the Christian faith.

It is important to note that my point here is not simply that religion/Christianity has shaped the arts, which is a patent truism. Christianity has not only provided the arts with subject matter from the stories of the Bible, especially the various events of Jesus' life, and those of the saints, predominantly Mary. In the West, for over a millennium (c.550–1550), Christianity was the—at times only—patron of the arts, and during this period, arts and architecture meant simply *Christian* arts and architecture, and the artists—architects, painters, sculptors, musicians and composers, masons and carpenters—were themselves pious Christians attempting to express their faith through their works.

Rather my point is that cultures in all their achievements have contributed in various and significant ways to the shaping of the very identity of Christianity. As a result, there are genuinely different Christianities, even though the general tendency is to refer to Christianity in the singular. To take architecture as an example, beside the familiar Romanesque, Gothic, Baroque, and Rococo styles, which were exported from Europe to other parts of the world, there are new building styles that are inspired by local, often non-Christian, cultures and even religious traditions. Furthermore, some churches, by the use of new materials such as concrete and glass and structural designs, are externally indistinguishable from secular buildings, such as the shopping mall-like megachurches. These architectural styles are not shaped, much less invented, by Christianity. Rather, with their diverse styles and locations, their beauty and power, they shape the identity and the future of Christianity by proposing new ways of understanding what the church should be in the postmodern world.

Much the same thing is to be said of contemporary arts in general. Christianity no longer shapes the arts—nor indeed can it do so—by providing them with subject matter and style, much less financial support. On the contrary, ironically, it is the arts that are shaping Christianity in novel ways as they become the new sites of the "other-worldliness," the "sublime," the "sacred," or the "spiritual," so that, as the French philosopher André Malraux has famously said, the art gallery is the cathedral of our time. Furthermore, in postmodernity, the arts are not simply trying to create two- or three-dimensional images, as Christian arts did in the past. Rather they seek to represent the whole life, blurring the borders between art and reality (think of "reality shows"), between art and religion, thus making Christianity as simply *a*—not *the*—way among many others to the "transcendent," the "spiritual," or "God."

It is also important to note that in speaking of the role of culture in shaping Christianity I am not referring to inculturation or contextualization as commonly understood, that is, the process of making use of the cultural resources of various peoples to express in ways understandable and appropriate to the audience the abiding and unchangeable truths of the Christian faith. Such a process is of course necessary, all the more now so since there has been a concerted effort by some high officials of the Catholic Church to roll back some of the post–Vatican II reforms.[23] However useful and necessary inculturation understood in this way may be, it still remains at the superficial level. A more appropriate term for this type of inculturation is *adaptation* or *accommodation*. Despite its eloquent rhetoric about the need of "incarnating" the gospel in the cultures, the church magisterium, including Pope John Paul II has been more concerned about how to be faithful to what it regards as the unchangeable Christian truths than to learn from the cultures and to let the cultures shape the church's ways of understanding and living the faith. The intention of adaptation is predominantly missiological, that is, how to use cultural forms to proclaim the gospel successfully. Underlying it are the metaphors of kernel and husk, or the deposit of the truths of faith and the manners of expressing them, as Pope John XXIII put it in his inaugural speech opening Vatican II. The kernel and the deposit are believed to be eternal, supracultural, and even acultural that can be "translated"—in its etymological meaning of being carried from one place to another—without undergoing any substantial change.

Such understanding of the Christian faith has now been shown to be ahistorical and naive, and worse, colonialist and imperialist. The claim for the supposedly supracultural character of the Christian faith

---

23. One of the best studies on inculturation that takes into account the critique of postmodernity is Gerald A. Arbuckle, *Culture, Inculturation and Theologians: A Postmodern Critique* (Collegeville, MN: Liturgical, 2010). A highly informative and up-to-date discussion of inculturation is Achiel Peelman, *Les nouveaux défis de l'inculturation* (Ottawa: Novalis, 2007).

masks the deeply ingrained Greek, Mediterranean, Latin, and Western shape of Christianity, and to impose it on other Christianities, despite the best intentions and protestations of Roman authorities to the contrary, is an exercise of naked power, as the recent enforcement of the Vatican-approved English translation of the Roman Missal has all too clearly demonstrated. This lack of recognition of cultures as sites of contest in power relations is of course not limited to the Catholic Church, but no doubt, given its hierarchicalism and the concentration of absolute power in the papacy and the Roman Curia, there is an inbred tendency within the Catholic Church to regard all teachings and administrative dispositions emanating from Rome, especially when written in Latin (the allegedly universal language), as "universal" (hence, supracultural and normative for the universal church) in contrast to the "particular" teachings and decisions of episcopal conferences and dioceses outside of Rome (hence, culturally bounded and binding at best only locally).

Beside cultural colonialism and imperialism, this model of inculturation as "translation" adopts an instrumental view of culture. That is to say, it makes use of only such cultural forms as are deemed suitable and helpful for the purpose of evangelization, "baptizing" them as it were for Christian purposes. In the process it decontextualizes, or to use Aloysius Pieris's arresting expression, "cannibalizes" these cultural elements, stripping them of their religious matrixes. As Pieris puts it, inculturation of Christianity as translation into Asia is often understood as the insertion of "the Christian religion minus culture" into an "Asian culture minus non-Christian religions."[24] Moreover, even the most successful, and widely celebrated, efforts at adapting Christianity to local cultures so far, such as those of Matteo Ricci in China, Roberto de Nobili in India, and Alexandre de Rhodes in Vietnam, were severely handicapped by their focus on the elite and dominant cultures, thus endorsing, though unconsciously, the power play in which rival, often minority, cultural and religious traditions had been marginalized.

In so doing, however, the church not only fails to become the church *of* (and not merely *in*) a country but also does injustice to both culture and religion as complex and interrelated patterns of meanings. It merely borrows (some would say, steals) superficially compatible building blocks of cultures (their whats) and invests them with Christian

24. Aloysius Pieris, *An Asian Theology of Liberation*, Faith Meets Faith Series (Maryknoll, NY: Orbis, 1988) 52.

meanings, ignoring and even discarding their cultural and religious meanings, instead of entering into a humble dialogue with them to learn from them. In other words, here the church is more concerned with shaping cultures and less, if at all, with letting itself be shaped by cultures. What occurs is a monologue where the church does all the talking and not the listening and the learning.

In contrast, genuine inculturation is a dialogue in which the church is actively and humbly listening to cultures to learn from and let itself be shaped by them. As Gerald Arbuckle puts it concisely, "inculturation is a dialectical interaction between Christian faith and cultures in which these cultures are challenged, affirmed, and transformed toward the reign of God, and in which Christian faith is likewise challenged, affirmed, and enhanced by this experience."[25] In brief, it is *both* Christianity shaping culture and culture shaping Christianity.

Interreligious Dialogue: An Imperative of Contemporary Religious Situation

That interreligious dialogue plays a key role in the process of the mutual shaping between culture and religion is evident. The religious situation of our age has been characterized in various ways, all serving to highlight the need for global connections and interfaith dialogue. Robert J. Scheiter speaks of a "new catholicity" uniting the global and the local and its implications for theology.[26] From his concern for the environment, the self-described "geologian" Thomas Berry speaks of the "Ecological" or "Ecozoic Age."[27] Ewert H. Cousins, picking up on Karl Jaspers's description of the intellectual and religious development in China, India, and Eastern Mediterranean (including Israel and Greece) between 800 and 200 BCE as the "Axial Age," argues that the twenty-first century ushers in the "Second Axial Age." Cousins does not deny the intellectual and religious achievements of the first Axial Age in terms of the individual's self-reflective, analytic, critical consciousness. However, he argues that this individual consciousness is being transformed by, to use Pierre

25. Gerald Arbuckle, *Culture, Inculturation and Theologians*, 152.

26. See Robert J. Schreiter, *The New Catholicity: Theology between the Global and the Local* (Maryknoll, NY: Orbis, 1997).

27. See Thomas Berry, *The Dream of the Earth* (San Francisco: Sierra Club Books, 1988).

Teilhard de Chardin's expressions, "complexity-consciousness" and the "convergence" of cultures and religions. In the Second Axial Age, while individuality must be maintained, it must be enriched by a deep sense of the convergence of all religions and of the connectedness with the ecology. Therefore, the Second Axial Age is brought forward not by "dialectical dialogue" but by "dialogical dialogue" (an expression coined by R. Panikkar) in which the partners-in-dialogue seek to understand each other, pass over into the consciousness of the other, and contribute to the complexification of the global consciousness.[28] From the perspective of spirituality, Wayne Teasdale discerns the coming of the "Interspiritual Age."[29] A lot more characterizations of our age, and from perspectives other than theology and spirituality, can be cited. Most if not all of them, diverse as they are, agree in highlighting the urgent need for dialogue among nations and religious traditions for the sake of justice and peace.

In the Catholic Church, the most authoritative text on interreligious dialogue is Vatican II's brief Declaration on the Relation of the Church to Non-Christian Religions (*Nostra Aetate*), in which the council declares that "the Catholic Church rejects nothing of what is true and holy in these religions. It has a high regard for the manner of life and conduct, the precepts and doctrines which, although differing in many ways from its own teachings, nevertheless often reflect a ray of that truth which enlightens all men and women" (no. 2). Vatican II goes on to say: "The church, therefore, urges its sons and daughters to enter with prudence and charity into discussion and collaboration with members of other religions. Let Christians, while witnessing to their own faith and way of life, acknowledge, preserve and encourage the spiritual and moral truths found among non-Christians, together with their social life and culture" (no. 2). These statements, groundbreaking as they were at the time, like the statement about culture in *Gaudium et Spes* cited above, sound, after the distance of almost half a century, too cautious and one sided. Vatican II and a host of postconciliar documents, especially by John Paul II and the Pontifical Council for Interreligious Dialogue, do assert the possibility of the salvation of non-Christians as individuals.[30] However, they do not and—I submit, cannot—fully

28. See Ewert Cousins, *Christ of the 21st Century* (Rockport, MA: Element, 1992).

29. See Wayne Teasdale, *The Mystic Heart: Discovering a Universal Spirituality in the World's Religions* (Novato, CA: New World Library, 1999).

30. For a collection of these documents, see Francesco Gioia, ed., *Interreligious*

appreciate and affirm the positive value of non-Christian religions *in and of themselves* rather than in their putative relationship to and derivation from Christ and the church. The basic reason for this inability is that these documents all judge non-Christian religions from the theological perspectives of Christ and Christianity, and to be more precise, from the commanding height of their claims for the universality, uniqueness, superiority, and normativeness of Christ and the church.

These claims have of course been seriously problematized by the postmodern understanding of culture and religion as analyzed above, including the "incredulity toward metanarratives," the unmasking of the insidiously pervasive presence of oppressive power in any "discourse," the postcolonialist and subaltern critique of religion, and the pressure, fueled by migration and globalization, of cultural and religious pluralism. Several contemporary Catholic theologians have tried to respond to these postmodern challenges by recasting certain basic Christian doctrines,[31] particularly Christology and ecclesiology, and in the process have developed a theology of religion that goes beyond the broadly synthetic, albeit ultimately unhelpful, categories of exclusivism, inclusivism, and pluralism. As a consequence, the nature, tasks, and methods of interreligious dialogue are reexamined in the light of the contemporary understanding of culture and religion and their mutual relationship.

Interreligious Dialogue in the Shaping of Culture and Religion

As expounded above, a radical revision in the understanding of culture and religion as well as the mutual shaping of their identity is afoot in postmodernity. How does interreligious dialogue affect this process of mutual shaping between culture and religion, in particular Christianity? Two aspects deserve notice. First, the boundaries between culture and religion, so clearly delineated in modernity, especially with the separation of church and State, have become, once again, exceedingly porous and flexible. Culture cannot be regarded as comprising the secular, and religion cannot be confined to the private sphere. Culture is a powerful

---

Dialogue: The Official Teaching of the Catholic Church from the Second Vatican Council to 2005 (Boston: Pauline Books & Media, 2006).

31. Notable among these Catholic theologians are Jacques Dupuis, Paul Knitter, Roger Haight, Michael Amaladoss, and Aloysius Pieris.

signal of transcendence, and religion has returned to the public square. Always the twain shall meet, in continuous mutual shaping and reshaping of each other. Consequently, interreligious dialogue is unavoidably intercultural dialogue and vice versa. Some recent attempts at separating these two modes of dialogue, on the pretext that the former deals with faith, which cannot be bracketed in dialogue without falling victim to the "dictatorship of relativism," whereas the latter deals with social-political issues, which can be subjected to negotiation for the common good, are unwarranted both theologically and practically.[32] Interreligious dialogue minus the cultural robs religion of its transformative power and strips culture of its innate self-transcendence. This is especially true of the countries of the global South where culture is deeply intertwined with religion. Intercultural dialogue minus the religious remains impotent and jejune and cuts culture off from the very source that gives it vitality and depth.

Second, thanks to interreligious dialogue, the walls separating one religion from another are fast crumbling both socially and existentially. One no longer lives in a religious bubble in which the claims of uniqueness and superiority of one's own religion above all others can blithely be made. One of the most interesting religious phenomena of our times is that of multiple religious belonging.[33] This need not be seen simply as New Age freelance dilettantism or cafeteria-style religion where one picks and chooses and consumes what suits one's religious needs and fancy. Nor is it predicated upon a relativist stance, religious or otherwise. Nor is it geared toward amalgamating diverse religions into a global religion. In multiple religious belonging, faith commitment and practice in one religious tradition are not abandoned in favor of another religious tradition (as in the case of "converts"). Rather it is the mature fruit of both intrareligious and interreligious dialogue in which one's religious life is deepened and enriched by the teachings and practices of another religion. There is of course "conversion," but the conversion

32. See Peter C. Phan, *Evangelization and Interreligious Dialogue: Compatible Parts of Christian Mission?* (Santa Clara, CA: Ignatian Center for Jesuit Education, 2010).

33. On this theme, see Catherine Cornille, ed., *Many Mansions?: Multiple Religious Belonging and Christian Identity* (2002; reprinted, Eugene, OR: Wipf & Stock, 2010); Peter C. Phan, *Being Religious Interreligiously: Asian Perspectives on Interfaith Dialogue* (Maryknoll, NY: Orbis, 2004) 60–81; and Gideon Goosen, *Hyphenated Christians: Towards a Better Understanding of Dual Religious Belonging*, Studies in Theology, Society, and Culture 6 (New York: Lang, 2011).

is not to another religion, thus acquiring a new "religious membership" (and as a result, allowing one to check a new box in religious surveys). Rather than conversion, it is a spiritual *transformation* that brings about a gradual elimination of the *self* in self-identity and a closer self-*identification* with others and the Other. Religious identity is not something definite and fixed; rather it is something-in-process, fluid, borderless, and evolving, shaping and shaped by culture and religion, in which interfaith dialogue plays a key role.

Spirituality of Interreligious Dialogue: A New Way of Being Christian

In order to be successful, interreligious dialogue requires certain attitudes toward the religious Other such as generous hospitality, expansive openness, profound respect, sincere humility, genuine willingness to listen and to learn and to change, and all-inclusive friendship. What is at stake is nothing less than a new spirituality, or a new way of being Christian. In her recent book, Catherine Cornille lists five of these: humility, commitment, interconnection/solidarity, empathy, and hospitality.[34] These virtues are of course not new; they can be found in any list of virtues urged upon Christians by New Testament writers, though not named as such (e.g., Gal 5:22–23; 2 Pet 1:5–7). What is new, however, is the recipients of these virtuous practices, that is, the religious Other, whom Christianity has for centuries condemned to hell. Interreligious dialogue has shaped thus a new ethos for what Raimon Panikkar calls "dialogical dialogue" or "dialogal dialogue," in which what is sought is spiritual *mutual* sharing and enrichment.[35]

In addition to this new dialogical ethos, interreligious dialogue has initiated a new spirituality. It is not a coincidence that in modern times interreligious dialogue was begun by and reached its depth with monastics, male and female. The names of Jules Monchanin, Henri Le Saux (Abhishikananda), Bede Griffith, Sister Vandana Mataji, Thomas Merton, Raimon Panikkar, Pierre-François de Béthune, Thomas Keating,

---

34. See Catherine Cornille, *The Im-possibility of Interreligious Dialogue* (New York: Crossroad, 2008).

35. See Raimon Panikkar, *Myth, Faith and Hermeneutics* (New York: Paulist, 1979) 241–45; and Panikkar, *The Intrareligious Dialogue* (New York: Paulist, 1978).

and countless others form the cloud of witnesses and pioneers in the Catholic Church's dialogue with other religions.[36]

As mentioned above, today we are experiencing a new way of being religious and spiritual, thanks to and for the sake of interreligious dialogue. While institutional belonging and personal commitment to and rootedness in a particular religious tradition or church remains essential, there is a deep consciousness of a transcultural and transreligious, indeed global, spiritual connectedness and of the possibility, indeed necessity of a global spirituality. As Wayne Teasdale puts it, "interspirituality, and the intermystical life it entails, recognizes the larger community of humankind in the mystical quest. It realizes that we all have a much greater heritage than simply our own tradition. It acknowledges the validity of all genuinely spiritual experience. Interspirituality honors the totality of human spiritual insight, whether or not it is God centered. To leave out any spiritual experience is to impoverish humanity. Everything must be included, that is, everything that is authentic and genuine, that springs from contact with the divine, however we know or conceive of this."[37] The genuineness of *inter*religious dialogue is conditioned by this *intra*religious dialogue shaped by inter*spirituality*. Multiple belonging is by no means a facile compromise or a painless feat of intellectual balancing between conflicting philosophical worldviews and religious loyalties, as the image of a butterfly fluttering from flower to flower might suggest. On the contrary, as Abhishikananda's diary reveals, it is a search for union with the divine through different religious faiths and practices, fraught with self-doubt, fear and trembling, ever elusive, provisional, and unfinished until, as Abhishikananda himself puts it, one reaches the "other shore."

This study investigates the mutual shaping between culture and religion/Christianity. It surveys the postmodern and postcolonial critique of both culture and religion. The study goes on to show how in this contemporary understanding of culture as ground of contest in relations and religion as conflictive sites of human self-transcendence Christianity has shaped culture and culture has shaped Christianity. Throw

---

36. See Fabrice Blée, *The Third Desert: The Story of Monastic Interreligious Dialogue*, trans. William Skudlareck with Mary Grady, Monastic Interreligious Dialogue Series (Collegeville, MN: Liturgical, 2011).

37. Wayne Teasdale, *The Mystic Heart*, 236. Teasdale goes on to say that this interspirituality is contemplative, intermystical, socially engaged, holistic, cosmically open, and integrative (236–41).

intrareligious and interreligious dialogue into the mix, and one can
see how a new theology of the Trinity, Christ, church, and mission has
emerged and how Christian identity has been molded by a new ethos
and a new mode of being religious/Christian. Being religious/Christian
today is necessarily being interreligious.

2

Forests, Food, and Fighting

The Vagaries of Christianity and Cultures

Robert J. Schreiter, CPPS

The Mutual Shaping of Christianity and Cultures

About a third of the world's population designate themselves of Christians. They are to be found on every continent, although they are the least numerous in Asia. The varieties of Christian faith and practice cover a wide spectrum of possibilities, from the stately rhythms of Orthodox liturgy to the enthusiastic acclamations of Pentecostal faith.

One of the reasons for the spread of Christianity around the world over the past two millennia has been its cultural adaptability. Lamin Sanneh has attributed this adaptability to its translatable character, i.e., the willingness to translate its canonical texts out of their original languages and, by so doing, enter into a prospective dialogue with the receiving culture. He contrasts this, for example, with Judaism and Islam, where the centrality of Hebrew and Arabic as originating languages (albeit for different reasons) restrain to some degree a corresponding adaptability.[1] Sanneh's thesis is quite suggestive, and provides perhaps one element that has to be taken into consideration in understanding how a religious tradition shapes, and is shaped by, the cultures it encounters. There are,

1. Lamin Sanneh, *Translating the Message: The Missionary Impact on Culture*, American Society of Missiology Series 13 (Maryknoll, NY: Orbis, 1989).

however, so many exceptions that can be pointed to in the history of Christianity that it cannot be seen to explain fully the cultural adaptability of Christianity.

Another, more theological, reason might be adduced. Central to the Christian faith is the doctrine of the Incarnation, where the second person of the Holy Trinity, takes on flesh and becomes a human being in Jesus of Nazareth. Jesus is considered at once the fullness of humanity, in that he assumed the fullness of human nature—"like us in all things but sin" (Heb 4:11)—yet at the same time a very specific human being, living at a specific time and place. Because the mission of Jesus Christ is intended for the totality of humanity, this opens the way to what Roman Catholics have come to call in the past forty years *inculturation.*[2] From the official point of view, inculturation entails the Gospel message of Jesus Christ entering a culture. As it does so, it is seen to affirm and lift up the positive elements of the culture (i.e., those in accord with the Gospel), while purifying the culture of those elements contrary to the Gospel. While this remains the official view, among Catholic theologians and practitioners in the field, the process is not so simple nor so unilateral (i.e., from the side of the missionary toward the receiving culture). Despite the differences in approach, the official acknowledgement of the role of culture in Christian faith since the Second Vatican Council (1962–1965), and especially since the latter 1970s, has opened up the possibility for a much closer examination of the relationship between culture and Christian faith. It is from within this context of a more complex field of discourse—that includes but goes beyond official Church discourse—that I want to explore the question regarding the intersection of interreligious dialogue and cultural adaptation and change, especially how "problematic" moments (i.e., encounters that raise questions about continuity and identity of a religious tradition) in inculturation raise opportunities for dialogue. These problematic moments of encounter remind us of how each religious tradition carries not only beliefs and practices, but also is shaped by the cultures in which they find themselves and operate. How these encounters are negotiated becomes a potential challenge to a religious tradition on a number of

---

2. For a recent overview of these understandings of inculturation see Gerald Arbuckle, *Culture, Inculturation, and Theologians: A Postmodern Critique* (Collegeville, MN: Liturgical, 2010).

levels: its historical integrity, its limits of adaptability, and its claims (if any) to universal relevance.

The presentation here will be in three parts. In the first part, I want to review some of the principal insights about the relations between Christianity and culture with respect to understandings of religious and cultural exchange that have been emerging over the past twenty-five years. This is intended as a kind of propaedeutic for moving into the second part. There I want to take three examples of encounter between Christianity and culture from the course of Christianity history that might be illustrative of the questions of how interreligious encounter shapes religions culturally. The propaedeutic reminds us that we are not beginning from a zero-point in our reflection. The three examples highlight different questions that arise in the course of the discussions about religious and cultural encounter. This will lead to a third part that tries to further the discussion about how cultures shape religions, as well as provide a brief look into the current context of globalization to see if any further clues can be ascertained about this encounter.

Christianity in Cultural Encounter

Christianity has seen as its mandate the bringing of the news of salvation from God through Jesus Christ to all the peoples and cultures of the world (cf. Matt 28:19–20: "Go therefore and make disciples of all nations, baptizing them in the name of the Father and of the Son and of the Holy Spirit, teaching them to obey everything that I have commanded you."). In the course of the nearly two millennia of its existence, the fervor with which this mandate was enacted has varied considerably. Different forces came to play upon both the motivation and the energy with which the mandate was carried out. Some of those forces were internal to the life of the Christian community; others were social and especially political forces that prompted Christian missionaries into greater action. In most of this—until the latter half of the last century—the message of Christianity was seen to be *replacing* the religious traditions it encountered, rather than offering either an enhancement or option to those traditions. From this point of view, the encounters of Christianity in Asia would come closest to what seems to be the guiding ideas here: where Christianity has had to accommodate itself to long established, literate religious traditions that can claim a history and complexity easily equal to that which Christianity is proposing. Elsewhere, the attitude was largely one of replacement.

But even with this mentality of replacing other religions, more sensitive leaders recognized that there was much good in the religions to be replaced, and often worked from an anthropology that recognized how much religious practice was embedded in cultural traditions and social relations. Most notable among these was Pope Gregory in his instruction to Augustine in 601, as the latter set out to convert the English: "The heathen temples of these peoples should be by no means destroyed, or the idols which are to be found in them. Take holy water and sprinkle it in these shrines, build altars and place relics in them . . . When this people see that their shrines are not destroyed they will be able to banish error from their hearts and be more ready to come to the places they are familiar with, but now recognizing and worshipping the true God."[3] Missionaries seeking a more nuanced approach to the peoples and the traditions they encountered have long appealed to this instruction to Augustine.

Without trying to rehearse all the outcomes of Christianity's encounters with cultures across time, I would summarize some of the reflections that have gone on concerning those encounters over the past quarter century in this way: From the point of view of Christian theology, they have had to do with different approaches to syncretism and the prospects of multiple religious belonging. From the point of view of the study of culture, they have had to do with the formation of new cultural identities using a variety of mechanisms.

Syncretism, from a Christian theological perspective, usually refers to the mixing of elements from two different religious traditions such that central elements of the identities of either or both are lost. Syncretism represents a "theologically untenable amalgam" of the two cultures, to quote the missionary anthropologist Louis Luzbetak. As such, the invocation of syncretism is, in Christian circles, a conversation stopper: when the pronouncement of syncretism is made, there can be no further discussion of the acceptability of the cultural presentation under discussion; an alternative must be sought.[4]

3. Gregory the Great, *Epistolae* 2:76, in *Patrologia Latina* 77:1215.

4. Louis J. Luzbetak, *The Church and Cultures: An Applied Anthropology for the Religious Worker*, The William Carey Library Series on Applied Cultural Anthropology (Pasadena, CA: William Carey Library, 1976). For a historical overview of the

Over the past quarter of a century, I and others have argued that, however important it is to maintain the integrity of Christian faith, such pronouncements are basically unhelpful to understanding the phenomenon.[5] This theological judgment does nothing to help us understand where the process of syncretic formation has seemingly gone wrong from a theological point of view; nor does it describe how that process differs from one that leads to theologically acceptable new formations. Here the work in the social sciences and in postcolonial studies has been helpful in uncovering a clearer picture of how these processes work. The dynamics of mixing, resistance, hybridity, and of other features that go into identity formations are more carefully examined. Postcolonial thinking has been especially sensitive too to the dynamics of power that are always at play in such encounters. A closer examination of the dynamics of intercultural communication also reveals that the goals of the two parties in the encounter may even be quite different in the communications that go on between them: the sender may want to be assured that the message sent is received and retained in the exact form the sender intended, whereas the receiver is trying to make sense of the message with the available resources of his or her own imaginary. The concern of the sender is possible syncretism; the concern of the receiver is achieving a synthesis within an existing mental universe. The encounter may likewise reveal elements of the message heretofore not evident to either or both of the parties.

There is a third set of concerns—alongside theological judgments and the parsing of cultural and communication dynamics—that has become more evident in the past fifteen years as well; namely, the perspectives of the observers of these processes. The perspectives of the participants were certainly in the sights of those studying such cultural encounters. But the prejudgments of the observers of the cultural encounter have now become much more clear. This is especially the case about the theories of religion that shape the observers' insights, as well as perspectives on the colonial encounter. When observing the colonized, resistance, for example, is presumed in much postcolonial

concept of syncretism beyond Christian theology, see, for example, Serge Gruzinski, *The Mestizo Mind: The Intellectual Dynamics of Colonization and Globalization* (New York: Routledge, 2002) 17–32.

5. Robert J. Schreiter, *Constructing Local Theologies* (Maryknoll, NY: Orbis, 1985) 144–58; Schreiter, *The New Catholicity: Theology between the Global and the Local* (Maryknoll, NY: Orbis, 1997) 62–83.

writing, and even a certain lack of agency on the part of the colonized. It is presumed, for example, that conversion is always coercive, and that everything the colonizer brings is unwanted. Uncovering presuppositions that have more to do with current Western academic culture and its biases concerning religion and Western culture itself, rather than the cultures under study, continue to raise issues to be examined and exposed.[6]

It seems to me that Christian theology—and interreligious dialogue—only stand to gain from a closer look at the dynamics of cultural encounter and the mixtures that occur as a result of such encounters. There is at this point in time no consensus in the supporting disciplines I have mentioned about the number and nature of these dynamics, nor a comprehensive theory that holds all of this together. Yet enough of a picture can be surmised to help address the questions posed in this volume. I will draw on a number of approaches here, supported by theorizing being done across the field. At the same time, I will give some priority to a semiotic understanding of culture as a useful entry point to look at issues of syncretism. I will be looking at how *messages*, conveyed by *signs*, circulate via *codes* in a culture. In the matter of religious encounter, more is involved than simply transferring messages through the same or similar signs. One has to engage the codes of the culture transmitting the message with the codes of those receiving the message. As I stated elsewhere: are certain cultural codes incompatible with certain religious messages, such that, a culture utilizing such incompatible codes could not be a suitable venue for the religious tradition trying to enter that culture?[7] I suggested then that this poses a dilemma for Christianity, at least. If the Christian message is intended to be for all people, what then of those who live by such "unsuitable" cultural codes? Do a culture's codes then have to be destroyed in order to save the culture? Or does the encounter with the "unsuitable" code raise more profound questions about the message itself? In the second of the examples I propose below, one has an instance, I believe, of the need to deal with such a question.

6. For a recent example of such work regarding theories of conversion and double belonging, see Joel Robbins, "Crypto-Religion and the Study of Cultural Mixtures: Anthropology, Value, and the Nature of Syncretism," *Journal of the American Academy of Religion* 79 (2011) 408–24.

7. Schreiter, *Constructing Local Theologies*, 149–51.

Three Examples of Cultural and Religious Encounter

I wish to turn to three examples from Christianity—past and present—to explore where cultural encounter (in what might be called "patterns of inculturation") has produced what some Christians would consider "problematic" outcomes. They are all instructive, in different ways, of both the limits of inculturation and the potential for interreligious dialogue. I will analyze the situations, in a general way, with the semiotic tools of sign, message, and code to highlight details of the encounter. Needless to say, the presentation and the analysis will be very cursory. The intention is not so much to convince the reader as to suggest some avenues for discussing cultural (in)adaptability and interreligious encounter.

Example 1: The "Pensive Christ" of Lithuania

When one travels through the countryside of Lithuania, one will frequently encounter in wayside shrines, in cemeteries, and in small chapels the figure of the "pensive Christ" (*rupintojélis*).[8] This is a carved figure of Christ, clothed and usually wearing a crown of thorns, sitting, resting his head in his right hand, and a look of sorrow or concern on his face. *Rupintojélis* translates as "concern," "anxiety," "solitude." He is usually seated in the carved out trunk of an oak tree. Besides its appearance in wayside shrines and cemeteries, the *rupintojélis* is also a popular devotional object found in homes. It is a deeply treasured image among Lithuanian Catholics.

Such a figure of Christ is neither original nor unique to Lithuania. It first appeared in the Low Countries, Prussia, and Poland in the second half of the fourteenth century. It was intended to depict the sorrowing Christ sitting as his cross was prepared for him on Calvary. The figure was brought to Lithuania during the evangelization of the Duchy in the fifteenth century.

Historians have suggested that its appearance in Northern Europe in the late medieval period was an imitation of earlier such figures dating from as far back as the Neolithic period. As a sculpted figure,

8. I have been told by some native speakers of Lithuanian that the "worried Christ" would be a better translation. They surmise that the "pensive Christ" grows out of the similarity of the image to Rodin's "TheThinker."

it appears in many parts of the world (one thinks of Auguste Rodin's famous sculpture, "The Thinker," from late nineteenth-century France).

Lowland Lithuanians enthusiastically accepted the Pensive Christ as they were converted to Christianity. Lithuania was the last part of Europe to turn to Christianity. The overlords in Lithuania had long vacillated between associating themselves with Orthodox or Latin Christianity, and finally chose the latter late in the fourteenth century. Conversion of the countryside took close to two more centuries, and Christianity and pre-Christian beliefs (an amalgam of Baltic and Indo-Aryan religiosity)[9] existed side by side during that period and even later. Their significant innovation with the image was placing the Pensive Christ in a hollowed-out trunk of an oak tree. Wandering woodcarvers (*dievdirbiai*) had long been a feature of Lithuanian folk culture, and they helped spread the image and the devotion to the Pensive Christ.

What does the image mean for Lithuanian Catholics? When asked, they will speak of their identification of their own suffering with that of the Pensive Christ in his passion. He has come to represent the suffering of the entire Lithuanian people as they struggled for their existence between Russia and Poland and, in the twentieth century, the struggle against both Fascism and Communism. They see the Pensive Christ as a distinctively Lithuanian figure, especially as he is depicted sitting in the hollowed-out oak tree.

One thing that is known about pre-Christian religion in Lithuania is that oak trees played a central role. Some claim that there was already an earlier figure depicted sitting in a hollowed-out oak trunk, and the Pensive Christ simply replaced him. (I have been unable to identify who this earlier figure was.) The oak tree, as symbolizing the "world tree," figures strongly in the old religions of Northern Europe from Great Britain[10] to the Yggdrasil tree of the *Eddas* of Nordic mythology, to Finnish, Slavic, and Hungarian mythologies, as well as in Siberia and the Americas.[11] Saint Boniface's felling of the Donar Oak in Fritzlar was the sign of

9. Literature on pre-Christian religions in Lithuania is scanty outside the Lithuanian language (and even inside it). Much of what I present here, especially on the Pensive Christ, is based on conversations with Lithuanians in the country itself as well as elsewhere.

10. Regarding Britain, see Thomas Ohlgren, "The Pagan Iconography of Christian Ideas: Tree-lore in Anglo-Viking England," *Mediaevistik* 1 (1988) 145–73. Ohlgren uses my discussion of syncretism to explore the iconography.

11. For a quick overview of the cultural spread, see the entry "Trees" in *The*

his converting the Franks to Christianity. At any rate, the Pensive Christ seated in the oak tree trunk is clearly an encounter between different religious traditions.

What are we to make of this? I would suggest two points worth discussion. The first has to do with the range of meanings given to situating the Pensive Christ sitting in the tree trunk. Different interpretations have come forward in my conversations with Lithuanians.

- Does this "encounter" between Christ and the tree trunk represent a "Christianizing" of the pre-Christian understanding of the oak tree as a site of divine presence?

- Does the hollowing out or opening of the tree trunk reveal a Christ at the "heart" of the oak tree, as already there before the missionaries arrived?

- If there was another figure in the tree trunk before, does Christ "replace" that figure?

- Should Christ and the tree trunk be seen as a symbiosis rather than a placing of one over the other?

- Does having Christ in the tree trunk change the meaning of the tree?

The second point of discussion has to do with the tree. Already in the New Testament, the cross is understood metaphorically as a kingly throne and as a cosmic tree. I have already referred above to the cosmic tree mythology found across northern Europe (but also found in Siberia and Mesoamerica). Indeed, this figure of the cross and the cosmic tree is found in Lithuanian iconography and sculpture as well. Here it raises some additional questions about the oak tree, the cosmic tree, as the cross of Christ:

- Does amalgamating the cross of Christ to cosmic trees help explain, from a Christian point of view, the cosmic dimensions of Christ's act of redemption?

- How does the cross, a sign of ultimate humiliation for its victim, change when the cosmic dimensions of the cross are emphasized? Does it turn the gaze of the viewer away from the horror of crucifixion?

Encyclopedia of Religion (2nd ed.), 14:9333–34.

- The cosmic tree connects and holds together the physical and spiritual dimensions of the universe in many of the mythologies in which it is represented. How does that square with the original meaning of the cross as the punishment for treason? In Mayan cosmology in Mesoamerica, the cross is a sign of the harmony of the universe. In the revival of Mayan religion in Mesoamerica, one frequently sees the Mayan cross displayed and people will identify it with the cross of Christ.

- Are there limits, therefore, to how many of the meanings of the cosmic tree can be taken over or identified with the cross of Christ (e.g., those of harmony, the order of the world)? Put another way, at what point does the Christian code of expiation/redemption/reconciliation clash with other codes of harmony, order, and the like?

Here we see signs (the suffering Christ figure, the oak tree) carrying messages (of salvation, of divine or cosmic order) circulating in a variety of cultural codes. Do the paradoxes in the Christian code of the drama of salvation get evened out in the codes of harmony of these other traditions? A parallel discussion could be found in equating the passion and resurrection of Christ with the Middle Eastern mythologies of the Dying God explored by the History of Religions School in the 1920s. In all of these instances to look at these cultural encounters only through a prescriptive lens of syncretism may obscure other elements in the picture: why the paradoxes of the Christian mythology of the meaning of the death of Christ are so hard to maintain in their tension, so that the cross moves toward one of the poles in the code at the expense of the other (an example would be the Crusades or the jeweled pectoral crosses of Catholic prelates).

Example 2: The Eucharist in Sixteenth-Century Mexico

My second example deals with the inculturation of the theology of the Eucharist in sixteenth-century Mexico. When the missionizing friars arrived in Mexico shortly after the conquest by Cortes in 1521, they were astonished by the complexity and the similarity of Aztec beliefs to Christian ones. A number of theories were proffered at the time to account for the similarities. One was that one of the apostles—either

Thomas or Bartholomew—had come to the Aztecs and educated them in the Christian faith, that had now become corrupted somewhat through the centuries. Others thought the Aztecs had been tricked by the devil into believing in a religion that was close to—but not quite— Christianity so as to deceive them.[12]

Franciscan friars were the first to arrive to undertake the work of evangelization. They were much taken by the Aztecs or Nahuas, as they were called. In their reforming spirit, they saw the possibility of establishing among these people something like primitive Christianity, uncorrupted by the decline among Catholicism in Spain or the dangerous rumblings of the Reformers north of the Alps. A number of them plunged into the culture of these recently conquered people in order to *inculturate* (the term had not been invented yet) the Christian faith, using the terms and categories of Aztec belief and ritual as much as possible. Chief among them was the Spaniard Bernardino de Sahagún and the Fleming Pedro de Gante. Sahagún has been called the "first anthropologist" for his systematic gathering of data on Aztec language, culture, and belief. He used native informants to confirm—and some believe, guide—his efforts at inculturation.[13]

Sahagún's intention to use Aztec signs to present the Christian message is most obvious (and some would say, problematic) in his presentation of the Eucharist. The Aztecs had a tradition of eating their god under the guise of a dough figure. Some of the friars saw this as a parody of Christian communion (another ruse of the devil?), but it was rooted for the Aztecs in a vision of the interconnectedness of all things. There was a chain of being, as it were, of elements of creation feeding other elements. Here corn was seen both as a foodstuff for human beings and symbolic of the interchange between humans and divine figures via sacrifice. The practices of human sacrifice and ritual cannibalism are well known. The theology behind this sacrifice was that humans were doing their part in this chain of being by feeding the gods through human sacrifice. Humans in turn were fed by the gods in ritual consumption of pieces of flesh of the human being sacrificed, but also through the consumption of the dough figure made from ground corn.

12. Fernando Cervantes, *The Devil in the New World: The Impact of Diabolism in New Spain* (New Haven: Yale University Press, 1994).

13. In what follows here, I am relying on Jaime Lara, *Christian Texts for Aztecs: Art and Liturgy in Colonial Mexico* (Notre Dame: University of Notre Dame Press, 2008).

In the early Christian Nahuatl texts, the eucharistic host is called the "little white tortilla" (*iztac tlexcaltzintli*). This was so not only because the tortilla served as the "daily bread" of the Aztecs—the term was also used in the translation of the Lord's Prayer—but because of the divine nature of corn itself: "It will be remembered that corn was a god in their pantheon and a multilayered figure of speech for sacrificial eating. As nourishment for human beings, it was the symbolic sustenance for all living entities, and in human sacrifice, people were metaphoric corn for other beings. In fact, the very act of making and kneading the corn dough, flattening it and spreading it out (*uememmana* or *tlemana*) was also the metaphoric meaning of the Nahuatl word for 'to sacrifice' a human being."[14] The drinking of Christ's blood in the Eucharistic sacrifice was likewise understandable to the Aztecs. Sacrifice was of course a central ritual act for them. However, the code of sacrifice for the Aztecs was different from the code of Christian sacrifice. In the Christian theology of the time, the term *sacrifice* itself revealed an understanding of the ritual. Sacrifice means, in Latin, "to make holy" or "do the holy thing." In the shedding of the blood of the victim—animal or human—this sinful and profane world is reunited with the divine and holy world of God. In the Aztec worldview there was no profane; all things were holy. The Aztec code of sacrifice, rather, was based on maintaining communion between the different realms of the cosmic order in which all of these realms are holy.[15]

The first missionaries were horrified at the practice of human sacrifice among the Aztecs. Yet they had to admit that their own theology of Christ's sacrifice was uncannily close to the Aztec concept, which would have to give them pause about their own theology. But rather than making them rethink their own theology, some of them resolved it by seeing Aztec sacrifice as a perversion of the "true" meaning of sacrifice revealed by Christ. Yet it remained impossible to separate Christian and Aztec notions of sacrifice in the minds of the neophyte Christians. This was only reinforced by the fact that the Nahuatl word for "altar" (referring to the stone upon which human beings were sacrificed) was taken over into Christian usage for the eucharistic altar.

One sees even in this very brief and general presentation of the understandings of the Christian Eucharist in sixteenth-century Mexico

14. Ibid., 141.
15. Ibid., 231.

that the message brought by the friars could easily circulate in Aztec codes of sacrifice, but with results that were certainly disturbing to the friars. On the one hand, the signs (the "divine tortilla," as the eucharistic host was called) in Aztec culture easily replaced the Christian signs. But as Lara points out in his own interpretation of this inculturation, the Aztec signs (Lara speaks of metaphors) set in motion a whole concatenation of metaphors and symbols that already had well-established linkages in Aztec codes, well before the Spaniards came. The Aztec signs could not be separated from this larger symbolic process, embodied in the cultural codes already present. Only after several generations could this in some measure be brought about.

For the purposes of our discussions here, one sees the power of cultural codes to direct cultural encounter. Messages entering the culture wishing to utilize signs present in the culture must negotiate the pathways that the cultural codes have already set out. Transferring the codes in which the message arrived into the new culture is a very uncertain process.

Second, the encounter of the message with a new cultural realm can set off indeterminacies in the communicated message itself. The encounter of the Spaniards with the ritual cannibalism of the Aztecs had to raise questions for the Spaniards as to what their own religious texts really meant, such as Jesus' injunction to eat his flesh and drink his blood if one wanted eternal life (cf. John 6:35–71). One only need think of the eucharistic controversies that were going on in European theology (about the Real Presence of Christ in the Eucharist, and whether the Mass was a sacrifice or merely a memorial of the sacrifice on Calvary) at the very time this drama was unfolding in Mexico. Alice Kehoe has suggested that the central role of the heart (removed from the body of the sacrificial victim and offered to the gods) in Aztec sacrifice had an influence on the development of Sacred Heart devotion in Counterreformation Europe. Certainly the move to represent the Sacred Heart of Jesus in European Christian iconography in a more anatomically correct fashion occurred around this same time; heretofore, a more symmetrical representation of the heart had been used. Here we may see an instance of reverse cultural influence.[16] Other correspondences and paths of influence might be traced around, say, the equation of the

16. Alice Kehoe, "The Sacred Heart: A Case for Stimulus Diffusion," *American Ethnologist* 6 (1979) 763–71. Cited in Lara, *Christian Texts for Aztecs*, 242.

eucharistic host with the sun in both Mexico and Counterreformation Europe in their respective Corpus Christi processions.[17]

In this second example, one sees different "problematic" issues arising in the encounter, where the signs and messages may seem similar, and even the surface reading of the codes as well. But the interconnections that make up the dense quality of the symbolic world change the circuitry along which the messages pass . . . or do they? Do they perhaps point to indeterminacies in the Christian doctrine of the Eucharist—especially about its "real" character that Christianity had not explored?

Example 3: Spiritual Warfare in African Pentecostalism

Pentecostal and charismatic forms are the fastest growing forms of Christianity in the world today. It is estimated that somewhere between 300 and 500 million of the 2.2. billion Christians today are of this persuasion. Broadly speaking, Pentecostals believe they are directly encountered ("seized" or "baptized") by the Holy Spirit, the result of which is manifested by the "gifts" of the Holy Spirit: ecstatic bodily behavior, speaking in foreign tongues hitherto unknown to them, prophesying (speaking on behalf of the Holy Spirit), and identifying and exorcising unclean spirits.[18] The name "Pentecostal" refers to an episode in the Acts of the Apostles, where the followers of Jesus, filled with the Holy Spirit, were able to speak in foreign tongues, such that people from different parts of the Mediterranean world could understand what they were saying. This happened on the Jewish feast of Pentecost (Acts 2:1–13). *Charismatic* has many different meanings. The term is used in the study of Pentecostalism to mean those Christians manifesting Pentecostal behavior who are not in independent Pentecostal congregations, but practice a Pentecostal-like faith within the historic churches of Protestantism, Catholicism, and Orthodoxy. For the sake of ease, I will simply use the term *Pentecostalism* to cover both Pentecostals and charismatics in this section.

Pentecostalism began more or less simultaneously in the first decade of the twentieth century in the United States, Chile, and India. Since

---

17. Lara, *Christian Texts for Aztecs*, 187–99.

18. For a good general introduction to Pentecostalism, see Allan Anderson, *An Introduction to Pentecostalism: Global Charismatic Christianity* (Cambridge: Cambridge University Press, 2004).

1970 it has grown very rapidly and is found around the world today. A great deal of attention has been given as to why it is being accepted so easily in many different cultures and settings around the world. Likewise, there is speculation about how it is tied to globalization itself.[19] Why it has grown so fast continues to be debated. Is it because it has a fairly simple set of beliefs that can be more or less rigidly maintained in different cultural settings? Or is it because it can connect with elements in the culture? Joel Robbins has suggested both factors may be at work, even in the same settings.[20]

For the purposes of our discussion here, I want to take an example that explores the second option, namely, of finding a particular cultural fit because of similarity in signs and codes. This is the practice of Spiritual Warfare among African Pentecostals.

"Spiritual Warfare" is a Pentecostal practice begun in the United States in the early 1970s that presents a worldview similar to the one found in the New Testament, especially in some of Paul's writings and in the Letter to the Hebrews. There the cosmos is seen as being governed more or less territorially by evil spirits. Spiritual Warfare consists of identifying those spirits, and then exorcising them in the name of Jesus, much as the followers of Jesus did in the New Testament. The exorcism is usually aimed at individuals or groups of people who need to be freed from the spirits' power; it does not mean that those spirits themselves are necessarily defeated definitively and robbed of their strength. An image here is of Christ ascending to the throne of God in the Letter to the Hebrews, passing through the *aiontes* or hegemonic realms of these evil spirits to offer the definitive sacrifice to God. Spiritual Warfare is controversial among Pentecostals themselves and not universally accepted, especially as to its cosmic geography.[21]

I want to introduce here just briefly a debate in Africa about Spiritual Warfare.[22] It should be noted that Spiritual Warfare is practiced

19. For Pentecostals' perspective on this, see Murray Dempster, Byron Klaus, and Douglas Petersen, eds., *The Globalization of Pentecostalism: A Religion Made to Travel* (Oxford: Regnum, 1999).

20. Joel Robbins, "The Globalization of Pentecostal and Charismatic Christianity," *Annual Review of Anthropology* 33 (2004) 117–43.

21. Paul Hiebert expressed doubt about spiritual warfare's biblical foundations as practiced today. See his essay on that subject in his *Anthropological Reflections on Missiological Issues* (Grand Rapids: Baker, 1994) 203–14.

22. I am depending here principally on insights from Ogbu Kalu, *African*

around the world by some Pentecostals. What is interesting about Africa (and one could make a similar case elsewhere, such as in Papua New Guinea) is that Pentecostalism is entering cultures where there is a strong belief in the ubiquity of good and evil spirits that control every aspect of life. Negotiating one's way through life entails propitiating these spirits at every turn. Hence, there is present a strong belief in the spirit world, with prescribed practices for making one's way through life. Some spirits are attached to territories; others to animals, plants, and human beings. Still others are now associated with social ills and the challenges of modernity.

The question here is: Does the introduction of the concept and practices of Spiritual Warfare lead to conversion of Africans to Pentecostal faith? In the acceptance of Baptism and receipt of Baptism of the Holy Spirit, Pentecostals abandon interaction with one set of spirits (such as ancestral spirits) but at the same time enhance their spiritual practices of dealing with the spirit world by calling upon Jesus or the Holy Spirit to exorcise those spirits. There is no unanimity about just how Spiritual Warfare is to be understood in the African spirit world.[23] (Spiritual Warfare as a practice began in the United States, where there is no widespread cultural belief in such a spirit world.) No doubt there are multiple answers to this question. Here the cosmological codes between Spiritual Warfare and indigenous religion seem to be very similar, allowing the message to pass easily through the same circuits. In other words, similar signs and codes may be one of the reasons that Pentecostal faith is spreading so rapidly in Africa.

At the same time, I think we are still in an early stage of understanding Pentecostal growth. Multiple theories have been put forward, indicating both the complexity of the phenomenon and our relative incapacity to get a solid hold on all the data. But the conundrums surrounding an adequate description and analysis of Pentecostalism illuminate a point I made above—namely, that the observer's own worldview

---

Pentecostalism (Oxford: Oxford University Press, 2008); and David Maxwell, *African Gifts of the Spirit: Pentecostalism and the Rise of a Zimbabwean Transnational Religious Movement* (Athens: Ohio University Press, 2009).

23. What is interesting as well is how Africans have "contextualized" this originally American product. Ezechiel Guti, the leader of the Zimbabwe Assemblies of God Africa, speaks of the "spirit of poverty" that includes all the things that are holding back development and prosperity for urban Africans. This is a spirit to be cast out. See Maxwell, *African Gifts of the Spirit*, 88–108.

probably plays a big role in what the observer is able to see and consequently improves or impedes a comprehensive understanding. Theories of religion and of cosmology come to play here in a significant way. As we look at ways that religions encounter one another in their various cultural forms, we must remain self-critical about what theories are shaping our own observations and judgments. In the case of African Pentecostals and the Spirit World, whether we believe that a spirit world is even possible; whether Christian faith is qualitatively different from other faiths or whether they are all of the same genre will make an obvious impact upon our conclusions—biases such as these are likely to play a role.

The Vagaries of Cultural Encounter

What emerges from these brief examples is the sheer complexity of the range of possibilities in cultural encounter. Jaime Lara's investigation, which provided the material for the second example, pays close attention to this question. In his conclusion, he notes a range of terms that have been used for the encounters themselves: "syncretic symbiosis, selective syncretism, cultural elision, intentional hybridity, synthesization, and guided syncretism."[24] These all refer to conscious efforts to bring the two religions and cultures into encounter. Others have noted the outcome as mixture: bricolage, creolization, hybridity, mestizaje, métissage, mélange. All of these terms bespeak the interreligious encounter as a kind of contamination of the "pure" original traditions, belying a naïve, vestigial "kernel-husk" approach to cultural adaptation. They also presume an understanding of the limits of orthodoxy or orthopraxis based upon a (theologically) determined sense of appropriateness. Christianity, for example, is likely to tolerate a more limited range of adaptations, especially as one moves toward the "center" of faith. Forms of Buddhism, however, may tolerate a wider range, since any such formulations are always at best penultimate in significance.

There are yet other terms for trying to manage and control the process, especially from the side of the party entering or invading the culture: guided tolerance, co-optation, legislation.[25] From the received or

24. Lara, *Christian Texts for Aztecs*, 262.

25. Robert J. Schreiter, *The New Catholicity: Theology between the Global and the Local* (Maryknoll, NY: Orbis, 1997) 78–79.

invading culture, on the other hand, there can be resistance and forms of subaltern behavior, utilizing the "weapons of the weak."[26] More recently, attention has been given to the agency of the weak, who may change the more powerful invader in more ways that one realizes.[27] There may be also a friendly symbiosis that allows the two to work together. One might note here in closing that all these approaches—mixing, the invading religion seeking to control, the invaded religion pushing back—make assumptions about the nature of cultural boundaries and their relative porous character.

Even the site of the encounter plays into all of this. Anthropologists such as Paul Rabinow and postcolonial theorists such as Homi Bhabha[28] have suggested that a new space—between the cultures—is the site of cultural encounter and negotiation. Lara himself takes up a similar position that has been found among students of Aztec religion: the *nepantla* (the middle).[29]

In a time of globalization and migration such as our own, these encounters have multiplied, and one can see the whole range of possibilities mentioned here being played out. Often these encounters are fleeting; at any rate, it will be some time before we are able to see how they solidify. At the same time, paradoxically, globalization has reduced the quantity of encounters as well, at least for the well-to-do. In what is called the phenomenon of hyperdifferentiation, the choices can be so many that some people can find niches for themselves to be only among like-minded others and rarely if ever encounter the alien other. We are seeing this phenomenon in North America and Europe, as well as in wealthy enclaves in urban settings in other parts of the world. At the same time, others are drawing boundaries around themselves ever more tightly in the hopes of remaining "pure."[30] As we think about religious

26. James C. Scott, *Weapons of the Weak: Everyday Forms of Peasant Resistance* (New Haven: Yale University Press, 1985).

27. Lara suggests that the informants of the friars may have changed the friars' theology more than the friars realized.

28. Paul Rabinow, *Reflections on Fieldwork in Morocco*, A Quantum Book (Berkeley: University of California Press, 1977); Homi Bhabha, *The Location of Culture* (London: Routledge, 1995).

29. Lara, *Christian Texts for Aztecs*, 258–60.

30. I explore this in more detail in "Inkulturation, Interkulturalität und Globalisierung," *Zeitschrift für Missionswissenschaft und Religionswissenschaft* 96 (2012) forthcoming.

and cultural adaptability, we need to attend to a host of factors at the semiotic, the cultural, and the theological levels.

3

"God Loves an Infant's Praise"

Cultural Borrowing and Cultural Resistance in Two Nineteenth-Century American Jewish Sunday-School Texts

Jonathan D. Sarna

Q. Who formed you, child, and made you live?
A. God did my life and spirit give.

Q. Who keeps you safely, can you tell?
A. God keeps me safe, and makes me well.

Q. Has God made known the way of truth?
A. The Bible is the guide of youth.

Q. What should you feel towards God above?
A. Honour and fear and grateful love.

Q. Does God know all you do and say?
A. Yes! and my thoughts, too, night and day.

Q. Have you evil thoughts within?
A. Yes, or I should not often sin.

Q. How do your thoughts their evil show?
A. By sinful words, and actions, too.

Q. And does not sin God's anger move?
A. Yes, for I sin against his love.

Q. Must you repent, with humble heart?
A. Yes! and from every sin depart.[1]

These charming questions and answers—remembered by students long into adulthood—appeared in one of the first Jewish Sunday School textbooks produced for America's Jews, Mrs. Eliezer [Rachel Peixotto] Pyke's, *Scriptural Questions for the Use of Sunday Schools for the Instruction of Israelites* (1843). Hundreds of young Jewish children mastered Mrs. Pyke's rhymes and went on to learn about the Bible from a catechism prepared by her sister, Simha C. Peixotto, titled *Elementary Introduction to the Scriptures for the Use of Hebrew Children* (1840). Both books, as we shall see, drew heavily upon Protestant Sunday School texts. They thus shed important light on the relationship between Jews, one of America's most prominent non-Christian religious minorities, and the dominant Christian (largely Protestant) culture that surrounded them. The books also provide a revealing case study of cultural borrowing and cultural resistance between minority and majority faiths.

The Sunday Schools for which both of these textbooks were prepared represented an important and controversial innovation in Jewish education. For most of diaspora history, young Jews acquired much if not all of their primary education under Jewish auspices: through Jewish schools, private tutors, and parental teaching at home. Classically, in Eastern Europe, elementary Jewish education was conducted in a Jewish language (Yiddish) and focused primarily on the acquisition of Hebrew, recitation of prayers, and the ability to read and translate biblical and rabbinic texts. In the New World, where Jews freely interacted

1. E. Pyke, *Scriptural Questions, for the Use of Sunday Schools for the Instruction of Israelites* (Philadelphia: L. R. Bailey, 1849 [orig ed., 1843]) 5. The wording reprinted in A. S. W. Rosenbach, "Early American Jewish School Books," *Hebrew Sunday School Society of Philadelphia 89th Annual Report* (Philadelphia: Hebrew Sunday School Society, 1927) 24, diverges slightly. I am deeply grateful to Dr. Arthur Kiron, the Schottenstein-Jesselson Curator of Judaica Collections at the University of Pennsylvania Library, for providing me with a scanned copy of this text.

with non-Jewish neighbors, and were heir to more cosmopolitan Western Sephardic Jewish educational traditions, greater attention was paid to general studies and educational skills. [2] The "publick school" of New York's only Jewish congregations, Shearith Israel, for example, hired a teacher in 1761 "to teach the Hebrew language and translate the same into English, also to teach English, Reading, Writing and Cyphering." [3] The school thus emulated the skills-based curriculum of the general community's schools, in a Jewish setting, with the addition of Hebrew. The goal was for young Jews to adapt to (and participate in) their new cultural environment while studying among people of their own kind and gaining the Hebrew competence needed to maintain Jewish cultural identity distinct.

The creation of state-sponsored nondenominational public schools spawned a revolution in American education and affected American Jewish education profoundly, paving the way for the creation of Jewish Sunday Schools. [4] Free charity-supported schools under religious auspices, such as the "publick school" at Shearith Israel, lost all of their public funding once the new public schools arose; few of them survived. Tuition-based private schools led by Jewish headmasters (such as Isaac Harby's school in Charleston and Jacob Mordecai's in Warrenton, North Carolina), as well as schools with more intensive Jewish religious curricula (like the boarding school that Rabbi Max Lilienthal would open in New York in 1848) struggled to compete. [5] For the burgeoning numbers

2. For a convenient survey, see the article on "Education, Jewish," in *Encyclopaedia Judaica*, 2nd ed. (Detroit: Thomson Gale, 2007) 6:162–214. Excellent primary materials and bibliography may be found in Simcha Assaf, *Mekorot le-toldhot ha-Hinukh be-Yisrael: A Source-Book for the History of Jewish Education from the Beginning of the Middle Ages to the Period of the Haskalah*, ed. Shmuel Glick, 3 vols. (New York: Jewish Theological Seminary of America, 2002) [in Hebrew].

3. Judah Pilch, ed., *A History of Jewish Education in America*, 3 vols. (New York: American Association for Jewish Education, 1969) 12; Jacob R. Marcus, *The Colonial American Jew, 1492–1776*, 3 vols. (Detroit: Wayne State University Press, 1970) 2:1056–68.

4. Some of what follows is drawn from Jonathan D. Sarna, "American Jewish Education in Historical Perspective," *Journal of Jewish Education* 64 (Winter/Spring 1998) 8–21. The best one-volume historical survey is Gil Graff, *"And You Shall Teach Them Diligently": A Concise History of Jewish Education in the United States, 1776–2000* (New York: Jewish Theological Seminary, 2008).

5. Gary P. Zola, *Isaac Harby of Charleston, 1788–1828: Jewish Reformer and Intellectual*, Judaic Studies Series (Tuscaloosa: University of Alabama Press, 1994) 49–54, 76–77, 175–79; Emily Bingham, *Mordecai: An Early American Family* (New York: Hill

of new Jewish immigrants from Central Europe, America's free public schools offered a ticket to advancement. But that ticket carried a hidden cultural cost. Public schools deprived students of the Jewish education required to preserve their heritage.

Two emerging and bitterly contested models of religious education competed for Jewish favor at this time. For the sake of simplicity, I label them the Protestant model and the Catholic model. The Protestant model, which books like Pyke's and Peixotto's came to reinforce, held that morality, universal values, patriotism, civics and critical skills all should be taught in state-funded public schools to a mixed body of religiously diverse students, leaving only the fine points of religious doctrine and practice to be offered in separate denominationally sponsored supplementary schools. The Catholic model, by contrast, insisted that the public schools really preached Protestant values, and that the only way to maintain a minority (dissenting) religious tradition was through a separate system of religious schooling, which Catholics organized and supported through their parishes (hence the term *parochial*).[6]

A highly significant internal Jewish debate took place between supporters of each model—appropriately so, since each reflected a different conception of American identity and a different strategy for maintaining a minority faith in the American setting. By the 1870s, the Protestant model seemed decisively to have won. Pragmatism, widespread hostility to what was perceived as Catholic separatism, and an apparently conscious Protestant effort to involve Jews in the shaping of urban education persuaded the majority of Jews that public schooling was patriotic and virtuous. One Jewish lay leader went so far as to describe public schools as "temples of liberty," portraying them as mini utopias, embodiments of the American dream, where "children of the high and low, rich and poor, Protestants, Catholics and Jews mingle together, play together, and are taught that we are a free people, striving to elevate mankind, and to respect one another."[7] Rabbi Isaac Mayer Wise, the great Cincinnati Reform Jewish leader, reported the positive Jewish attitude toward public schooling to the US Commissioner of Education in 1870, likely

---

& Wang, 2003) 37–43; Morton J. Merowitz, "Max Lilienthal (1814–1882)—Jewish Educator in Nineteenth-Century America," *Yivo Annual* 15 (1974) 46–65.

6. Sarna, "American Jewish Education in Historical Perspective," 11.

7. Lloyd P. Gartner, "Temples of Liberty Unpolluted: American Jews and Public Schooling, 1840–1875," in *A Bicentennial Festschrift for Jacob Rader Marcus*, ed. Bertram W. Korn (New York: Ktav, 1976) 157–89, quote from 186.

in response to bitter Catholic opposition to his city's decision (which Wise favored) to prohibit "religious instruction and reading of religious books, including the Holy Bible" in the public schools. "It is our settled opinion here," he declared to the commissioner, "that the education of the young is the business of the State and the religious instruction, to which we add Hebrew, is the duty of religious bodies. Neither ought to interfere with the other."[8]

By the time Wise made that declaration, the American Jewish community had come up with a Protestant-inspired solution to the problem of how to provide a Jewish religious education to those who attended public schools during the week. Fearing that such Jews might be lost to their faith, and worried particularly about their falling prey to professional missionaries, who targeted Jews, or to well-meaning neighbors, who likewise sought to save them from "perdition," a remarkable group of Jewish women resolved to "follow the example of other religious communities." They established, in 1838, the Hebrew Sunday School Society of Philadelphia for the Instruction of Children Belonging to the Jewish Faith.[9] The increasing numbers of Jewish immigrants flooding into the country coupled with the economic depression that commenced in 1837 likely explains why the women acted when they did. The fact that the Sunday School was undemanding, free, lay led, and headed by pious women of impeccable American credentials likely explains how they managed to succeed.[10]

The prime mover behind the Jewish Sunday School was Rebecca Gratz, one of the foremost Jewish women of her day. Wealthy,

8. Lloyd P. Gartner, ed., *Jewish Education in the United States: A Documentary History*, Classics in Education 46 (New York: Teachers College Press, 1969) 85–86. For the context, the case of *Minor v. Board of Education*, see Tracy Fessenden, "The Nineteenth-Century Bible Wars and the Separation of Church and State," *Church History* 74 (2005) 796–809; and John D. Minor, *The Bible in the Public Schools* (New York: De Capo, 1967 [orig. ed. 1870]).

9. It was incorporated twenty years later; see *The Constitution and By-Laws of the Hebrew Sunday School Society of Philadelphia, Incorporated 1858* (Philadelphia: L. R. Bailey, 1859). On the Sunday school, see Graff, *"And You Shall Teach Them Diligently,"* 16–21; Dianne Ashton, *Rebecca Gratz: Women and Judaism in Antebellum America*, American Jewish Civilization Series (Detroit: Wayne State University Press, 1997), esp. 121–69; and Joseph Rosenbloom, "Rebecca Gratz and the Jewish Sunday School Movement in Philadelphia," *Publications of the American Jewish Historical Society* 47 (1958) 71–75.

10. Lance J. Sussman, *Isaac Leeser and the Making of American Judaism*, American Jewish Civilization Series (Detroit: Wayne State University Press, 1995), 99.

native-born, deeply cultured, unmarried, and closely associated socially with elite Protestant women in her native Philadelphia, Gratz served as a bridge builder between majority and minority religious cultures. She upheld Jewish tradition and belonged to the Sephardic Mikveh Israel synagogue in Philadelphia while also cultivating friendships and philanthropic ties across religious lines.[11]

Philadelphia, of course, was the city where America's Protestant Sunday School movement began in 1790 and where the American Sunday School Union was founded 34 years later.[12] Gratz, who seems to have closely familiarized herself with these Protestant efforts and earlier ones in England borrowed from them heavily. She too opened Sunday School, at no charge, to children of all social classes, whether synagogue members or not. She too enlisted women, most of them single, as volunteer teachers. She too tacitly accepted the Protestant division of learning into universal morality (taught in public schools) and particularistic forms (reserved for Sunday School). She too focused heavily on essentials of faith and upon the Bible. She too led her students in simple hymns—indeed, upon the table where she taught, a student recalled, rested a copy of "Watts' Hymns," presumably one or another edition of Isaac Watts *Hymns and Spiritual Songs: Original and Selected, for the Use of Christians,* a classic Protestant hymnal.[13] Finally, she too drilled her charges through catechesis: she or her colleagues posed questions, and students responded with memorized answers.

Historically, catechisms, especially those setting forth essentials of the faith, played but a minor role in Jewish education. "In Judaism," Alexander Altmann explains in the *Encyclopaedia Judaica*, "the need for a profession of belief did not arise and rabbinic synods saw no necessity

11. The best biography is Ashton, *Rebecca Gratz.*

12. Anne M. Boylan, *Sunday School: The Formation of an American Institution 1790–1880* (New Haven: Yale University Press, 1988); Robert W. Lynn and Elliott Wright, *The Big Little School: Two Hundred Years of the Sunday School,* 2nd ed. (Nashville: Abingdon, 1980); Barton E. Price, "Education: Sunday Schools," in *Encyclopedia of Religion in America,* eds. Charles H. Lippy and Peter W. Williams (Washington, DC: CQ Press, 2010) 2:672–77.

13. Rosa Mordecai, "Rebecca Gratz and America's First Jewish Sunday School," in Jacob R. Marcus, *The American Jewish Woman: A Documentary History* (Cincinnati: American Jewish Archives, 1981) 136; Selma L. Bishop, *Isaac Watts's Hymns and Spiritual Songs 1707: A Publishing History and A Bibliography* (Ann Arbor: Pierian, 1974); on Watts and his significance for Protestant hymnody, see Stephen A. Marini, *Sacred Song in America: Religion, Music and Public Culture,* Public Expressions of Religion in America (Urbana: University of Illinois Press, 2003).

for drawing up concise formulas expressing Jewish beliefs. Theologically speaking, every Jew is born into God's covenant with the people of Israel, and membership in the community does not depend on creedal affirmations of a formal character."[14] Traditional Jewish education, as a result, focused on knowledge of the Torah and of Jewish law; not on professions of belief. With the onset of modernity in German-speaking lands, however, Jews came to interact more with Christians and sought to explain Judaism to them. So the importance for a Jew to be able "to carry the principles of his religion on the tip of his tongue" became increasingly evident. Protestant education in Germany, following the example of Luther and Calvin, had long placed great emphasis on precise knowledge of the catechism. In response, Jews formulated catechisms of their own—notwithstanding criticism from those who labeled such works foreign to the spirit of Judaism.[15]

With the opening of Jewish Sunday Schools, the call for suitable Jewish catechisms and other texts rang out in America. Initially, following British precedent, Jews employed Christian Sunday school texts, and teachers carefully pasted pieces of paper over "answers unsuitable for Jewish children." The books had the appearance, so the antiquarian bookseller A. S. W. Rosenbach recalled, "of having escaped with the penciling of the censor." At the same time, the censorship inevitably helped students to appreciate how much their religion and Christianity differed.[16] Fortunately for those who did the pasting, the Peixotto sisters,

14. Alexander A. Altmann, "Articles of Faith," *Encyclopaedia Judaica*, 2nd ed. (Detroit: Thomson Gale, 2007) 2:529–32.

15. Michael A. Meyer, *The Origins of the Modern Jew: Jewish Identity and European Culture in Germany, 1749–1824* (Detroit: Wayne State University Press, 1967) 125–27; Jacob J. Petuchowski, "Manuals and Catechisms of the Jewish Religion in the Early Period of Emancipation," in *Studies in Nineteenth-Century Jewish Intellectual History*, ed. Alexander Altmann, Philip W. Lown Institute of Advanced Judaic Studies, Brandeis University: Studies and Texts 2 (Cambridge: Harvard University Press, 1964) 47–64; Jay Berkovitz, *Rites and Passages: The Beginnings of Modern Jewish Culture in France, 1650–1860*, Jewish Culture and Contexts (Philadelphia: University of Pennsylvania Press, 2007) 219–21; for opposition, see Noah H. Rosenbloom, *Tradition in an Age of Reform: The Religious Philosophy of Samson Raphael Hirsch* (Philadelphia: Jewish Publication Society, 1976) 187–91; and *Israelite* 1 (1854) 13.

16. Rosenbach, "Early American Jewish School Books," 19; Rosa Mordecai, "Rebecca Gratz and America's First Jewish Sunday School," in Jacob R. Marcus, *The American Jewish Woman: A Documentary History* Cincinnati: American Jewish Archives, 1981) 137; for the British precedent, see Todd M. Endelman, *The Jews of Georgian England 1714–1830* (Philadelphia: Jewish Publication Society, 1979) 239.

both of them teachers under Rebecca Gratz, soon produced acceptable Jewish volumes that displaced their Protestant counterparts, remaining staples of the Sunday School for decades. In time, numerous other Jewish catechisms appeared in the United States—at least fifteen prior to 1900.[17]

The Peixotto sisters' textbooks, when compared with their Christian counterparts, highlight the twin themes of borrowing and resisting that underlay the whole Jewish Sunday School enterprise. Pyke's *Scriptural Questions,* akin to its counterparts prepared for Protestant schools, opened with a "prayer." Though unattributed, it was likely written by Rebecca Gratz herself (which would make it an unusual antebellum example of an American Jewish prayer written by a woman),[18] and it read as follows: "O God, give unto us the help we need; give us bread to eat, and raiment to put on, and instruction to understand thy mercies; may we be grateful for all thy goodness; may we be dutiful to our parents; honest in all our dealings; true in our words and actions; affectionate in our behaviour to one another; attentive to our teachers; and above all, ardent and devout in adoring thee alone, the God of our fathers, Abraham, Isaac and Jacob; enlighten our faith, that we may daily repeat the acknowledgment of thy unity. Hear, O Israel, the Lord our God is one Lord. Blessed be the name of the glory of his kingdom for ever and ever. Amen."[19]

Strikingly, this prayer brings together various themes from the traditional Jewish prayer book, beginning with simple petitionary prayers. It then moves on to reiterate universal ethical teachings found in Jewish tradition but also regularly repeated in public schools and in Protestant Sunday schools (duty, honesty, truth, affection and attention to teachers). The last and most important part of the prayer, however, consists of a ringing affirmation of what made Jews and Judaism distinctive in the American setting: first, the insistence upon ethical monotheism ("adoring thee alone") without Jesus or the Holy Spirit; and second, the pride

17. For editions of the textbooks and a listing of other catechisms, see Robert Singerman, *Judaica Americana: A Bibliography of Publications to 1900,* 2 vols. (New York: Greenwood, 1990).

18. Rosa Mordecai, in Marcus, *American Jewish Woman,* 137, describes Miss Gratz reciting "a prayer of her own composition, which she read verse by verse" every Sunday. Sarah Ann Hays, Gratz's niece, likewise describes "a prayer written . . . by herself, which combined 'all prayer'" (ibid., 98).

19. Pyke, *Scriptural Questions,* 3.

in belonging to a people that traces itself back, genealogically, to "our fathers Abraham, Isaac and Jacob."

The prayer concluded with the recitation, in the King James translation, of the opening lines of what Jews call the *Shema* (Deuteronomy 6:4–9): "Hear (*Shema*) O Israel, the Lord our God is one Lord." The *Shema* was reputedly recited in the ancient temple of Jerusalem (along with the Ten Commandments), and generations of Jews have pronounced it twice a day in their prayers, as well as nightly upon retiring, and for the final time upon their deathbed. Its six opening Hebrew words, easily remembered and transmitted to children at a young age, became "the preeminent expression of monotheism in Judaism" as well as the quintessential expression of Judaism's "most fundamental belief and commitment." Because of their emphasis on God's oneness, these words also came to serve as a powerful Jewish response to Christianity, a daily reminder from the Bible that Jews believe in one God alone and not in the trinity.[20] In America, the *Shema* continued to serve all of these functions, and even Jews who read no Hebrew knew its opening words by heart. Reciting these words underscored for children in Jewish Sunday School what distinguished them from their Christian counterparts. Indeed, for some Jews these words became known as the "the watchword of our faith."[21]

It was not just the content of the opening prayer, however, that distinguished Jewish Sunday Schools from Protestant ones, but also the prayer's tone. Protestant schools opened either with the Lord's Prayer, from the New Testament, or with christological prayers unsuited to Jewish schools. Many of the prayers, seeking to spark a conversion experience on the part of the children, made reference to the need for atonement from sin. "Forgive the sins of all those who are penitent," one such prayer from the 1830s declares, "create and make in us new and contrite hearts, that we, truly lamenting our sins, and acknowledging

20. Jeffrey H. Tigay, *Deuteronomy*, JPS Torah Commentary (Philadelphia: Jewish Publication Society, 1996) 438–41; Louis Jacobs, "Shema, Reading of," in *Encyclopaedia Judaica*, 2nd ed. (Detroit: Thomson Gale, 2007) 18:453–56.

21. The formula "Blessed be the name of the glory of his kingdom for ever and ever" was recited, in Temple times, following the mention of God's name, and was incorporated into the recitation of the *Shema*. Functionally speaking, the formula substitutes for "Amen." The Sunday School prayer nevertheless concludes with Amen, in accordance with what had, by then, become a universal norm. For the phrase "the watchword of our faith," see especially Michael Carasik's comments online, on his *The Bible Guy* blog: http://mcarasik.wordpress.com/category/sacred-or-secular/.

our unworthiness may obtain of thee, the God of all mercy, perfect re-
mission and forgiveness through Jesus Christ our Lord." Often, in Protestant Sunday School prayers, the children were prayed over, rather than
prayed with. Many a Protestant Sunday School opening prayer included
words and ideas far beyond the level of students' comprehension.[22] The
prayer that opened Pyke's *Scriptural Questions,* by contrast, avoided all
of these pitfalls.

Scriptural Questions moved on to religious pedagogy with its best-
loved (and best-remembered) section: "Answers in Rhyme." Designed
for those in the "infant school"—ages four to seven—it began with the
line already quoted: "Who formed you child and made you live," usually attributed to Pyke herself. In fact, the entire catechism, it can now
be shown, was selectively borrowed and adapted from "A Catechism
in Rhyme," known to Protestants on both sides of the Atlantic.[23] Pyke,
influenced by the traditions of the Protestant Sunday School but determined to adapt those traditions to the needs of her Jewish charges,
chose her verses carefully, copying some and resisting others. In general, in conformity with Jewish tradition and with the theology of her
Philadelphia synagogue doubtless in mind, she admitted verses that
promoted belief and confidence in God ("God keeps me safe, and makes
me well"). But those that referred to original sin ("Have you an evil heart
within? Yes; I was even born in sin"), a doctrine largely alien to Judaism,
she banished. Banished too were verses that denied free will ("Have you
the power to change your heart? No; it is prone from good to start")
and that threatened the wicked with "everlasting flames in hell." Fire
and brimstone, a staple of Protestant pedagogy in the first half of the
nineteenth century when children were seen as "little adults needing

22. Samples and a critique are found in Alexander V. Griswold, *Prayers Adapted
to Various Occasions of Social Worship for which Provision Is not Made in the Book of
Common Prayer* (Boston: Dow, 1843 [orig ed. 1835]) 15–26, quote is from 25–26; see
also "Prayer in Sunday School," *The Sunday School Teachers' Magazine and Journal of
Education* 18 (1867) 137.

23. I have found two full versions of this Protestant catechism, one in *The West-
minster Assembly's Shorter Catechism, With Scriptural Proofs* (1847) online: http://con-
tinuing.wordpress.com/2011/05/25/a-catechism-in-rhyme/; and the other in Norman
MacLeod, *The Christian Guest* (London: 1859), 300. For mentions of other versions,
see Arlo A. Brown, *A History of Religious Education in Recent Times* (New York: Abingdon, 1923) 59 [quoting a copy in the library of the American Sunday-School Union]
and Richard G. Pardee, *The Sabbath School Index* (Philadelphia: Garrigues, 1868) 128.
In several versions the opening line reads "Who made you, child, and bade you live"?

conversion," was largely resisted by Jewish educators.[24] In one case, Pyke deftly swapped "God" for "Jesus" ("*God* loves an infant's praise") and managed to preserve the "answer in rhyme." In another, she amended "The Holy Spirit, God of Truth" to "My God, the only God of Truth." Most christological verses, however, she excised completely, including "Who then can peace and pardon give? Jesus who died that we might live," and the final verse of the Protestant catechism, "Where will good children ever be? In heav'n, their Saviour Christ to see." In place of the stark Christian message of reward and punishment, her conclusion reasserted the uplifting monotheistic message that she hoped Jewish children would forever remember: "And how may you his grace receive? In one true God I must believe."

Pyke's focus on faith in God, rather than upon the performance of ritual commandments, reflected not only Protestant emphases, but also theological trends within modern Judaism in the early nineteenth century. Most Jewish catechisms in Germany (where some 50 catechisms were produced between 1799 and 1832) carried the same emphasis.[25] The Sunday School was by no means a Reform Jewish institution—indeed, Rebecca Gratz expressed forceful opposition to Jewish religious reform in Charleston[26]—yet it did reflect the religious spirit of its times. As a result, Pyke's catechism devoted no attention to the Jewish calendar or lifecycle, and a full chapter to the Ten Commandments. Protestant catechisms focused upon these as well (and had done so since Luther), so this provided yet another opportunity to highlight religious similarities and differences.

For the most part, since Jews and Christians shared the Ten Commandments in common, Pyke's catechism harmonized perfectly with its Protestant counterparts. Both proceeded commandment by commandment ("Which is the first commandment?" "Which is the second commandment" etc.). Both set forth the text of each commandment from the King James Bible. And both interpreted the commandments in similar if not identical words ("avoid all false, rash, unjust and unnecessary

24. Rosenbach, "Early American Jewish School Books," 24–25. Following the publication of Horace Bushnell's influential *Christian Nurture* (1847), perceptions of childhood gradually changed in Protestant circles, and Sunday School curricula changed with them; see Boylan, *Sunday School*, 133–65.

25. Rosenbloom, *Tradition in an Age of Reform*, 189–91.

26. Rebecca Gratz to Miriam Gratz Cohen (March 29, 1841) in Marcus, *American Jewish Woman*, 101.

oaths").[27] But for all that Pyke borrowed from her contemporaries, she also resisted language that departed from Jewish tradition. So, for example, when her catechism asked "Which is the first commandment?" the correct answer given is "I am the Lord thy God, who brought thee out of the land of Egypt, and out of the house of bondage; thou shalt have no other God before me." Protestant youngsters, by contrast, were taught that the first twenty-two of these words formed but the "preface to the ten commandments."

Pyke concluded her brief, eighteen-page catechism with a hymn, opening with the words "We are but young, yet we may sing." Like so much in her pamphlet, this too was borrowed. "We Are But Young" is actually a beloved Sunday School children's hymn reprinted in no fewer than sixty-seven Christian hymnals.[28] What distinguished Pyke's version from all the rest, was the hymn's complete de-Christianization. She dropped a stanza beginning "We are but young, we need a guide / Jesus, in thee we would confide." She also replaced "The gospel news, the heavenly word," with "From the true God, the Heavenly word." While she (inadvertently?) preserved an echo of the early nineteenth-century Protestant emphasis on hell and its torments—"If we despise the only way / Dreadful will be the judgment day"—she closed, as per Jewish tradition, on an uplifting note:

> We are but young; yet God has shed
> Unnumbered blessings on our head:
> Then let our youth, and riper days,
> Be all devoted to his praise.[29]

Pyke's catechism, as it came to be known, illustrates central themes of "interreligious dialogue" in America of the 1840s. The country's 15,000 Jews, eager to succeed economically and win acceptance but wary of

27. Pyke's comments also duplicate, often word for word, the interpretation of the Ten Commandments in standard Catholic catechisms; see *A Short Abridgement of the Christian Doctrine Newly Revised and Augmented for the Use of the Catholic Church in the Diocese of Boston* (Boston: Donahoe, 1873) 28–33.

28. For a listing, see the website http://www.hymnary.org/.

29. Pyke, *Scriptural Questions*, 18. By contrast, in *Sunday-School Hymns* (Philadelphia: American Sunday School Union, 1856) 104 (hymn 136), the hymn ends with, "Dreadful will be the judgment day." Later hymnals end it, as Pyke does, with the more uplifting stanza. For evidence that this hymn was sung by Sunday school children in Columbia, South Carolina, see *Occident* 2 (May 1844); online: http://www.jewish-history.com/occident/volume2/may1844/columbia.html/.

losing their distinctive identity in the process, struggled mightily to find an appropriate balance between "fitting in" and "standing out." The very establishment of a *Hebrew* Sunday School, patterned on its Protestant counterpart but distinct from it, embodied this tension, which we have characterized here as one between "cultural borrowing" and "cultural resistance." Pyke's catechism, produced by one of the school's most dedicated teachers, provides a closer look at how this tension worked itself out in curricular terms. On the one hand, the volume appropriated its tone, its form, and much of its content from Protestant Sunday School materials. Its focus upon faith, ethical behavior, and the Ten Commandments, as opposed to ritual practices and rabbinic teachings, demonstrated to all who read it that Judaism could adapt itself to a Protestant religious agenda. On the other hand, the volume also made perfectly clear where Judaism resisted Protestantism's teachings. More than anything else, what defined Jews at that time was that they were "not Christian" (just as what defined Protestants was that they were "not Catholic").[30] Consequently, Pyke vigilantly held the line against Christology in any form and did her best to banish other theological teachings deemed unacceptable. Even as her book reassured Jews that they could fit into American Protestant culture, it subtly warned them not to convert.

Pyke's sister, Simha Peixotto,[31] clarified this agenda in her book, first published in 1840 and "carefully revised" in 1854 titled *Elementary Introduction to the Scriptures for the Use of Hebrew Children.* The title itself was illuminating. Since 1836, Protestant children had been raised on the American Sunday School Union's *Child's Scripture Question Book* (revised 1853). While not identifying itself as a *Protestant* child's introduction to Scripture, that in fact was what the book was. It employed the King James translation, introduced youngsters to christological interpretations of the Hebrew Bible, followed the Protestant canon, and, of course, included the New Testament as part of Scripture. Jews, meanwhile, criticized the King James translation, cherished their own interpretive traditions of the Bible, ordered the biblical books differently, and

30. Jonathan D. Sarna, *American Judaism: A History* (New Haven: Yale University Press, 2004) 108.

31. For a brief sketch, see Henry S. Morais, *The Jews of Philadelphia* (Philadelphia: Levytype, 1894) 151.

denied Scriptural sanctity to the New Testament.[32] So even as the Bible served as a common sacred text for Jews and Christians in America, and many aspects of the American Sunday School's textbook were unobjectionable from a Jewish perspective, "Hebrew children" still needed a "scripture question book" of their own. Simha Peixotto's volume looked to fill that void.

What makes her book so revealing for a study of "cultural borrowing" and "cultural resistance" is that she used the American Sunday School Union's textbook as her model, and even received permission to borrow many of its questions and answers. Unlike her sister, she provided full credit to her source: "An acknowledgment is due to the American Sunday School Union for the liberality they have manifested in permitting us to make their "Child's Scripture Question Book" the basis of this production, and I, therefore, return them publicly my thanks for their kind permission."[33] This expression of thanks is in many ways remarkable, for the American Sunday School Union maintained a traditional, supersessionist view of the Jews as a benighted "race" in need of salvation. In 1845—five years after the first edition of Peixotto's work had appeared—the ASSU published a text titled *The Jew at Home and Abroad*, replete with comments highly objectionable to the American Jewish community. The volume concluded with a "Prayer of Gentiles for the Jews," presumably intoned by teachers and students together, that summarized the book's theological message:

> O God of Israel, hear the plea
> We Gentiles urge, in faith, to Thee
> For those who still thy calls refuse,
> Our elder brethren, the Jews.
>
> We view them blinded now by sin,
> Until our fullness be come in;
> Oh, hasten, Lord, that day of grace,
> And save and bless the Jewish race.

32. See Jonathan D. Sarna and Nahum M. Sarna, "Jewish Biblical Scholarship and Translations in the United States," in Ernest S. Frerichs, ed., *The Bible and Bibles in America*, The Bible in American Culture 1 (Atlanta: Scholars, 1988) 83–116.

33. Simha C. Peixotto *Elementary Introduction to the Scriptures for the Use of Hebrew Children* (Philadelphia: Collins, 1875 [1854]) v. Interestingly, Peixotto did not make use of the twenty-one engravings that embellished the Protestant original. No reason is provided for this omission, but it may reflect Jewish sensitivity toward including "graven images" in a textbook dealing with the Bible.

> May Jews and Gentiles join to sing
> The praises of their heavenly King;
> And trusting in God's only Son
> As Christians, be for ever one.[34]

Still, and notwithstanding these sentiments, the Society liberally permitted Peixotto to borrow and modify *Child's Scripture Question Book* so as to produce a textbook that, ironically, aimed to perpetuate (and even strengthen) the faith and people prayerfully described as "blinded by sin!" The ambivalences and complexities of Jewish-Christian relations in early America—contradictions between offensive portrayals of the "mythical Jew" and liberal treatment of the "Jew next door"[35]—are illuminated by this surprising exchange, which explains why characterizations of interfaith relations so often defy easy generalization.

Peixotto's book, revised and approved by Isaac Leeser, the foremost American Jewish religious leader of the day,[36] sheds light in other ways on Christian-Jewish relations at that time. Whole sections repeat almost word for word the same wooden questions and answers found in the Protestant volume, especially concerning fundamentals that Jews and Christians easily agreed upon.

> Q. What is the first book in the Bible called?
> A. Genesis
> Q. What is the meaning of the word Genesis?
> A. Creation
> Q. Of what does the first book give an account?
> A. Of the creation[37]

Yet from the first lesson, the two presentations also disagreed about matters large and small. The Protestant text, for example, began by describing the Bible as the book children should "prize above others." The Jewish text, seeking to underscore the Bible's *particular* significance for Jews, described it as "the book in which are contained the laws

34. *The Jew at Home and Abroad* (Philadelphia: American Sunday School Union, 1845) 178.

35. Jonathan D. Sarna, "The 'Mythical Jew' and the 'Jew Next Door' in Nineteenth-Century America," in *Anti-Semitism in American History*, ed. David Gerber (Urbana: University of Illinois Press, 1986) 57–78.

36. The best biography is Sussman, *Isaac Leeser and the Making of American Judaism*.

37. Peixotto, *Elementary Introduction*, 7; *Child's Scripture Question Book*, 5–6.

constituting the Jewish religion." The Protestant text taught the story of creation. The Jewish text added that God "alone" was responsible for creation, a subtle polemic against Christian trinitarianism. The Protestant text listed Adam and Eve as the first man and first woman. The Jewish text appended a Hebrew etymology ("Adam . . . Because he was formed from the ground, which in Hebrew, is called *Adamah*"), a reminder of the Bible's original (holy) language. The Protestant text identified the serpent with Satan (based on Revelation 20:2) and the "seed of the woman" with Christ. The Jewish text accepted neither interpretation and deleted both of them. In short, from the very first lesson, the Jewish text borrowed only selectively from the Protestant original.[38] It substituted Jewish interpretations for Christian ones, and sought to ensure that Jewish children identified the Bible as a Jewish book and the source of Jewish law.

A line-by-line comparison of the Protestant and Jewish texts, which cannot be undertaken here, would recover a full-scale early American example of interreligious debate or "dialogue" concerning the Bible. It may be presumed, indeed, that Jewish and Protestant children engaged in such "dialogues"—for better and for worse—when they interacted in public school and discussed the meaning of the Bible based on their Sunday school lessons. A few examples demonstrate the point. The Protestant text stressed a universal Christian message. It therefore skipped over God's promise to Abraham of the land in Genesis 13 and the covenant of circumcision between God and Abraham in Genesis 17. The Jewish text, unsurprisingly, devoted significant space to these episodes, teaching children about the land promised to the Jewish people (Gen 13:14–15), how Jews would ultimately be "as numerous as the dust of the earth," and about the "EVERLASTING covenant," between God and Abraham's descendants, the capitalized word a none-too-subtle polemic against Christian supersessionism. It repeated these lessons later in discussing God's promise to Isaac (Genesis 28), underscoring Jewish chosenness, the promise of multitudinous offspring, and the role of Israel in history ("through us the nations would learn that the Eternal alone is God"), all themes about which the Protestant text was silent.

38. Compare Lance J. Sussman, "Isaac Leeser and the Protestantization of American Judaism," *American Jewish Archives* 38 (1986) 3: "The main thrust of the movement to accommodate traditional Judaism to American society involved the adaptation of select features of American Protestantism which brought Jews into the mainstream of religious life in nineteenth-century America but did not violate Jewish religious law."

The Jewish text also explained the "ordinance of circumcision" and its continuing relevance, another subject that its Protestant counterpart understandably skipped over. "What," Jewish children were asked, "is the penalty should any male among us (the descendants of Abraham) not keep this covenant?" The lesson closes with the uncompromising answer still ringing in students' ears: "It is written that his soul shall be cut off from among his people. *Gen.* xvii.14."[39]

Nothing so obviously distinguished Jews from Christians in nineteenth-century America as the Jewish Sabbath, observed on Saturday, while the Christian Sabbath was observed on Sunday. In teaching children the story (Exodus 16) of the manna which was not collected on Saturday in the wilderness, Simha Peixotto devoted two full paragraphs to a defense of this Jewish institution, her words focused not only on the past but on the present, and aimed not only at Jewish children but also at their parents, many of whom violated the Jewish Sabbath in order to keep their six-day-a-week jobs and feed their families.[40]

> Q. What are we to infer from this [the story of the manna]?
>
> A. That we, the decendants [sic] of Israel, shall consider ourselves bound to keep the Sabbath holy, wherever we may be, always preparing on the sixth day for the seventh, and not do the slightest work on that day on any pretence whatever . . .
>
> Q. What should the keeping of this manna teach us?
>
> A. It is to teach us that we like, our ancestors, should know that it is in the power of the Creator to remove all our difficulties, and to supply all our wants when we cry unto Him in time of need. It is also to teach us that we should never permit poverty to cause an infringement of the Sabbath; for the God who gave us a law will ever take care of its adherents.[41]

By contrast, the Protestant text, far less interested in contemporary implications of biblical laws (other than the Ten Commandments) for children, and perhaps uncomfortable with the switch of the Sabbath from Saturday to Sunday, dealt briefly and matter-of-factly with the details

---

39. Peixotto, *Elementary Introduction,* 17–20, 25; compare *Child's Scripture Question Book,* 10, 14. God's promise to Moses (Exodus 3) is likewise ignored in the Protestant text and emphasized in the Jewish one (47).

40. Sarna, *American Judaism,* 23–24, 70, 162–65.

41. Peixotto, *Elementary Introduction,* 58–59

of the biblical story, mentioning "the Sabbath," but ignoring its day-of-the-week completely. "How were they supplied [with manna] on the Sabbath," Protestant children were asked. "By gathering twice as much as usual on the preceding day."[42]

Here and throughout its pages, the Protestant *Child's Scripture Question Book* taught the Bible in the *past* tense, as a set of stories from ancient times. By contrast, Peixotto's *Elementary Introduction to the Scriptures* taught the Bible as a *living* text, full of continuing relevance for Jews. For example, in teaching the laws of the three pilgrimage holidays (Exodus 23), both books began with almost identical questions about how often the Israelites were "to keep a feast to the Lord." But Peixotto soon switched to the present tense ("Is this a feast much regarded among our people?"), and noted ongoing observances of these holidays, which she assumed children were generally familiar with. The Protestant text had none of this. Similarly, in teaching the Book of Leviticus, Peixotto devoted space to the Jewish dietary laws ("birds and animals which may be eaten, and such as may not be eaten") and to the Jewish New Year (Rosh Hashanah) and the Day of Atonement, subjects of abundant continuing relevance to the Jewish people. *Child's Scripture Question Book* dismissed Leviticus in less than half a page, as consisting principally of "laws concerning the Levites."[43]

For *Child's Scripture Question Book*, the most significant parts of biblical books were those that could be interpreted christologically. For this reason, it devoted a full page to a two-verse biblical story concerning the "serpent of brass" that Moses erected to bring relief to the afflicted people of Israel (Num 21:8–9). "Of whom was the brazen serpent a type?" it asked. The answer, of course, was "Christ," relying upon a proof text from the Gospel of John (3:14–15). Peixotto passed over this entire biblical story in silence. The Protestant text likewise lavished attention on prophets like Isaiah, whom it depicted as the "evangelical prophet . . . because he prophesied so much concerning Christ and his kingdom." It devoted two full chapters to Isaiah, one of them opening with the question "Under what names is Christ mentioned by Isaiah?" Peixotto forcefully resisted this line of interpretation. She devoted but

42. *Child's Scripture Question Book*, 33.

43. Ibid., 36, 38; Peixotto, *Elementary Introduction*, 63–65, 69–70.

half a chapter to Isaiah, much of it a thinly veiled rebuttal of Christian interpretations of his message.[44]

Both books concluded their treatment of the Hebrew Bible with Malachi, the "last book of the Old Testament" in the Protestant canon and, in Jewish tradition, the last of the prophets. Jewish and Christian interpretations of Malachi diverged radically—so much so that, in summarizing his message, Peixotto borrowed scarcely one word from her Protestant counterpart. While the Protestant text depicted Malachi as foretelling the coming of John the Baptist, "to prepare the way before Christ," she depicted a Malachi who came to "reform the people," and who foretold the coming of "Elijah the prophet." The final lines of the Protestant text pointed children toward "the birth of Christ." For Peixotto, meanwhile, messianic time meant "the time that the Jews will be restored to their former glory." Her final line, recalling her explanation of the Bible in her opening lesson ("the book in which are contained the laws constituting the Jewish religion.") led her to a quite different verse from Malachi than her Protestant counterpart trumpeted. "Remember ye the law of Moses my servant," she concluded "to whom I commanded in Horeb for all Israel statutes and judgments (3:22)."[45]

In the twentieth century, the two-hour-per-week Hebrew Sunday School fell under withering criticism from Jewish educators. More intensive supplementary schools with an Hebraic focus, as well as Jewish all-day schools, came to dominate the Jewish educational field. Textbooks like those produced by the Peixotto sisters were forgotten.[46] To look back at those books, however, is to gain new appreciation for how mid-nineteenth-century American Jews, looking to educate their children religiously, studied the ways of their Protestant neighbors, borrowed educational texts from them, and yet also resisted those neighbors, by focusing on what made Jews different and distinct. In the process of reading Protestant texts and recreating them as Jewish texts, something of an interreligious dialogue took place. It helped to clarify where Jews and Christians resembled one another, and where they differed.

---

44. *Child's Scripture Question Book*, 43, 80–83; Peixotto, *Elementary Introduction*, 77, 157–58.

45. *Child's Scripture Question Book*, 96; Peixotto, *Elementary Introduction*, 174–75.

46. Jonathan B. Krasner, *The Benderly Boys and American Jewish Education* (Waltham, MA: Brandeis University Press, 2011) esp. 27–28.

4

Hinduism, Interreligious Dialogue, and Acculturation in North America

Deepak Sarma

There is no period in the Gregorian calendar more demanding and transformative for diaspora Hindus than the weeks leading up to and culminating with Christmas. In daycares and schools, in workplaces and civic spaces, on television and in the digital media in North America, Hindus are constantly reminded about the holy days of Christians.[1] Whether an actual interreligious or comparative theological dialogue between a Hindu and a Christian occurs, internal and imagined ones are unavoidable. An examination of the effect of these interactions on the diaspora Hindu community illuminates the degree to which Hindus have experienced acculturation.

In what ways, then, have members of the diaspora Hindu community adapted to these contexts and cultural environments, to "Christian

1. Though not all North Americans are Christian, it is certainly the case that the dominant paradigm in North America is Christianity. For this reason I will use "American culture" and "Christian culture" interchangeably.

privileging,"[2] and to the "creedal intrusion"[3] inevitable in the days and weeks leading up to Christmas? How have members experienced acculturation? How have Hindus, and how has Hinduism, been integrated and assimilated into the North American Christian environment? And have these processes resulted in changes to Hindu theological paradigms?[4] Or, is there something about Hindu doctrine or about the demographics of the Hindu immigrants themselves that makes doctrinal changes possible and passable? In this brief article I will examine these and other questions concerning the intersection between interreligious dialogue and cultural adaptation and change as it pertains to the Hindu diaspora in North America.[5]

Though at first glance, terms like *diaspora* and *acculturation* seem as if they do not need to be defined, they are widely used across a number of different disciplines and have thus acquired a variety of meanings and usages. To avoid confusion I will offer stipulative definitions of *disapora* as well as stipulative definitions of terms that pertain to the cultural psychology of immigrants. In offering these stipulative and formal definitions I do not intend to reify or to suggest that they perfectly characterize behaviors and practices of communities and people. Actual communities and people are likely to be somewhere between these categories and to combine elements from each. These definitions, then, are

2. Warren J. Blumenfeld, "Christian Privilege and the Promotion of 'Secular' and Not-so 'Secular' Mainline Christianity in Public Schooling and in the Larger Society," *Equity and Excellence in Education* 39 (2006) 195–210. Blumenfeld explains that Christian privilege refers to the ways that Christianity "reiterates its values and practices while marginalizing and subordinating those who do not adhere to Christian faith traditions." 195. For more on this, see the articles in *Investigating Christian Privilege and Religious Oppression in the United States*, Warren J. Blumenfeld, Khyati Y. Joshi, and Ellen E. Fairchild, eds., Transgressions: Cultural Studies and Education (Rotterdam: Sense, 2009).

3. Tom Flynn, *The Trouble with Christmas* (Buffalo: Prometheus, 1993) 156.

4. There are complexities about the term *Hindu*, and I will not address them here. For more, see Sarma "Hindu Leaders in North America?" *Teaching Theology and Religion* 9/2 (2006) 115–20.

5. For an analysis of similar issues, see Raymond B. Williams, "Sacred Threads of Several Textures: Strategies of Adaptation in the United States" in Raymond B. Williams, ed., *A Sacred Thread: Modern Transmission of Hindu Traditions in India and Abroad* (Chambersburg, PA: Anima, 1992) 228–57. See also the articles in *Religious Reconstruction in the South Asian Diasporas: From One Generation to Another*, ed. John R. Hinnells (New York: Palgrave Macmillan, 2007).

intended to be useful as heuristic devices that may shed light on the transformations of Hinduism and Hindus in North America.[6]

Diaspora Hindus in North America

By "diaspora Hindus" I mean first generation immigrants of Indian heritage and their offspring who trace their roots to India, consider India to be an ancestral homeland, and who identify themselves as Hindu.[7] While there are diaspora Hindus throughout the world, in this analysis I will limit diaspora Hindus to those found in North America. Among first generation immigrants, I refer exclusively to those who were permitted entry into the United States in 1965, after significant changes in US immigration policies and elimination of ethnic quotas.[8] These immigrants were almost entirely men and skilled professionals (engineers, scientists, and medical doctors) whose spouses accompanied them or came soon after.[9]

6. To reiterate, there are many scholars in cultural and ethnic studies, in psychology, sociology, and elsewhere, whose work has focused on these definitions themselves, their construction, their viability, and so on. My intention is not to situate myself in this methodological morass, though it may be unavoidable. Rather it is to use these categories as a means to an end, namely to shed light on the Hinduism in North America.

7. I do not wish to address the issues concerning the differences between ethnic identity and Hindu identity here. For more, see Kirin Narayan's "How Native Is a 'Native' Anthropologist?" *American Anthropologist* 95 (2003) 671–786, for one of the first treatments of the ambiguities of these categories. For more on the history and uses of the term see Steve Vertovec, "Religion and Diaspora," in *New Approaches to the Study of Religion*, ed. Peter Antes, Armin W. Geertz and Randi Warne, 2 vols., Religion and Reason 42–43 (Berlin: de Gruyter, 2004) 1:275–304; and Martin Baumann, "Diaspora: Genealogies of Semantics and Transcultural Comparison" *Numen* 47 (2000) 313–37. See also Rajesh Raja and Chita Sankaran, "Religion and the South Asia Diaspora," *South Asian Diaspora* 3/1 (2011) 5–13. Those in the community who explicitly and aggressively reject or deny their relationship with India are still in this set of people.

8. For more on this group, see Padma Rangaswamy, *Namaste America: Indian Immigrants in an American Cosmopolis* (University Park: Penn State University Press, 2003); and Maxine Fisher, *The Indians of New York City: A Study of Immigrants from India* (New Delhi: Heritage, 1980). While they are certainly an important group I do not wish to consider Sikh immigrants who entered the United States in the late nineteenth and early twentieth centuries. For more on the Sikhs and other earlier immigrants see Joan Jensen, *Passage from India: Asian Indian Immigrants in North America* (New Haven: Yale University Press, 1988).

9. For a list of the number of Indian immigrants see Fisher, *The Indians of New York City*, 12.

Among subsequent-generation Hindu immigrants it is important to distinguish between those who were born after the first wave of immigration, between approximately 1965 and 1978, and those who were born in later years.[10] The tribulations confronted by the first group differ significantly from those experienced by the offspring of later immigrants. By 1978 the population of Indians in the United States had reached sufficiently high numbers such that these newer immigrants did not face the same demands and challenges as did their predecessors. Indian Americans, for example, who were born in the early 1990s and who are entering college in 2012 face and faced significantly different scenarios than their antecedents, who may have been among the first students of Indian origin in their colleges and universities, not to mention in their elementary and junior high schools. The second group also has grown up in a context where yoga is familiar and tolerated, if not accepted, by most non-Hindu North Americans. There are many other examples of assimilated Hindus and the incorporation of Hindu practices and beliefs in American popular culture. In short, those born in North America after 1978 grew up in a world where Hinduism had already been somewhat acculturated and assimilated. These younger generations have also grown up in the digital age where cultural and geographic distances have been reduced and where webcams have made intercontinental video calls possible.

While there is significant debate in immigrant studies and other disciplines about the meaning and usage of the terms *acculturation*, *assimilation*, *integration*, and *separation*, I will rely on the definitions offered by Bryan S. Kim in his "Acculturation and Enculturation of Asian Americans: A Primer."[11] Kim states that "acculturation" is "the process of adapting to the norms of the dominant culture." "Assimilation" is an "adaptation status in which individuals absorb the culture of the dominant group while they reject the norms of the heritage culture." "Integration" is an "adaptation status in which individuals are proficient

10. I am grateful to Joshi for her delineation of the second-generation into these categories. For more on these groups see Khyati Y. Jhoshi's *New Roots in America's Sacred Ground: Religion, Race, and Ethnicity in Indian America* (New Brunswick, NJ: Rutgers University Press, 2006) 5–7.

11. The definitions that follow are taken verbatim from Bryan S. Kim, "Acculturation and Enculturation of Asian Americans: A Primer," in *Asian American Psychology: Current Perspectives*, ed. Nita Tewari, Alvin N. Alvarez (New York: Psychology Press, 2009) 110.

in the culture of the dominant group while they retain proficiency in the heritage culture." "Separation" is "an adaptation status in which individuals are not interested in learning the culture of the dominant group and maintain only one's heritage culture." "Bicultural competence" refers to the "skill with which individuals are able to successfully meet the demands of two distinct cultures."

Again, these terms are ideal types and are useful categories within which to locate individuals and communities. As already mentioned, members of the Hindu diaspora cannot avoid engaging in interreligious dialogue with Christians during the latter quarter of the Gregorian calendar, which includes November and December. Whether this involves actual and informal conversations or consists of internal, self-reflective dialogues, interreligious dialogue and comparative theology is inevitable and inescapable when one is frequently enjoined to "Have a Merry Christmas" or even to "Enjoy the Holidays."[12] What effect do these conversations, intended, invited, or otherwise, have on practicing Hindus? Are such instructions merely a covert form of "cultural imperialism?"[13] Does it demand acculturation? Does it lead to assimilation?

With all of the marketing of merriment and conspicuous consumption, it is hard for diaspora Hindus not to feel left out, lacking, or deprived, and to become hyperaware of their minority status.[14] This is especially true for the children of immigrants who have integrated and who are painfully aware of gift exchanges in schools and classrooms before Christmas and the plethora of presents that Christian classmates have received (either after Christmas vacation is over or by observing the curbside evidence the day after Christmas). Christian classmates are stupefied that their "poor" and "downtrodden" Hindu friends have not received any gifts (confirming unfortunate stereotypes about poverty in India), and (seemingly delinquent) Hindu parents are forced to answer

12. Although it is certainly the case that not all people who identify themselves as Christians in North America are comfortable with the model of Christmas that has been, and is, heralded by the media, this capitalist/commercial model is the one with which most Diaspora Hindus are familiar.

13. Blumenfeld, "Christian Privilege and the Promotion of 'Secular' and Not-so 'Secular' Mainline Christianity in Public Schooling and in the Larger Society," *Equity and Excellence in Education* 39 (2006) 195–210.

14. For parallels in the Jewish community, see June Andrews Horowitz "Negotiating Couplehood: The Process of Resolving the December Dilemma among Interfaith Couples," *Family Process* 38/3 (September 1999) 304.

to accusations of injustice and child abuse from their confused children, many of whom have assimilated into mainstream American culture or have achieved some degree of bi-cultural competence, and whose sentiments are confirmed from watching the original animated version of "How the Grinch Stole Christmas."[15]

Hindu families and communities are forced to confront these issues annually and the impact is unavoidable. Joshi explains: "Faced with Christian normalcy and feeling the normal childhood yearning to fit in with peers, many [Hindu, Muslim, and Sikh] students were embarrassed to be associated with their own families and ethnic communities. Some avoided learning about their home religions."[16] How have Hindus responded to these demands and complexities? Has it facilitated the assimilation of the second generation?

The December Dilemma for Jews and Hindus

Such complexities are not new in North America, and all immigrant communities have addressed related issues to some degree, though not all have had to address religious ones. Jews in North America, for example, who immigrated in greater numbers in the mid nineteenth century, have faced similar issues of acculturation and assimilation that are also exemplified during the confluence of Christmas and Hanukah. In her 1971 article titled "the December Dilemma," Esther Jacobsen Tucker bemoans the sale of "A Hanukah menorah in the shape of a Christmas Tree" and worries about the subversion of the meaning and devaluing of Hanukah.[17] Regarding the particular timing of Hanukah, Lawrence Hoffman writes: "To be sure, my Jewish festival of Chanukah, which falls about the same time as Christmas, is now being hyped as a sort of Jewish equivalent—as in 'Chanukah bushes.' It doesn't matter when Chanukah falls. Since it is pegged to the Hebrew calendar, it may occur any time from late November to late December. Regardless of which it

15. This 1966 animation of Dr. Seuss's illustrated children's story appears predictably on American television during the Christmas season.

16. Khyati Joshi, "Because I Had a Turban," *Teaching Tolerance* 32 (2007) 46.

17. See, for example, Esther Jacobsen Tucker's amusing and informative piece, aptly titled "The December Dilemma," *Reconstructionist* 37/9 (1971) 16–20.

is, people wish me a "happy holiday" around December 25, as if real holidays ought to happen then.[18]

Jewish communities have responded to this dilemma in a variety of different ways that has indexed, in part, the degree to which Jews have acculturated, assimilated, and integrated, into the religious fabric of America. Joselit writes: "At different times and in different circumstances, the [American Jews] were given to ignoring, retaining, modifying, adapting, inventing, reappropriating, and reconstructing tradition."[19] In order to appease their children some Jews, for example, sought to give greater importance to Chanukah and to change gift exchange from symbolic to actual. One result of this form of acculturation has been a Chanukah retail industry with requisite gift giving to celebrate the rededication of the second temple in Jerusalem in 165 BCE by the Maccabees after its desecration by the Syrians.

All, however, have not embraced this. According to Joselit, "Many within the Jewish community lamented Chanukah's 'transfiguration' into a 'Jewish Christmas,' deriding both the process and the end product as a pallid and inappropriate imitation of non-Jewish practices or, worse still, as a 'back-door means to participation in a Christian festival.'"[20] There has thus been internal debate in the Jewish community in North America about the degree to which Jews should assimilate or integrate and, for some, Jews have had to reflect critically on the identity of Judaism and Jews and on the validity of establishing and accepting essential Jewish practices.[21]

Has the Hindu community in North America responded in similar ways to the norms of American culture? To what Blumenfeld refers to as "Christian privileging," namely "marginalizing and subordinating those who do not adhere to Christian faith traditions"?[22]

Hindus have responded to the challenges of living in American Christian-centric society in several ways. First, they have become

18. Lawrence Hoffman, "Being a Jew at Christmas Time," *Crosscurrents* (Fall 1992) 363.

19. Jenna Weissman Joselit, *The Wonders of America: Reinventing Jewish Culture, 1880–1950* (New York: Hill & Wang, 1994) 4.

20. Ibid., 241.

21. See, for example, the reflection on these issues in Tucker.

22. Blumenfeld, "Christian Privilege and the Promotion of 'Secular' and Not-so 'Secular' Mainline Christianity in Public Schooling and in the Larger Society," *Equity and Excellence in Education* 39 (2006) 195.

acculturated and have recontextualized Divali, a festival that occurs on the day of the new moon between mid-October and mid-November, as an opportunity to exchange gifts, as a pan-Indian celebration that serves as a unifying nationalist event, and as a celebration of the victory of "good" over "evil." Second, like those in the Jewish community mentioned by Tucker, some Hindus have embraced the practice of purchasing and decorating a "Christmas" tree, sometimes renamed by Hindus as "Holiday" tree.[23] This practice, which involves assimilation, includes the distribution of gifts on Christmas morning and may include a narrative about Christmas Eve, and accompanying references to Santa Claus. Third, diaspora Hindus have made visits to the Hindu temple an annual pilgrimage, both on Christmas Day and sometimes on New Year's Day. Fourth, some Hindus, as an act of acculturation or at times of separation, have adopted a celebration of the Hindu god Gaṇeśa, called "Pancha Ganapati," invented by Satguru Sivaya Subramuniyaswami, founder of the *Hinduism Today* magazine, as a response to, and substitute for, Christmas.

Divali in America

Divali (the Festival of the Garland of Lights) is a tradition that is celebrated by most Indians in the diaspora, regardless of religious, ethnic, regional, and other contextual differences. It is easily acculturated and recontextualized because so many Indian religious traditions share it, yet differ on the narratives associated with it. Jains, for example, celebrate Divali yet associate it with the achievement of *nirvāṇa* by the Mahāvīra.[24] Sikhs celebrate Divali as the liberation of Guru Hargobind from Gwalior where he had been imprisoned.[25] The differences among Hindus are largely regionally based. Some Hindus, for example, observe it as the celebration of the victory of Kṛṣṇa over the demon Nāraka, while others celebrate the return of Rāma, the divine protagonist of the

---

23. While the link between Christmas and the Christmas tree is relatively new, it has become a significant aniconic symbol of the birth of Christ in North America. By suggesting that there is a link I do not intend to make doctrinal claims about Christianity.

24. Paul Dundas, *The Jains*, Library of Religious Beliefs and Practices (London: Routledge, 1992) 217.

25. Hew McCleod, *Sikhism* (London: Penguin, 1997) 152.

Rāmāyaṇa, from fourteen years of exile.[26] The variation in its significance and origins makes it an ideal candidate for unifying Indians, for creating a new and more ecumenical narrative among Indians, and for framing an acceptable Indian nationalism. In this way, Indians in India have also had to acculturate and assimilate in response to the Divali practices and beliefs/narrative of the dominant Hindu group. When reflecting on the Hindu diaspora in Singapore Rakesh Rai and Chitra Sankaran explain, "At different times of the year, religious festivals and processions—*Diwali, Dusshera, Thaipusam* and *Vaisakhi* for example—would take centre-stage, reinvoking memories and re-affirming their collective connection to a remembered 'ancestral homeland.'"[27] While the other festivals have been celebrated throughout the Hindu diaspora, the malleability of the Divali narrative and its pan-Indian nature has made it syncretistic. Divali is thus especially useful as a method for diaspora Hindus to invent and institute an imagined community.[28]

The narrative that is often offered with the public in North America is that Divali is a celebration of good over evil. While thinking of Divali in terms of the dichotomy may seem, at first glance, somewhat useful since it places Hindu paradigms in a Christian context, exemplified in the symbolic language of the Gospel of John and the mainstream conceptions of Satan,[29] there is tremendous ambiguity in Hinduism concerning the nature and status of "evil" in light of the doctrine and mechanism of *karma.* In the Hindu world, agency is problematized given the tendency that an individual might have towards acting in a certain way—largely due to her/ his *prārabdha* (latent) *karma.* According to this perspective, one's choices are an amalgam of natural and contextual proclivities. Individuals are thus bound by *puṇya* (meritorious *karma*) and *pāpa* (demeritorious *karma*). What is popularly rendered as "evil" is merely the manifestation and exhibition of *pāpa karma.* No one, therefore, is inherently "evil" as may be the case in the Christian context. There is no "Satan" figure in Hinduism who motivates or lures the impressionable. While the appropriation of Christian language here

26. Julius Lipner, *Hindus: Their Religious Beliefs and Practices,* Library of Religious Beliefs and PRactices (London: Routledge, 1994) 295.

27. Rajesh Rai and Chitra Sankaran, "Religion and the South Asia Diaspora," *South Asian Diaspora* 3/1 (2011) 8.

28. For more on imagined communities, see Benedict Anderson's *Imagined Communities: Reflections on the Origin and Spread of Nationalism* (New York: Verso, 1983).

29. See John 1:5–9.

is certainly evidence of acculturation, it may also indicate assimilation, an "adaptation status in which individuals absorb the culture of the dominant group while they reject the norms of the heritage culture."[30]

As already mentioned, one Divali narrative pertains to the *Rāmāyaṇa* and celebrates the return of Rāma from exile and the defeat of Rāvana, the demon king, antagonist, and purportedly "evil" character.[31] But is Rāvana evil, as per the Christian paradigm? Evidence from Valmīki's paradigmatic retelling of the *Rāmāyaṇa* suggests otherwise. For example, Hānuman, the monkey devotee of Rama, admonishes Rāvana: "You, sir, are learned in righteousness and polity and have hoarded up a great treasure of asceticism. A wise man like you should not be holding the wife of another man against her will."[32] And, furthermore, and most relevant here, Hānuman explains the mechanism of Rāvana's *karma*: "The fruits of righteousness may not coexist with those of unrighteousness. Each one gives rise to its own fruits; and righteousness is unable to outweigh unrighteousness. There is no doubt that you, sir, have reaped the fruits of your early righteousness. But you must now swiftly suffer the consequences of your unrighteousness."[33] Clearly from these passages Rāvana is not "evil" and the triumph of Rama over Rāvana is not one of good over evil. Rather he is merely manifesting his *pāpa karma*.

Using the term *evil* and the dichotomy good/evil thus ignores these ambiguities and embraces the paradigms of the dominant religious culture, namely Christianity. Nonetheless, this Christian-perfumed narrative is acceptable to all Indians, whether they are religious or secular, and, perhaps equally importantly, it is acceptable to their Christian neighbors whose sensibilities agree with this simple (and simplistic) narrative. The nature of the Hindu narrative changes as a direct result of conversation, invited or otherwise, with Christianity.

30. Kim, "Acculturation and Enculturation of Asian Americans: A Primer," in *Asian American Psychology: Current Perspectives*, ed. Nita Tewari and Alvin N. Alvarez (New York: Psychology Press, 2009) 110.

31. This issue has also been examined in the mainstream media in India. See, for example, "Ravana: Evil Incarnate or Man of Virtue" by Jayanth Kumar Rath, *Hindustan Times* (October 4, 2008); online: http://www.hindustantimes.com/News-Feed/HTNEXTstories/Ravana-An-evil-incarnate-or-man-of-virtues/Article1-342317.aspx.

32. Vālmīki, *Rāmāyaṇa* 5.49.15. Translation from Robert Goldman and Sally J. Sutherland Goldman, *Rāmāyaṇa Book Five* (New York: New York University Press, 2006) 403.

33. Ibid., 5.49.29.

The juxtaposition and comparison of Divali with Christmas and the resultant morphing of Divali is both a product of Indian/Hindu imagination as well as those of non-Indian Christians. Acculturation and assimilation are enhanced and encouraged when the Christianized retelling is retold and confirmed by non-Hindus. Well-known Hollywood actress Julia Roberts, for example, compares Christmas and Divali stating that both "are festivals of lights, good spirits and death of evil."[34] Her comparison and approval is embraced by many Hindus and helps to further acculturate and assimilate Hinduism, to make it a more acceptable bulge on the American landscape.

This assimilation is intensified significantly when recent American presidents have participated directly or indirectly in Divali celebrations. In October 2011 President Obama, for example, wished all people a happy Divali and lit Divali lamps.[35] In his speech he explains, "Diwali is a time for gathering with family and friends and—as we experienced in India—celebrating with good food and dancing. It is also a time for contemplation and prayer that serves as a reminder of our obligations to our fellow human beings, especially the less fortunate."[36] He also offered an explanation that employs the already adapted version about the meaning of the holiday: "The holiday is also known as the 'festival of lights' and a traditional candle—or 'Diya'—is lit to symbolize the victory of light over darkness. It's also an occasion to share what one has with others who are less fortunate. Service—or 'seva'—to others is a key value of Diwali."[37]

In both these official proclamations and acknowledgements Obama has recontextualized Divali such that it coheres with mainstream American Christian sensibilities for Christmas, with American civil religion, and even with the narrative that helping a fellow American is a great American tradition.[38] Sharing with the less fortunate is not a key value

34. "Christmas & Diwali the Same: Julia Robets," *Hindustan Times* (November 3, 2010). Online: http://www.hindustantimes.com/Lifestyle/CelebWatch/Christmas-amp-Diwali-the-same-Julia-Roberts/Article1-621774.aspx/.

35. Matt Compton, "Diwali at the White House," *The White House Blog* (October 26, 2011), online: http://www.whitehouse.gov/blog/2011/10/26/diwali-white-house.

36. Ibid.

37. Paul Monteiro, "Marking Diwali at the White House," *The Office of Public Engagement Webpage* (October 27, 2011); online: http://www.whitehouse.gov/blog/2011/10/27/marking-diwali-white-house.

38. Online: http://www.time.com/time/magazine/article/0,9171,908900,00.html/.

in Divali, as Obama incorrectly suggests. It would appear that Divali, in Obama's eyes, shares a great deal with Christmas. The dominant narrative has thus supplanted any Hindu ones. Hindus who embrace this narrative have certainly become assimilated and absorbed into the culture of the dominant group while rejecting the norms of their heritage culture. While it is possible to add meanings without losing those that were part of the original tradition, in this case the original meaning has become less important than the new one. This is reminiscent of the phenomenon of the "Pizza Effect," first characterized by Swami Aghenanda Bharati in his article "The Hindu Renaissance and Its Apologetic Patterns," which is a reacculturation that occurs when cultural exports are reappropriated by the culture of origin.[39]

The relationship between the Hindu communities and Obama is mutually beneficial: both imagined communities and narratives are confirmed and conformed.[40] The end result is that Divali is officially acculturated and has become representative of an imagined American ideology and supportive of American civil religion.

Though Divali is a public festival in India, until recently it was celebrated in the privacy of homes and temples in North America. In light of its continued acculturation it has moved into the public eye.[41] Celebrants often hoard fireworks made available for Independence Day in America to be used during Divali parties which occur in suburban homes, Indian cultural centers, and the like.[42] They invite neighbors, colleagues, and local political dignitaries to observe and participate in the extravagant pyrotechnical event. With the recent increased population of students of Indian and Hindu origin in colleges and universities in North America, there have been equally elaborate and extravagant Divali celebrations, which are often among the most popular and well-attended events on campuses. Divali's popularity and prominence is

39. See Agehananda Bharati, "The Hindu Renaissance and its Apologetic Patterns," *Journal of Asian Studies* 29/2 (1970) 267–87.

40. See Prema A. Kurien, *A Place at the Multicultural Table: The Development of an American Hinduism* (New Brunswick, NJ: Rutgers University Press, 2007) 188–89, for more on Hinduism and the U.S. government.

41. See Henry Johnson with Guil Figgins "Diwali Downunder: Transforming and Performing Indian Tradition in Aotearoa/ New Zealand," in *Sociology of Diaspora: A Reader*, ed. A. K. Sahoo and B. Maharaj (Jaipur, India: Rawat, 2007) 2:913–37.

42. See Sunil Bhatia's *American Karma: Race, Culture, and Identity in the Indian Diaspora*, Qualitative Studies in Psychology (New York: New York University Press, 2007) for an ethnographic account of a Divali party in Connecticut.

further evident in its mention in American sitcoms, such as in "The Office" and in "Outsourced."[43] Do Hindu watchers of these programs learn Hindu doctrine from these retellings? Are these instances of the so-called Pizza Effect? Clearly an Americanized Divali has become part of the American religious and popular landscape. In some cases, then, Hindu Americans have successfully integrated Divali into American culture.

Hindu Christmas

Many diaspora Hindus now celebrate Christmas. Inundated by Christmas cheer and pressured by their children, Christmas has become part of the lives of diaspora Hindus. Ironically, the importance given to Christmas can become an opportunity for acculturation.

Some have decided to celebrate Christmas superficially, as if it were a mere commercial holiday. They purchase Christmas trees, gifts for one another, and encourage their children to enjoy the Santa Claus myth, in the same way that they may encourage their children to enjoy (and benefit from) the tooth-fairy myth. They classify Christmas as a secular, commercial festival for children, in the same way that Father's Day, for example, is a festival for fathers.[44] Many non-Hindus in America too have come to see the celebration of Christmas as a secular American winter festival. They call the tree a "Holiday tree" despite the fact that the only related holy day is Christmas.

Some argue, though, that it is impossible to make Christmas secular and that claims that it is secular are evidence of the degree to which one has become acculturated, if not assimilated. Other Hindus utilize Hindu, specifically Vaiṣṇava, theology to reconfigure, reinvent, and reimagine Christmas to be a Hindu tradition. Vaiṣṇavas believe that Viṣṇu has *avatāras* (incarnations which appear and act in the world in order to defend *dharma* and his devotees. They characterize Christ to be an *avatāra* of Viṣṇu, thus rendering Christianity just another sect

---

43. *The Office*, season 3, episode 6: "Diwali." Directed by Miguel Arteta. Written by Mindy Kaling. First aired on NBC Nov. 2, 2006. *Outsourced*, season 1, episode 8: "Home for the Diwalidays." Directed by Linda Mendoza. Witten by Vera Santamaria. First aired on NBC, Nov. 11, 2010.

44. Thanks to Peter Haas for this language.

of Hinduism.[45] In the same way that the North American narrative of Divali is suffused with Christian motifs, the narrative of Christmas is impregnated with Hindu sensibilities.

It is not surprising that the retail world has reacted to these potential markets in North America by making available Hindu ornaments that can be used on Christmas trees.[46] Though the intended consumer of these "Hindu-flavored" tree ornaments is likely non-Indian, New Age, yoga practitioners, it overlaps with diaspora Hindu families. The Christmas tree, a popular symbol of Christmas in North America, though, is reappropriated by Hindus and spiced with Hindu flavors. The retail world confirms and acculturates this Hindu Christmas, paralleling the confirmation conferred by actress Julia Roberts and President Obama of the modified Divali.

No matter what narrative is given about the relevance of Christmas (secular, Vaiṣṇava, or what have you) many Hindu parents believe that they have to accept and celebrate it given the pressures of their immediate surroundings and the shame that they will likely feel if they do not permit their children to have fun in these prescribed ways. Christmas celebration has become another *dharmic* obligation.

Christmas Pilgrimages

Many diaspora Hindus make it a point to visit the local Hindu temple on Christmas Day. For those who see Christ as an *avatāra* of Viṣṇu, a trip to the temple is no different than a visit to celebrate Kṛṣṇa-*jāmṣṭamī* (the birth of Kṛṣṇa). For those who do not believe Christ to be a part of the Hindu pantheon their trip to the temple may be a chance to take advantage of the vacation day and to teach their children about Hinduism. Some temples, such as the Pasadena Hindu Temple, include Christmas Day in their "Schedule of Events" even though no special

---

45. This hermeneutical strategy seems structurally similar to the theological strategy deemed *inklusivismus* by Paul Hacker. Hacker characterized *inklusivismus* as a strategy by which religious traditions were subsumed under one religious tradition, namely Advaita Vedānta. See Hacker, "Religiöse Toleranz and Intoleranz im Hinduismus," in *Kleine Schriften*, ed. L. Schmithausen (Wiesbaden: Steiner, 1978).

46. See "Best Hindu Decoations for Christmas." Online: http://www.squidoo.com/hindu-decorations-christmas/. Trees, of course, are not by themselves Christian symbols.

event is planned.[47] The inclusion of a Christian holiday in their calendar signifies its importance in diaspora Hinduism and signifies the degree to which acculturation has occurred.

This adaptation (or acceptance) of the Gregorian, rather than Hindu, calendar is further exemplified by the importance that is placed in many temples on New Year's Day (according to the Gregorian calendar). Many Hindu temples in North America include celebrations of the god Gaṇeśa on New Year's Day. Gaṇeśa is especially appropriate as he is worshipped as the god of beginnings and obstructions. Such temple events exemplify acculturation.

In both of these cases, Hindus make pilgrimages to the local temples on days that are holy in the Gregorian/Christian calendar, and certainly not in the Hindu calendar. Gregorian New Year's Day has been accepted, to some extent, as the beginning of the New Year and as a moment when the Hindu god Gaṇeśa should be revered. Though this may merely be a convenient moment for Hindus, its inclusion in the temple calendars suggests that Hindus are obliged to recognize Christmas and New Year.

Removing the Obstacle of Christmas by Replacing It

It is not without irony that Pancha Ganapati, a festival celebrating the god Gaṇeśa, who is responsible for both the placement and removal of obstacles, has been invented and prescribed by Satguru Savaii Subramuniyaswami, founder of the *Hinduism Today* magazine, as a response to and substitute for Christmas and as a method for resisting the dominant culture.[48] The authors of the webpage titled "Pancha Ganapati: The Family Festival of Giving," in which this celebration is promoted states: "Think of this as the Hindu Christmas, a modern winter holiday full of family-centered happenings, but with five days of gifts for the kids, not one. From December 21 to 25 Hindus worship Lord Ganeśa, the elephant-headed Lord of culture and new beginnings. Family members work to mend past mistakes and bring Gnash's blessings of joy and

47. Online: http://www.pasadenahindutemple.com/10.html. This site also includes "Thanks giving" [sic] in this list.

48. *Hinduism Today* is a publication of the Himalayan Academy in Kauai, Hawaii. Though this publication is not located in North America, it is read by many members of the North American Hindu Diaspora. It is for this reason that I think that it can be included in this study.

harmony into five realms of their life, a wider circle each day: family, friends, associates, culture and religion."[49] Information about the origins of Pancha Ganapati is also addressed:

> How did this festival begin? In 1985, Satguru Sivaya Subramuni-
> yaswami, founder of HINDUISM TODAY magazine, conceived
> of and introduced Pancha Ganapati during the thirty days of the
> Markali Pillaiyar home festival. With five days of gift giving at
> the time of year when Christmas is widely celebrated, it offers
> Hindu families, especially in the West, a meaningful way to par-
> ticipate in the holiday season without compromising their Hin-
> du values. Their children receive and give gifts just as do their
> non-Hindu friends. Adults can fulfill the season's social custom
> of sharing gifts and greeting cards, as well as accepting them
> from relatives, neighbors, friends and business associates.[50]

And, finally, the site includes explicit directions on how to keep the celebration Hindu: "How is the Hindu tone maintained? While the fes-
tival occurs at Christmas time, Hindus celebrate Pancha Ganapati in a distinctly Hindu way, without Christmas trees, Santa Claus or symbols of other religions. Greeting cards are Indian in design and content, con-
veying Hindu wisdom from scripture. Hindu music and bhajans take the place of Christmas carols."[51] Pancha Ganapati is the archetypal ex-
ample of the intersection between interreligious dialogue and cultural adaptation and change as it pertains to the Hindu diaspora in North America.[52] The cultural adaptation is kept to a minimum and the event is made into an opportunity to inculcate and thus maintain what are imagined to be the social norms of Hinduism.

Conclusion

In this brief paper I have employed stipulative terminology to examine the changes that have occurred and are continuing to occur in North American Hinduism and the North American Hindu diaspora. As suggested, these changes were and are the product of a number of different

49. http://www.hinduismtoday.com/modules/wfchannel/index.php?wfc_cid=48.

50. Ibid.

51. Ibid.

52. Paul Younger offers other examples of similar responses in "Guyana: Invented Traditions," in his *New Homelands: Hindu Communities in Mauritius, Guyana, Trinidad, South Africa, Fiji, and East Africa* (Oxford: Oxford University Press, 2010) 55–94.

factors, internal and external. North American Hinduism has had to unify and amalgamate what was diverse and divergent. Pan-Hindu and pan-Indian festivals have arisen from imagined commonality. North American Hinduism has also had to accommodate itself to a largely Christian world, leading to an incorporation of a Christian sense of time (the Gregorian calendar, marking Saturday or Sunday as a day for worship, and so on).

The most significant changes have occurred because of the centrality of Christmas in North American public and civic culture. The Christmas "holidays" forced most Hindus in America to be or become public about their private lives and beliefs. Hindus have adopted some Christmas customs in what they believe to be secular forms (Holiday tree), have incorporated Christmas beliefs into Hinduism (Christ as an *avatāra* of Viṣṇu), and still others have invented a parallel Hindu festival to be celebrated at or around the same time (Pancha Ganapati).

Such changes are inevitable and unavoidable for any immigrant community, religiously based or otherwise. Transnationality and globalization have made these challenges and changes all the more complex. Now that members of the North American Hindu diaspora can maintain ties with India with great ease and can participate in Hindu celebrations in India "virtually," the changes that were demanded of, and initiated by, earlier immigrants are not so pressing or crucial. That is, technological changes made possible by the internet such as Skype and other voice over Internet Protocol services have allowed diaspora Hindus to enjoy festivities in real-time in India, thus making the actual distances less relevant and less impeding. In this connection, it may be that the internet makes possible and permits a more globalized form of Hinduism that need not always adapt to the nuances of the local culture within which the immigrant Hindu finds her-/himself.

5

The Misplaced Immediacy of Christian-Buddhist Dialogue

James Heisig

Buddhist-Christian dialogue stands at the frontier of Christian history as a radical test of Christianity's commitment to inculturation. Like much of interreligious dialogue, it has thrown a *sabot* into the theological apparatus, confounding its foundations with new questions about the uniqueness of its revealed truths, the inspired authority of its sacred texts, and the universality of its way of salvation. For Buddhist participants in the dialogue, at least here in East Asia, most of this confusion has seemed peculiarly Christian and has not perturbed their self-understanding in the least. For the most part, they have stood by as theologians scrambled to make room for claims of other religions inconsistent with their own and to grant legitimacy to a worldview that did not include the essentials of their own creed. The Buddhist enthusiasm in discussions with theologians was by and large caught up in the adventure of appropriating the moral and religious insight hidden in the rich but unfamiliar coding of Christian symbols, not in rethinking any claims to uniqueness or universality in a religiously plural world.

Although the numbers of Buddhist participants in the Buddhist-Christian dialogue have never been very large and the dialogue has attracted more suspicion than encouragement by the Buddhist establishment, the spirit of tolerance among this new breed of Christian thinkers struggling to shake free of old apologetic habits and to grapple with questions of common interest was seen as a welcome change. Yet as the methodological preoccupations of the theologians grew more intense, the welcome began to wear thin. As precepts, guidelines, norms, and entire theologies of dialogue were being packaged in the academies of the West, differences of opinion among Christian thinkers on the aims and limits of interreligious encounter hardened and then splintered in every direction. Nothing of the sort took place in the Buddhist world in East Asia, where it looked as if Christianity had become distracted from what had seemed such a promising turn of history. The *sabotage* of the dialogue had in fact left Buddhists out of the picture; contact with the territory suffocated under a surfeit of maps. Christian theology came to be so overwhelmed by derivative debates over the nature of doctrinal truth claims in a religiously plural world that the immediacy of *contact* had been displaced by *talk about contact*. In time, it became clear to Buddhist participants that the Christians preferred to talk to themselves.

From the time Christian dialogue with Buddhism in East Asia began in earnest, around the early 1980s, there was no want of critics complaining that it was a Christian initiative of suspicious motivation.[1] The courtesy of putting "Buddhist" before "Christian" did little to cloak which side was in control of the venture. Everyone agreed it was a Christian initiative, but the critics were mostly wrong about the motives. Fears of covert evangelization turned out to be unfounded. Fears of inequity were not. As a test of Christian theology's commitment to inculturation, the Buddhist-Christian dialogue has failed in a way none of us could have foreseen: the Christian encounter with Buddhist thought was brought to its knees as the idea of dialogue itself was transformed into an *ancilla theologiae*. Advances in epistemological and hermeneutical awareness have frightened many Buddhist partners away from the dialogue with Christian theologians precisely because they have been experienced as an expropriation of the agenda of dialogue. Still, the

---

1. This concern among Buddhists was voiced already from the inaugural meeting of the Inter-Religio network of dialogue centers in East Asia, which took place in 1982 (see *Inter-Religio* 1), and was repeated frequently at future meetings. For example, in 1983 there was a campaign among the Buddhist in Thailand against Christian overtures to dialogue, accusing it of masquerading a new wave of evangelization. See Seri Phongphit, "The Impact of Interreligious Encounter in Thailand," *Inter-Religio* 5 (1984) 16–21.

stream of theological publications in the West taking up some aspect of the dialogue with Buddhism in East Asia flows on merrily, apparently oblivious of the fact that the wellspring has been reduced to a dribble.

In the case of Japan, the Buddhist-Christian dialogue has managed to survive in philosophical forums where equity is determined primarily by the religious neutrality of the context. Normative questions of the role of comparative theology, theology of religions, and scriptural reasoning do not get in the way for the simple reason that they rarely arise.[2] No doubt, most of the participants are out of touch with the ongoing theological debates of the West, and those who are in touch tend not to take part in the forums or otherwise engage directly in dialogue. The creativity and timeliness of those debates is undeniable, but so is their overwhelmingly Christian stamp. I have drawn two meters of books on theological hermeneutics from our library shelves at the Nanzan Center for Religion and Culture in Nagoya and find that none of them take seriously the kind of interreligious dialogue going on in Japan, and that where they do, the dialogue is stripped of its qualification as "interreligious." This is unfortunate not only because the experience in Japan differs from the dominant approach of interreligious research in the Christian West, but also because the fate of the dialogue within Japan is another unacknowledged sign of what I am calling the misplaced immediacy of the dialogue in general.

Formal Buddhist-Christian dialogue in Japan has diminished over the past several years in the number of participants and the regularity of the encounters. Dialogues focused on Christian theological questions, as I have said, have been few and inconsequential. Now even dialogues set up on a more neutral, philosophical basis, which were once at the forefront of interreligious dialogue around the world, are witnessing the ageing of its participants and a marked disinterest among the younger generation of Buddhist and Christians. The academic output on interreligious matters in countries with a strong Christian culture has continued to flourish. The reasons for this are not entirely clear, but the overall

2. One need only peruse the published papers of the past thirty years of meetings of the Japan Society for Buddhist-Christian Studies to realize how different the agenda of this, the principal and most longstanding series of dialogues I know of in East Asia, has been. The ten volumes of dialogue with the principal religious traditions of Japan published by the Nanzan Institute for Religion and Culture show a similar tendency to shift the focus away from the questions that preoccupy Christian theologians in the West.

impression is that as far as a revised self-understanding of the respective traditions is concerned, formal dialogue has borne too little intellectual fruit outside of the meetings themselves.

Meantime, overtly religious philosophy and philosophy of religion have experienced a resurgence in Japan. Despite the decline of these approaches in Europe and the Americas, the reevaluation of native Japanese philosophical resources has resurrected the question of whether the way the lines between philosophy and religion have been drawn in the modern era are not a function of a different, and on this point alien, religious culture. The renaissance of Japanese philosophy, which at first stimulated interreligious dialogue, has since turned away from it. This cannot be attributed to a lack of interest in religious questions or to a lack of openness to other traditions. Few intellectual environments can compare with Japan in terms of religious pluralism and tolerance. Waning interest in established religion, except as a guarantee of the continuation of traditional rituals, is not a satisfying explanation either. True, interreligious gatherings abroad continue to include representatives of the Buddhist establishment, but their repercussions in Japan are all but nonexistent. The assumption behind the attendance is that the dialogue is a foreign initiative that requires a Japanese presence, little more. The reasons, I am persuaded, lie in a rupture of contact with the immediacy of dialogue, exacerbated by a theological deadlock over understanding the emergence of religiously plural cultures in predominantly Christian countries.

The Immediacy of Dialogue

I understand the dialogue between religions in its immediacy to be something as different from political dialogue as it is from theology, comparative religions, global ethics, or even the "lofty, unbiased, and benevolent search for the truth." [3] Put the other way around, it is precisely in mediating the dialogue through these frameworks that its distinctive quality gets bleared. Unless a more immediate dialogue can be

---

3. The remark is from Jan Van Bragt, with whose writings on the Buddhist-Christian dialogue I am in full sympathy. See my essay on his thought, "The Pontifical Thought of Jan Van Bragt," *Bulletin of the Nanzan Institute for Religion and Culture* 32 (2008) 9–27.

acknowledged as the primary analog, dialogue in the derivative senses has no choice but to define itself in analogy to some other paradigm.

Let us be clear about this primary analog. It is not the kind of Buddhist-Christian dialogue that takes place between particular religious traditions represented by trained specialists but between persons brought up in a particular tradition and driven by the need to bring a fuller religious inheritance to bear on questions of existential or moral importance to them. This definitive, if generally informal, dialogue is not the outreach of an established faith or its believers to those of other faiths, for whatever motives. It is a response to a mood or inclination brewing in society and culture at large, concentrated in individuals of different faiths who join to give it expression and explore its meaning. It has its own authority which can never be expropriated in full by the institutional keepers of tradition. The particular authority of dialogue shows up precisely in the cracks that tradition experiences under the constant pressure of lived religious culture. To bring dialogue under the control of existing institutions or doctrinal systems while ignoring this immediacy is to risk twisting it to other purposes. Thus, as far as religious establishments and doctrinal tradition are concerned, the "aims" of dialogue need always to be grounded in an immediate dialogue that is "aimless" yet committed.

It may be naïve to suppose that Christianity or Buddhism could survive at the borderlands of this primary dialogue without historically and culturally specified institutional "centers." But formal dialogue between them carried out in a prearranged setting with invited participants must not be seen as the defining model of dialogue. It is rather one more expression of the felt need to pose religious questions against a backdrop wider than one's own tradition. The primary analog for formal dialogue does not entail the obligation to insure that one's own tradition is properly explained to those who do not share it, let alone an engagement with apologetics at points of difference. To borrow the expression of the Japanese philosopher Tanabe Hajime, the defining impulse of interreligious dialogue is to discuss matters of common concern as a *gewordener Buddhist* or a *gewordener Christ,* and at the same time as a *werdender Christ* or a *werdender Buddhist.* Brought up in the fund of symbols, ideas, and moral values of Christianity and having appropriated them to one degree of another, we dialogue with our Buddhist counterparts in order to wrestle with those concerns, and in the process mutually to enlarge the range of symbols, ideas, and values that make our questioning reasonable. Institutional affiliations and loyalties, defense of the faith, and even the search for a shared foundation of beliefs are preoccupations that are not necessary to, and generally do not even belong to, the primary analog of dialog.

I do not mean that that concerns with fidelity and orthodoxy are not significant, but only that they represent only part of Buddhist-Christian dialogue *subsequently and analogically*. Similarly, religious politics may dictate, for example, disinviting Tibetan Buddhists from an interreligious gathering that includes mainland Chinese Buddhists. But by that very gesture, whatever other value it may have, the gathering has ceased to be a primary analog of interreligious dialogue. We may go yet a step further and claim that if the "question of common interest" is an interinstitutional problem that requires cool heads for a joint decision, after the model of political arbitration by specialists, and if the success of the dialogue is measured in terms of a specific outcome, it is no longer interreligious dialogue in the immediate sense. Similarly, a religious fundamentalism committed to the conquest of false beliefs may restrain itself before unbelievers for the sake of politeness, but it cannot enter into dialogue in the definitive sense we are speaking of here. At the same time, simply checking one's religious identity at the door in the name of intellectual objectivity may enhance the intellectual objectivity of the discussion, but it forfeits the interreligious quality of the dialogue.

The primary analog of dialogue, therefore, is rational discussion without a specific goal and without the burden of institutional pressure, but *with* the religious identity of the participating individuals. It is, in a word, a voyage of discovery, not a voyage to an identifiable destination. This is the immediacy of dialogue that has been devalued under the weight of Christian theology and the severity of the limits imposed on Christianity's adaptation to other religious cultures. Religion is always and forever encoded in its culture and epoch. Any pretense to transcend them works against the religious impulse no less forcefully than the ecclesiastical bureaucracies it wrestles with for the control of orthodoxy. Insofar as the primary dialogue fades out of the picture, it no longer marks a frontier for the church to pursue but is exiled to the realms of the *extra ecclesiam* where it is tolerated and permitted, with varying degrees of magnanimity, by those pursuing dialogue enthusiastically as well as by those apprehensive of its consequences.

Theologies of Religion and Dialogue

The misplaced immediacy of the Buddhist-Christian dialogue, as I have already suggested, is due in part to the nature of the Christian theological involvement. During the last decades of the twentieth century, the Buddhist-Christian dialogue held out the promise of stimulating Christian theology and slowly disarming it of its cultural bias, but creative efforts in this direction have been marginalized and diluted by theoreticians of dialogue. While the latter flourish, dialogue founders. It will not do to lay too much blame on theology, but as Joseph O'Leary has stated, "Theology of religions since Rahner's time has continued to theorize about the religions with little effort to become directly acquainted with them, as if the religions posed a threat to the neatness and completeness of the theologian's metaphysical system."[4] The slow dissolution of the theology of liberation is instructive in this regard. All too often the assumption has been that theology is the *method* and liberation the *object* to which the method is applied. In the case of Catholic theology, this means reflecting on social "liberation" by means of scripture and the doctrinal tradition. The sources of the tradition are thus brought to bear on the meaning, ethical consequences, ritual expression, pastoral praxis, and spiritual dimensions of the liberation of human beings from social injustice. The wider aim is for theology to help believers incorporate the theory and practice of liberation into their religious faith and at the same time to help infuse ongoing efforts at liberation with Christian values.

I am not saying that the assumption is wrong, only that it is half of the picture. To borrow an image from Xenophon, theological reflection in liberation represents the *anabasis* of Christianity's self-understanding as it strains itself in the march up country in order to extend its tradition into new territory. The equally, if not more important task is the *katabasis,* the return home. Far from being a retreat, the *katabasis* is a reversal of method and object, of the subduer and subdued. The theory and praxis of liberation there serve as a *method* to be applied to theology as its *object*. In other words, the theology of liberation is a theology reformed by reflection on liberation. Only with a new hermeneutic for reading scripture and tradition is the theology of liberation complete and its first phase justified. The same may be said not only of the way

4. Joseph O'Leary, "Rahner and Religions," *The Japan Mission Journal* 64 (2010) 62.

philosophy finds in religion "something that resists becoming an object of philosophy,"[5] but also of the way philosophy and theology deal with women, ecology, suffering, and in fact a whole range of other moral and cultural concerns. In the case of the theology of religions, the reflexive nature of the process brings us to the core of the challenge that the dialogue among religions presents to Christianity's commitment to inculturation: arrived at the outermost frontier of its *anabasis* into contemporary cultures, it can no longer return home unreformed.

The choice to exclude this second aspect to the theology of religions, as is evident in the tendencies of Joseph Ratzinger's *Dominus Jesus*, is a death notice to the immediacy of dialogue among religions. The opinions expressed there reflect earlier assertions issued in his role as Prefect of the Congregation for the Doctrine of the Faith, making it clear that no scriptures of any religion at any time in history may be considered "divine revelation" or even "complimentary" to the Old and New Testaments; that no other religion by itself is a way of salvation or even "complementary" to the salvation gained through the Christian church due to their "omissions, insufficiencies, and errors regarding fundamental truths about God, man, and the world."[6] Clearly this goes beyond merely preserving one's own tradition to voice a condemnation that prohibits theology from learning anything essential from any other religion, at any time or any place. If there is no essential enrichment to be had from another religion, if the only nobility of doctrines that are not Christian is that granted them by Christianity, and if the only

5. I refer here to Paul Tillich's 1925 essay on "The Philosophy of Religion," in James L. Adams, ed. and trans., *What Is Religion?* (New York: Harper & Row, 1973). It was not until his last published lecture that Tillich recognized that the same can be said of the objects of theological reflection, and that this would entail a complete recasting of his own systematic theology "The Significance of the History of Religions for the Systematic Theologian," in J. C. Bräur, ed., *The Future of Religions* (New York: Harper & Row, 1966).

6. Taken from "Notification on the book *Toward a Christian Theology of Religious Pluralism* (Maryknoll, NY: Orbis, 1997), by Father Jacques Dupuis, SJ," signed, Joseph Cardinal Ratzinger. I would note a curious remark by the Benedictine, Pierre de Béthune, a leading figure in the inter-monastic exchange since 1978. After explaining at length the enrichment that his encounter with Buddhist monks has brought to his own life as a monk, he adds this surprising proviso: "I have never regarded it as an opportunity to *complement* or even replace my Christian faith," corroborating the language of the Notification—one has to assume—with tongue in cheek. Pierre François de Belthune, *Interreligious Hospitality: The Fulfillment of Dialogue*, Monastic Interreligious Dialogue Sereis (Collegeville, MN: Liturgical, 2010) 158; emphasis added.

true religious culture is that of Western, theological Christianity, then dialogue has no choice but to become a camouflage for apologetics.

More often, however, the exclusion functions as a tacit assumption, even in approaches that claim to be open to relativity in the truth claims of religion. Thus, we have generous approaches as different as of Paul Martinson, Paul Knitter, and Jacques Dupuis, for each of whom Christian theology is allowed to carry out its reflection on other religions pretty much as before except that it relinquishes its claim to being the one and only ultimately valid truth. The effort to justify, on theological grounds, the truth of other religions as something independent of the truth of the Christian faith is not unimportant, but neither does it stop at the methodological level. When it comes to including competing truth claims in the reformulation of Christian ideas, the grounds for appeal take leave of received theological method. This undertaking, as we see in the work of thinkers like Raimon Panikkar, Yagi Seiichi, John Keenan, and Frank Clooney, is a far more exacting task. It involves actually wrestling with the texts and incorporating ways of thought from other religions that in their turn may also require the restoration of neglected elements of the Western theological tradition, even elements previously dismissed as heretical. These efforts do not impede the dialogue or fit it out with the kind of theological constraints that an exclusionist approach does. Still, they do not yet qualify as dialogue in the strict sense we have been using it here. They are not even necessarily a response to actual dialogue as much as they are a response to the challenge that the dialogue poses to theology. In a word, we need to relocate the theology of religions outside of the dialogue altogether in order to understand the full import of the questions that the dialogue presents to the ongoing inculturation of the established churches.

The "theology of dialogue," that is, theological reflection on inter-religious dialogue, presents a special problem and raises an important question about the way the theology of religions is conducted. Insofar as theological theories of dialogue stress the virtues and spiritual discipline needed to encounter the "other," there is every reason to draw on the more benevolent side of Christian spirituality in order to disown the dark side of intolerance and persecution that has accompanied it throughout history. Obviously, such reflection is primarily a matter for the Christian believer and offers no divinely sanctioned right to impose its newly elaborated guidelines on those of other faiths. The grounds for asserting such guidelines may be advanced in general philosophical terms, but their religious foundations need to be discovered in each faith on the grounds of its own tradition. In other words, Christian theology can talk about *Christian* motives for encountering other religions in dialogue, but it has no claim to authority where other partners in dialogue are concerned. What is more, there is no basis for taking the step from prescribing the motives for interreligious dialogue to prescribing its content, as natural as that step may seem theologically. During dialogue in the primary and immediate sense, theological norms are suspended, and are restored again only after the dialogue is over. If not, dialogue becomes the maidservant of theology.

Even as theology of religions continues to assert its own norms into the dialogue, which happens far more than is recognized, much of its academic output is composed with no experience in dialogue and often no demonstrable concern with the actual teachings and interpretative methods of the religions being theologized about. Incompetence in the contents of other religions is not even necessarily held to be an obstacle to the study of the theology of religions.[7] In this respect, the kind of thinking that Catherine Cornille has promoted with her series of Christian Commentaries on Non-Christian Texts is an indispensable ingredient in the advance of the theology of religions. But the venture remains incomplete until these commentaries reach those who hold the text as authoritative, and until Christian sacred texts are in turn commented on by those who do not hold them as authoritative. This, as I understand it, is the burden of the "scriptural reasoning" initiative that has been active for the past several years at the fringes of theological academia.

Here again, the dormancy of the theological establishment in Japan and its neighboring countries is altogether regrettable. In the same way that the arrival of Buddhism crystallized the native religions of

7. For example, pontifical faculties of theologies in Japan, where theology of religions has been required by Rome for over twenty-five years, have not been allowed to include study of the actual living religions around them from believers or experts, but only from Catholic theologians whose task is to instruct them on the proper way to reflect on and assess those religions. When I personally met with the authorities at the Roman Curia a few years ago to suggest that this amounts to teaching prejudice, there was agreement that the regulations were illogical, but none of those in attendance would take the responsibility to grant us permission to rectify the situation in our faculty. I was advised to pursue the matter through correspondence, but two years of follow-up letters to the Curia were never answered or even acknowledged.

Japan into the pursuit of a unified identity, the arrival of Christianity has raised to the surface numerous questions submerged in Japanese religion. Buddhism has absorbed a great deal of Shinto and native spirituality ever since Kūkai in the ninth century, just as Shinto has tried at times to identify Buddhism as a stage in its own evolution. The fact that Christianity has failed to take this historical process into its self-understanding is in large part responsible for its irrelevance in Japanese society today. Its theoretical tolerance of the religious world that surrounds has proved impotent, and its practical intolerance has not, since the seventeenth century defined itself as more than simple prejudice.

Be that as it may, Buddhist participants in the Buddhist-Christian dialogue face a quite different set of problems. Their encounters with Christians have been marginalized by the Buddhist establishment in East Asia and—apart from notable comments by the Dalai Lama—received little formal recognition by religious leaders. Even those Buddhists who have been most active have rarely stepped up to take the leadership in their own communities where the dialogue has met with indifference or wariness of the institutional agenda of the Christian churches. Indeed, I cannot ever recall having heard a criticism that the Buddhist representatives were usurping the agenda, controlling the logic, defining the questions unilaterally, or laying down norms for what it means to "enter into dialogue." It is not enough that Christian participants take seriously complaints that the dialogue is not truly Buddhist-Christian, but "Christian Buddhist-Christian." The very fact that there is nothing like a Buddhology of non-Buddhist religions, nor any noticeable movement in such a direction, should by itself alert Christian theologians to the question of whether their methods are as essential to the dialogue as they have thought them to be. By the same token, one would expect Buddhists engaged with Christian theologians to be far more forthright than they have been in lamenting the lopsided concentration on "doctrinal" questions to the detriment of the rest of the Buddhist reality.[8]

Nevertheless, the nonformal, immediate, and for the most part theologically naive dialogue between Buddhist and Christians, which I have proposed as the primary analog of the dialogue, shows little sign

---

8. The response of Buddhists in the West is another matter, which I am not qualified to take up. Indications are that many of the criticisms raised in this paper have struck a promising chord in those circles. See, for example, John Makransky, "Thoughts on Why, How, and What Buddhists Can Learn from Christian Theologians," *Buddhist-Christian Studies* 31 (2011) 119–33.

of demise and strictures by the Christian establishment have had no visible impact on it.[9] The number of Christian believers who have avoided dialogue out of fidelity to theological positions taken by the churches is negligible, whereas the number of those who have discovered the urge to dialogue with Buddhist beliefs through contact with believers continues to grow. This fact alone underscores the derivative nature of interinstitutional dialogue among religions. It reminds us of the existential roots of such encounters, the locus from which they ascend and to which they must, in the end, descend if they are to be complete.

Dialogue and Culture

It is time we returned to the problem with which we began: the relationship between the Buddhist-Christian dialogue and Christianity's commitment to inculturation. The first thing to notice is how freely the methods and vocabularies of theologies of culture and inculturation on the one hand, and theologies of religion and dialogue on the other, flow in and out of each other. It is hard to distinguish one from the other in practice, and much of the argumentation and wording can be transposed from one to the other with little or no loss of meaning. This suggests that a level of abstraction has been achieved at which foreign cultures and religions can become objects of theological reflection at one remove from the particular relationship between them. This process of distillation is particularly noticeable in attempts to lay out the available "models" for choosing interreligious dialogue, multiple belonging, inculturation, evangelization, and the like. Reliance on this

9. From the other side, the theological captivity of the dialogue has produced a considerable literature of inbred debate that has lost touch with the religious reality that has set them their questions. I would single out, as an extreme example of this, the more than 600 pages of *Catholic Engagement with World Religions,* edited by Karl Becker and Ilaria Moralia (Maryknoll, NY: Orbis, 2010). I could not find a single reference to the role that the Christian faithful at large played in bringing interreligious dialogue to the attention of theologians. Nor is there any mention of theologically informed Catholic monastics like the Benedictine Pierre de Béthune (see note 6), the Trappists Jef Boeckmans and Kevin Hunt, or the Jesuits Enomiya la Salle and Robert Kennedy who became teachers of Zen or even *rōshi* while remaining in their own religious communities. Nor is any theological weight given to the formal inter-monastic exchange that has been going on since the late 1970s. The closest the volume comes is a brief treatment of the mystical tradition, but this is the mysticism of literature, not of living experience. Some Asian counterparts are listed, but without any reference to the content of their thought.

kind of categorical distinction easily overlooks the fact that the claim to comprehensiveness rests on a reification of the lived, concrete reality it has set out to explain.

I leave this charge in its crude, uncritical form to raise a still more general point. It seems to me that the slide into secondary, mediated dialogue—one grounded in talk about dialogue—belongs to a wider malaise that theology has contracted from the intellectual mood of the age: the habit of allowing criticism and critique of criticism to obstruct the primacy of performance. It is an example of what George Steiner aptly termed "life in a secondary city,"[10] where interpretation loses sight of its performative nature. As a translation of meaning from one frame of reference to another, the critical quality of interpretation is not limited to the deliberate application of a set of epistemological tools to selected texts. It is inherent in all cultural activity, however hermeneutically unconscious it may be. Interpretation is also an act of moral engagement of the present context with a received past. There is no such thing as a "pure," timeless, epoch-transcending content, let along any context-free, neutral standpoint from which it can be identified and evaluated. Nor is there any universally accessible "experience" from a variety of interpretations may be said to emerge. Experience is already itself an act of interpretation, perhaps closer to music to than to literary criticism, as Steiner suggests, because it is *only* accessible through interpretation and at the same time renders language about it lame.

Interreligious dialogue is primarily a form of performative interpretation, whose moral dimension is broader than the search for cooperation among different religions in tackling one or the other ethical crisis. Even where that moral dimension is left out of the discussion, it is already present in the implicit goal of instructing the faithful with regard to the plurality of religious traditions. In this regard, it has to be said that reactions in the Christian West *against* a positive assessment of this plurality have been the more effective. Compared with the epistemological sophistication of theologies of dialogue, fundamentalism and Biblical literalism would not seem to have a leg to stand on, and yet by all accounts they are running better among the faithful than the methodologically advocates of dialogue are. And yet both sides share the same misplacement of the dialogue by making it primarily an object

10. See the opening essay of his *Real Presences: Is There Anything in What We Say?* (London: Faber & Faber, 1989).

of theological examination, refusing true primacy of place to the masses of "uneducated faithful" whose turn to other religions for inspiration was what prompted theology towards dialogue in the first place. The "immediacy" of that dialogical temper is the result of too many factors to allow for a simple judgment. It may indeed be closer to the "spirit of the age" than the theological responses seem to be, but it is not for that reason above criticism. Dialogue reflected about, for all the fervor and timeliness of the encounters, is still cut and dried in comparison to the strange flowers that have been growing wild in the carefully tended gardens of Christian tradition. Unless this new religious music is accepted as a living interpretation of that tradition, it cannot be understood for what it is, let alone appropriated into theological discourse.

Accordingly, when we say that the immediacy of dialogue can only be present in the dialogue itself, not in reflection on the nature, rules, and limits of dialogue, we mean that it is a critical performance of faith that precedes theological judgment on its content and norms of engagement. The inverting of this precedence, as we have been suggesting, has infected the dialogue as well as the larger Christian commitment to inculturation.

The notion of "culture" undergirding the theologies of inculturation that began in earnest in the 1980s was not substantially different from that found in missiologies a generation before or in the documents of Vatican II. As with earlier sociologies and anthropologies, a culture was understood as a cluster of inherited patterns of thought, speech, symbols, and customs more or less circumscribed geographically and often identified with a particular "people." This notion of culture has had a relatively short and stormy history, even shorter than the notion of religion, but one thing has remained fairly consistent in both: the closer one approached the "center" of the circle, the more stable and recognizable the patterns; the further out one ventured to the periphery, the weaker and less representative these patterns. Intercultural exchange was therefore pursued as close to the respective centers as possible. A Japanese Nō troupe from Tokyo performing at Lincoln Center in New York, an exhibition of Picasso's paintings in the National Gallery of Moscow—these were the paradigms of "cultural" events. This model carried over to the study of foreign cultures and languages, whose authenticity was guaranteed by certified specialists trained in authorized "centers."

Theologians devoted to the "incarnation" of the gospel in cultures not informed by Judeo-Christian tradition accepted this substantialist model of culture in the attempt to establish points of contact and identify the "accidental" elements of Christian culture that could be adapted or dispensed with in order to make their beliefs more universally understood. While the debates about where to draw the line between the essential and the incidental were going on, the steady flow of foreign migrants into the Christian West was slowly eroding the last vestiges of the *Kulturkreis* mentality. The shock of cultural pluralism gave way to awareness that the idea of a center had been an ideological fiction all along. The violence wrought by this fiction on the "dominant culture's" denomination of "minorities," "subcultures," "countercultures," and otherwise "marginalized groups" found a voice whose echoes are with us still. The idea of a culture-neutral gospel adaptable to a variety of cultures has already been laid to rest, and efforts to identify a *Leitkultur* that could be fused with a gospel *kerygma*—again on the model of two "core" elements in encounter—have not proved enough to salvage it.

The dialogue among religions belongs to this story of the Christian notion of culture waking up from its ideological slumber. Buddhist-Christian encounters, it should be recalled, were also structured on the assumption of exchange between "centers." Those unlearned in their tradition, and eventually those untutored in the proper etiquette and disposition for dialogue, were not held to be sufficiently "representative" of the Christian reality. Ironically, time and again in international congresses, serious theologians and Christian scholars of religion entered freely into dialogue with Buddhist partners whose true Christian counterparts would have failed the qualification. This, in itself, made it plain that the hermeneutical problem was predominantly of Christian origin. In any case, the place of dialogue in the secondary city was assumed to be the principal judge of what constituted authentic dialogue.

The primary analogue of intercultural transformation, I mean to argue, lies at the periphery, on the borderlands where the boundaries of one world touch on another. It matters little that we no longer think of this image exclusively in geographical terms, that multicultural experience has come down to the neighborhood level. The point is the same: those who straddle customs, languages, and modes of perceiving reality through marriage, work, and the activities of daily life *as a lived habit* are better suited as immediate paradigms of intercultural encounter than events staged as temporary experiences.

The same may be said of the religious aspects of cultural life. Consideration of ways in which intercultural habits are formed and transformed may not address the kind of questions that formalized interreligious dialogue is concerned with, but it remains the primary analog for consideration of what dialogue should be. The irony is that those who control the norms for Buddhist-Christian dialogue exclude the de facto dialogue that has always been part of religion's interaction with culture, well beyond the reach of institutional strictures. This exclusion occurs for basically the same reasons that made dialogue unacceptable to religious authorities in the past, namely, maintaining the semblance of control. Formal dialogue is drained of its life's blood when it forgets that dialogue at the periphery is where interreligious culture is to be sought in its immediacy.

In its adaptation to Japanese culture, for example, Christianity has yet to shake free of its colonial mission. Obviously, when a religion as profoundly marked as Christianity is by the peculiar conditions of the history that produced it is universalized and transported to a culture with a historical structure as different as Japan's, it is apt to become highly abstract and frozen in time. That is, unless there is a reorientation as profound at the original orientation. To exempt a culture's religious past from the inculturation of Christianity is to trivialize the culture as a whole. The dialogue with Buddhism has held out this challenge to Christianity in Japan and its neighboring countries of East Asia. When the dialogue loses sight of this challenge, as I believe it now has, it risks becoming no less misplaced than dialogue in the West.

Critics of "multiple belonging," both Christian and Buddhist, tend to take as their prime exemplar those who inhabit the center and trifle with the periphery, insisting on monogamy as the only form of fidelity to a tradition. Religious promiscuity has always been closer to the historical reality. The idea of "block-universe" traditions belongs to the same ideological fiction that has sustained dominant cultures in their domination. Christians who claim multiple belonging for themselves are quick to point this out, but they tend to take themselves as examples to demonstrate the point, and often to retain the bias of the encounter of cultural "centers." For example, Panikkar's idea of "intra-religious dialogue" as the encounter in one's own person of two traditions of which one has previously established historical-critical consciousness sets the standard beyond the reach of the masses of people who actually lead multireligious lives in the immediacy of their lives. Religious genius that he was, he was not a paradigm for interreligious, intercultural existence. The primary analogy can never be intellectuals who engage in dialogue with themselves or with others in the rarefied air of academic debate. It must be the habitual *mestizaje* of ordinary believers who have been thrown by birth or circumstances into an environment at the periphery in which they cannot breathe if they identify exclusively with any of the dominant traditions as defined by their centers.[11] When formal dialogue loses touch with these roots in ordinary, immediate, interreligious experience, it has no way out of the methodological obsessions that bring Buddhist-Christian encounters to a standstill.

Buddhism and Dialogue

The Buddhist neglect of second-level reflection on dialogue is not all for the best. Christian formulations of the problem may be alien and hard to reconcile with a very different religious reality, but there is much in the Buddhist tradition to support a self-critical approach to the encounter with other religions. Here again, it is principally the Christian partners in dialogue who have called on Buddhist concepts to broaden their understanding of the effect of dialogue on Christian tradition. But the challenge has not been met by Buddhist attempts at a hermeneutics of dialogue, and it is not my place to predict what shape it would take. What we can say is that the principal focus would fall not on doctrine or on distinction between faith and belief. There are indeed some Buddhist establishments that have tethered their image to a preoccupation with orthodoxy, but the weight of the tradition clearly falls on ritual and awakened praxis.

Hints of a Christian hope for a Buddhist initiative are present in the turn of some Christian proponents of religious pluralism away from doctrinal questions and towards a religiously motivated collaboration for the welfare of the human community and the natural environment.

11. For an attempt to carry the sociology of creolized identity over into the religious sphere, see Xavier Gravend-Tirole, "Double Commitment: *Or* The Case for Religious *Mestizaje* (Creolization)," in D. Cheetham, U. Winkler, O. Leirvik, and J. Gruber, eds., *Interreligious Hermeneutics in Pluralistic Europe: Between Texts and People*, Currents of Encounter 40 (Amsterdam: Rodopi, 2011) 415–35.

Even where this is not tied to a pragmatic norm for the evaluation of competing truth claims, that question lurks continually in the background. A comment by Joseph Ratzinger on the back cover of the recently published Italian translation of Paul Knitter's *Without Buddha I Could Not be a Christian* makes the point sharply: "Knitter opts for a radical simplification of interreligious dialogue and grounds it on a single principle that ends up rendering it ineffective: the primacy of orthopraxis over orthodoxy. This way of elevating praxis above knowledge is clearly a Marxist legacy."[12] Given the content of the book, the conclusion is academically irresponsible, but it typifies the kind of emotional reaction that the word *praxis* elicits among those in the Christian establishment obsessed with the rational defense of orthodoxy. Despite Knitter's attempts over more than twenty years to shift the focus of interreligious dialogue over to praxis, his ideas have constantly been dragged back into the debate over orthodoxy. Part of the reason is that Knitter himself has used his approach as a critique of orthodoxy, without which orthopraxis cannot get a foothold in theology. Buddhist praxis comes at praxis from a different perspective, one that does not get stalled in defending truth-claims.

There is, of course, no guarantee that a Buddhist theory of dialogue would do a better job of keeping in touch with what we have been calling the immediacy of religious experience, and insofar as it does not, it could not be expected to fare much better than Christian theories. But at least its commitment to do so is at the heart of its teachings, as is its commitment to keep the rational exposition of its doctrines subservient to the awakened mind and its incarnation in present history.

Critical strategies for restoring theories of dialogue and inculturation in a religiously plural world to their primary analog (one thinks at once of Lindbeck's view of religion as a comprehensive cultural-linguistic framework, and Ricoeur's arguments against the bias that sacred texts can only be rightly understood by religious insiders) are not absent, but in the Christian world they end up becoming the focus of methodological debate more often than they stimulate the restoration. It seems naïve to suppose that similar strategies from the Buddhist side would meet with any better reception. Still, the task remains: if we could accurately describe the place in which people stand when they live and

12. *Senza Buddha non potrei essere cristiano*, trans. Paolo Zanna (Rome: Fazi, 2011).

act interreligiously and interculturally, and accept this description as a primary analog, we would be in a better position to reflect on how the pursuit of norms to govern the dialogue between religion and culture has become estranged from its lived reality. Obviously, the mere fact of interreligious or intercultural *mestizaje*, however widespread, does not qualify it as normative for any of the religions or cultures involved. It is simply a foundational datum for interpreting and evaluating points at which the spirit of the age has overflowed the banks of tradition. At the same time, the more successful the aberration from prevailing norms, the more those norms themselves need to be included as an object of reform. This is in fact what we see going on in Christian theology. The problem is that the rationale for reforming the tradition has systematically excluded that foundational datum from the discussion and replaced it with philosophical principles, biblical hermeneutics, and theological debate.

If Buddhist participants in the Christian-Buddhist dialogue are to be encouraged to contribute their own understanding of a culturally and religiously plural society, they will have to come to grips more critically with the religious reality of our times and question more seriously the Christian captivity of the whole adventure. I am reminded that nearly thirty years ago, when Nishitani Keiji discussed with us the publication of the English translation of his book *Religion and Nothingness*, he was adamant that it not be submitted to a theological publishing house. His fear was that the association of a book of predominantly Buddhist religious philosophy with Christian theology would weaken its message. Try as we might to persuade him otherwise, he was put off by the kinds of questions that prevailed among the many Western theologians who came to "dialogue" with him. He was more interested in serious philosophers but also in religious-minded people who could no longer identify with the institutional religion in which they had been brought up. Buddhism, he often said, had become a kind of "geological relic" that had drifted away from the vital religious concerns of the modern world. It needed its own "theology," which could only be built from the ground of contemporary experience up. To judge from the current state of the Buddhist-Christian dialogue, it is hard to see that things have changed much since then.

If I have abridged the historical complexities of Christian theology's encounter with other religions almost to the point of caricature, and have broadsided its misplacement of interreligious immediacy, it is only because I feared that entering directly into the methodological fray would eclipse the simple conviction I meant to express. The recasting of Christianity's self-understanding in a religiously plural world is not a mere intellectual exercise to be taken or left *ad libitum*. To borrow an expression from William James, it is a live, forced, and momentous option—at all levels of Christianity. And even if the number of those who respond is small and the religious establishment continues to eye the fruits of interreligious dialogue with distrust, interreligious habits have already taken root among growing numbers of believers who otherwise count themselves faithful to the Christian tradition. After all, it was there that that the interreligious dialogue began and there that Christianity's future lies.

6

Does a Bodhi Tree Grow in Brooklyn?

The U.S. Engagement with Buddhism

Thomas P. Kasulis

In discussing the relation between religion and culture, I will focus my discussion on Zen Buddhism and Christianity in the United States. Before I do so, however, I want to stress something both obvious and easily forgotten. When teaching my Introduction to Comparative Religion lecture course, I typically begin with a comment like this:

> This is a course in world religions. Yet, it is crucial to remember there is no such thing as Buddhism; there is no such thing as Judaism; there is no such thing as Islam; there is no such thing as Hinduism; there is no such thing as Christianity. Religions do not believe this or that; nor do they do this or that. Religions are neither things nor agents. Yet, although there is no such thing as Buddhism, Judaism, Islam, Hinduism, or Christianity, there are Buddhists; there are Jews; there are Muslims; there are Hindus; and there are Christians. In those religious people, not in the abstraction of religion, we find real beliefs, intentions, and agency. The "study of religion" is, in the final analysis, a misnomer. We will be studying not religions, but religious people. And what do we know about people? They each exist in specific times and places and in social and political contexts. They have native languages and are enculturated in native cultures or are acculturated into diasporic cultures. In any sampling of religious people

(and for some religions in this course our sampling will be in the hundreds of millions or even more than a billion), we will find some religious people—like all people—who are primarily intellectual and others more pragmatic; some who depend on creativity and others on regimen; some with the intention to transform themselves spiritually and others with the intention of controlling others; some who are hypercritical and others who are uncritically accepting; some who are duplicitous and others who are sincere. To study religion is to develop a lens through which we can see the variety within our common humanity.

Since I teach in a department of comparative (cultural) studies, I sometimes give the same spiel about culture. Culture is not a thing either; it has no inherent agency. Rather, it is a repertoire of possible forms of thinking and acting made available to people through enculturation. It lays out the field or stage on which people play out their language games or enact their forms of life. Culture is intrinsically no more an agent or domineering force of oppression than is the chessboard in a game of chess. A chessboard delimits some possibilities, but it does so in a way that leaves open an infinity of options to be chosen freely by the true agent, the chess player. Culture no more determines behavior than the chessboard determines the outcome of the chess match. If culture becomes oppressive, the oppression lies in the oppressive people within that cultural context, not the culture itself.

Preliminary Comment on Culture, Religion, Agency, and Borrowing

The point of these rather simplistic preliminary comments is to remind us that we are not considering the interaction of two agencies—religion and culture. Religions do not borrow from each other. Religious *people* borrow. And perhaps *borrow* is not even the right word. It can be seriously misleading to think of religion as an object with defined boundaries across which ideas or practices can be borrowed or lent. At its worst this is more than misleading—it is an Abrahamic assumption about inside and outside deriving from the notion of a jealous God who commanded: "*I* am the Lord thy God; thou salt not have strange gods before me."[1] One thing I do *not* want to do in this discussion is to let such

1. Outside the Abrahamic sphere, traditions are more likely either to deny there is

an assumption from the outset color our analysis of religion, culture, and borrowing. I have met many Americans over the years who identify themselves as "Zen Catholics" or "Jewish Zen Buddhists," for example. To overlook that phenomenon is to miss something, maybe even to miss *the* point: religious people determine their own religious identities from the array of possibilities available in their spiritual culture. Furthermore, the notion of borrowing suggests a level of self-consciousness among religious people that I suspect does not fit the experience of most of them. It is often only the act of historical scholarship that, after objectifying or even essentializing the domains of particular religions, identifies what idea, value, or practice went from where to where.

An analogy may help. Consider the cooking technique of stir-frying as part of present-day American cuisine. Where did it come from? Chinese cooking probably. But is that exactly right? The other day I watched a short-order cook scramble up for my breakfast some corned-beef hash. Is not hash a kind of stir-frying? Was its technique borrowed from China? Or consider the Japanese dish sukiyaki. Most Japanese eat it as a native food without realizing it historically originated as an attempt to mimic the stews introduced by the Portuguese in the sixteenth-century (and given the reality that most of the ingredients for Portuguese stew—tomatoes, potatoes, beef, and some seasonings—were unavailable in Japan). Of course, the Japanese did have their own kind of noodle soups (themselves developed through interaction with Korea and China) that served as the base out of which they developed the new concoction.

What do the food analogies show? For stir-frying, it shows that the basic technique had a correlate in US cooking before the Chinese influence, but it was a little-used technique. The impact of Chinese cooking was to present an extraordinary variety of what could be stir-fried. Undeniably, stir-frying would not have gained its popularity in American cuisine without the Chinese influence, but it was not something totally new that Chinese cooking introduced to the United States. It resonated with something already there in US cooking, but took it to a much more sophisticated and wide-ranging set of applications. Similarly, sukiyaki might not have been invented without the exposure to Portuguese stew, but again, sukiyaki came about by taking something already well known

---

a god (or any single central God) or, if there is such a God, to claim the "strange gods" are really manifestaions of that central God.

to Japanese cooking and expanding it to an application never conceived in Japan before the interchange with Western people and their cooking.

My proposal is that we think of this resonance-with-something-already-there as a paradigm for religious borrowing. Rather than thinking of borrowing across religions as being like my going to your house and borrowing a power tool I do not have, it is more like my seeing you use a tool in better way or for a different purpose than what I have used my similar tool for. Or perhaps I do borrow your tool, but not because it is something totally unlike what I have, but rather a better, more useful version of it. For example, I may have only general use drill bits for my power drill, but I borrow yours with the counter-sink feature.

Both points discussed thus far may help us understand intercultural and religious dialogue. To begin, religions do not engage in dialogue; religious people do. And people maintain their religious identity if and only if it somehow works for them, not because they accept its ideology whole cloth. So, interreligious dialogue is between people who are examining "what works for me in my tradition" with "what works for you in your tradition." Interreligious dialogue should be more like cooking for each other than sharing recipes. It is about showing through embodied engagement, not intellectual repartee. When this point is forgotten, when dialogue is construed in terms of comparing catechisms as holistic bodies of doctrine, interreligious dialogue often fails, shifting its focus from embodied beliefs and practices to disembodied analyses of rarefied philosophical positions such as kenotic theology or Mādhayamika dialectic, many of which are often totally unknown to most adherents of the religious tradition to which they belong. Merely because intellectuals are the ones who most commonly engage in interreligious dialogue, it does not follow that the dialogue need restrict itself to the intellectual dimensions of religion. Interreligious dialogue should, above all, be interpersonal dialogue with all of the richness the term "personal" evokes.

Moreover, for interreligious dialogue to get off the ground there must be a common base from which to take off. Dialogue cannot begin with an assumption of absolute otherness. There has to be something in the other that is familiar. Absolute otherness is seldom engaging since it presents no challenge to my way of thinking, feeling, and acting. What is totally other is ignored or discounted as being bizarre or just plain crazy. What is truly unnerving is not the encounter with absolute otherness, but instead, the encounter with what seems familiar but which is somehow also deeply alien. The response to the unnerving can be either rationalized aggression or intriguing fascination. The former leads to dogmatic apologetics or inquisitional aggression; the latter to dialogue. If we think in terms of Rudolf Otto's *mysterium tremendum* and *mysterium fascinans*, we can say there is something holy in true dialogue with people from other religious traditions.

Therefore, in thinking about Zen Buddhism and US culture I will draw for my narrative and analysis from my own experience with people who in one way or another have negotiated, or inspired others to negotiate, their identities as being Buddhist while also being American or even while also being Christian American. I am not interested in how Buddhism influenced American culture or how American culture influenced Buddhism. That puts the question in the wrong way, yielding to the assumptions of scholars who make a profession of drawing boundaries that distinguish one religion from another or one culture from another. (Think of old-style comparative religion textbooks that have global maps with each country colored according to its dominant religion.) My focus is not religion or culture, but rather, religiously encultured people. If Buddhism has influenced American Christian culture, it is because Buddhists not Buddhism influenced the thinking and values of a significant number of American Christians. And if American Christian culture has influenced Buddhism, it is because American Christians not Christianity influenced the thinking and values of a significant number of Buddhists. The narrative that captures my attention, therefore, is not one of the Dharma coming to the West nor of the Westernization of the Buddhist Dharma. Instead, it is the story of D. T. Suzuki, Thich Nhat Hanh, and the Dalai Lama; the story of Alan Watts, Henry Steel Olcott, Thomas Merton, and Robert Thurman. In truth, however, the real "data" behind my narrative are not even those well-known names, but instead, my interpersonal encounters over the past four decades among those who have been influenced by such people. I have engaged many who have negotiated their Buddhist, Christian, and American identities in a variety of ways. I have witnessed some of both their struggles and their moments of insight and transformation. I have myself been influenced by them and, if their own accounts are true, some of them have been influenced by me.

Let us now turn to the analysis itself. For the sake of historical context, let us first consider how Zen Buddhist and American identities came to coexist in a significant number of people. For the sake of brevity, we will focus on the paramount figure in this interreligious, cross-cultural encounter, D. T. Suzuki (1870–1966), and the changing ways readers in the English-speaking world have read his works over the past century.

D. T. Suzuki: A Century of His Readers

A corpus of writings as well as interpersonal exchanges can spur an interest in a particular kind of interreligious or cross-cultural dialogue. A case in point is the way the writings (and later the personal interactions) of D. T. Suzuki made Zen Buddhism a household word in the United States. In evaluating the impact of a book or series of books, however, it is important to remember that reading itself is dialogical: the agency of influence resides in the book-as-read, not the book itself. Here again, Suzuki is particularly relevant since the evaluation and impact of his writings shifted from generation to generation. This shift is especially noteworthy because when I look with detachment at Suzuki's writings, I am struck by how remarkably little he modified his basic message over more than six decades of writing in English.[2] His diction shifted slightly—the word *unconscious* appears in his works only after his personal encounters with C. G. Jung and Erich Fromm, for example. The topics varied a bit as well. Yet, he never really changed his mind about the nature of Zen and its importance. By comparison, when I examine the cultural impact of those writings, the ways they were interpreted by his English readers, I am also struck by its variation over time. That is, while Suzuki's basic message remained constant, the readings of his work differed remarkably. The readers' evaluations ranged from the starry-eyed admiration of the Beats and hippies of the '50s and '60s to the cold, reptilian stare of the cynical postmodern critical theorists of the '80s and '90s. As a preliminary to analyzing Buddhist American identities and the nature of interreligious dialogue in the US context, let us consider a few major features of these different readings of Suzuki over time.[3]

2. For this discussion, we need not consider Suzuki's writings in Japanese since they have had minimal impact on the formation of American Buddhism.

3. For a somewhat more complete overview, see my "Reading D. T. Suzuki Today," *The Eastern Buddhist* 38/1&2 (2007) 41–57. The purpose of that essay was to analyze how Suzuki has been read over the years by his English-reading audiences as a prelude to my suggestion about how we might fruitfully read Suzuki today.

1897–1909: Reading Suzuki as Bearer of the Wisdom of the East

Suzuki first came to the United States at the invitation of Paul Carus, the philosopher-publisher who founded both the Open Court Press and the journal *The Monist.* Carus had really wanted to bring to Illinois Suzuki's Zen Master, Shaku Sōen (1859–1919), whom he had met at the World Parliament of Religions in 1893, but the master was too busy with responsibilities at home in Japan and so he recommended Suzuki. After serving as Carus's assistant translator, houseboy, and gardener for a few years, Suzuki's own agenda eventually became clear—to introduce Zen Buddhism to the West and, when the time was right, to proselytize it. One challenge he faced was that most of the English-reading audience at that time was aware of only one kind of Buddhism, the early Buddhism of India preserved in texts written in Pali and assumed to be still alive as the Southeast Asian Theravāda tradition. This lacuna in knowledge about northern forms of Buddhism reflects the agenda of the British Pali Text Society and the London Buddhist Society. Many major members of the two learned societies, for whatever personal reasons, presented Buddhism more as a philosophy than a religion.[4] The Pali tradition better fit that interpretation than did the Mahāyāna tradition with its marvelous imagery and elaborate rituals.

Suzuki responded by publishing in 1909 his *Outlines of Mahāyāna Buddhism* (1907). It opened with the following statement of purpose: "The object of this book is twofold: (1) To refute the many wrong opinions which are entertained among Western critics concerning the fundamental teachings of Mahāyāna Buddhism; (2) To awake interest among scholars of comparative religion in the development of the religious sentiment and faith as exemplified by the growth of one of the most powerful spiritual forces in the world. The book is therefore at once popular and scholarly."[5] The references to "sentiment," "faith," and

---

4. Based on hints in their own writings, we can surmise that some wanted to avoid direct conflict with Christianity (one could be philosophically Buddhist while still being a practicing Presbyterian or Anglican, presumably). Others were anti-ritualism or mistrustful of religious faith. Moreover, it is worth recalling that "the study of religion" was in its infancy as a field of scholarship at the time and it was the philosophers—including such notables as Hegel, Schopenhauer, Nietzsche, and the American Transcendentalists—who played a major role in bringing Buddhism to the notice of a Western audience.

5. Daisetz Teitaro Suzuki, *Outlines of Mahayana Buddhism* (Chicago: Open Court 1908) v.

the "spiritual" suggest Suzuki's efforts to undermine the then current Western impression that Buddhism is more a philosophy than a religion. Yet, given his audience's jittery attitude toward religion, he did not want to trigger any unnecessary negative reactions.[6] So, how could he advocate the spiritual side of Zen without using the word *religion*?

At around this time, Suzuki read William James's *Varieties of Religious Experience* (1902) and he found a way out of his dilemma. He would disagree with the interpretation of Zen as philosophy by characterizing enlightenment as an *experience* rather than a kind of *knowledge*. Up to then, Buddhism in the English-speaking world had been characterized mainly as aiming toward an insight into the way things are without dependence on faith, institutions, or ritual. Even Suzuki's Zen master, Shaku Sōen (1859–1919), had made efforts in his lecture at the 1893 World Parliament of Religions to claim Buddhism was more "scientific" than mystical or religious. He focused his remarks on the general idea of conditioned co-production as an empirical understanding of the causal interconnectedness among all things without reference to any transcendent agency. By contrast, Suzuki seemed to favor James's quasi-phenomenological focus on consciousness and the experiential dimension of spiritual life. By this process, the idea of "Zen experience" came to be central in the English-language discourse about enlightenment. It was Suzuki's way to disassociate Zen from rational analysis, empiricism, and philosophical speculation.

With his emphasis on spiritual experience, Suzuki eventually found conversation partners among theologians (like Alan Watts and Thomas Merton), humanistic psychologists (like Erich Fromm and C. G. Jung), and literary writers (like the Beats). Western philosophers generally showed disinterest or even disdain. From this point onward, among the Buddhist traditions practiced in the West in the first half of the twentieth century, Theravāda came to be associated with enlightenment as knowledge, Zen with enlightenment as experience.[7]

6. Until neologisms were created in the late nineteenth century to translate the Western words *philosophy* and *religion*, the distinction did not exist in the Japanese language. Hence, the whole controversy had to seem a bit odd to Suzuki at the time.

7. There are dozens of English books published over the past 120 years on Indian, southeast Asian, and Tibetan Buddhism that have the word "Buddhism" and "knowledge" in the title. I know of only one with "Zen" and "knowledge" in the title, however: Andrew Cooper's *IQ: The Zen of Knowledge* (Prince George, British Columbia: Urizen, 2002). It is a book of poetry. Conversely, there are at least a couple of dozen books in

Back in Japan during the 1920s and '30s: Reading Suzuki in the Era of the New Japan

Suzuki's writings gained even more attention in the English-speaking West after he returned to Japan and founded the English-language journal, *The Eastern Buddhist*, under the auspices of The Eastern (rather than London) Buddhist Society. With its victories over both Russia and China as well as its fortunate alliances in the First World War, Japan had by the 1920s assumed a prominent role in world politics and many Western readers wanted to know more about the culture. Suzuki responded with his three volumes of *Essays on Zen Buddhism* (1927, 1933, 1934). More significant, knowing the Western fascination with the Japanese arts dating back to the mid-nineteenth century, Suzuki wrote his highly influential *Zen in Japanese Culture* in 1938.[8] The book even included a chapter on the martial arts and the Western audience generally came to accept Suzuki's thesis that Japanese culture was rooted in Zen. The result was that through Suzuki, there was an increasingly strong link in the Western readers' mind among Zen, religious experience, and aesthetic expression. [9] After 1939 until the end of the war, Suzuki published only works in Japanese for a Japanese audience. After the war, however, he would appeal to a new generation of American readers.

English with both "Zen" and "experience" in the title.

8. This first edition was published in Japan by the Eastern Buddhist Society as *Zen Buddhism and Its Influence on Japanese Culture*. In the 1959 edition, Princeton University Press published a new version for the Bollingen Foundation with the title *Zen and Japanese Culture*.

9. This is not to imply that there was no link between Rinzai Zen Buddhism and the arts before Suzuki. Starting in the Japanese late medieval period, Rinzai Zen adapted from China the Five Mountain system of institutional affiliation and ranking. The "Five Mountain" temples became centers for studying the (mainly Chinese style) arts of poetry, calligraphy, landscape painting, and garden design. This artistic turn was less the influence of Zen on the arts (as Suzuki claimed) than a rebirth of Japanese admiration for things Chinese. It was, in fact, this same cultural shift in focus that led to the blossoming of Japanese Confucian studies starting in the late fifteenth and early sixteenth centuries. This led to the "conversion" of many Zen monks and samurai Zen laity to Confucianism.

The 1950s, '60s, and '70s: Reading Suzuki in the Age of Aquarius

Suspicious of the military-industrial complex, disdainful of the anonymity in the corporate world, and incensed over the Vietnam War, the disaffected youth of the hippie, beat, and student counterculture generation sought the freedom of self-expression and creativity. They devoured the republication of Suzuki's books in English.[10] Whereas the postwar G. I. Bill had brought a generation of former soldiers to the university as a means to securing a good career, their children went to college to "find themselves." The students of the '60s did not seek knowledge of facts and skills of a trade, but rather, the wisdom and ecstasy found in "peak experiences." Suzuki's characterization of Zen fit the bill perfectly and he added to his corpus of writings books dealing with the training of the Zen monk, the creative artistic expression of Zen Master Sengai, a comparison of Buddhist and Christian mysticism, and an encounter with the humanistic psychoanalysis of Erich Fromm.[11]

The Zen Boom of the 1960s inspired a generation of college students and many took up the practice of meditation in newly founded Zen centers, a number led by masters from Japan. Some of the more serious student-practitioners (Gary Snyder being an early example) found their way to Japan in the 1960s and '70s to engage Japanese Zen in its home environs: to practice Zen in the monastery and to study Buddhism in the university. This pilgrimage spawned a brood of American and European buddhologists. Many of those buddhologists returned

---

10. Oddly enough, Suzuki's rise in popularity also served the interests of that same military-industrial complex and capitalist elite. By 1950, Japan's relation to the United States had shifted from archenemy to loyal economic and political ally. The United States held up Japan as the capitalist and democratic success story of East Asia in opposition to both China and North Korea, as well as being an anchor in the US Pacific Rim defense policy. In that context, Suzuki served as a cultural ambassador of the new image of Japan: aesthetic rather than military, creative rather than dogmatic, with just a smattering of the enigmatic to keep the old-guard orientalism alive. This American image of Japan flourished until its rise as a major economic competitor in the late 1970s when it became viewed as a culture of "economic animals" working as "robots" in service to "Japan Incorporated," a resurrection in some ways of Arthur Koestler's 1960 critique in *The Lotus and the Robot* (London: Hutchinson, 1960). Of course, by then, Suzuki had been dead for a decade.

11. The earliest psychoanalytic connection for Suzuki's writings was C. G. Jung's foreword to the German translation of *Introduction to Zen Buddhism* in 1939. When the new English edition came out in 1949, it included Jung's foreword.

from Japan disillusioned, however. They had discovered that the Zen monastic trainees were mostly sons of Zen temple priests who, often against their preference, were undergoing training so they could carry on the family business. Finding present-day Zen on its deathbed as a vibrant tradition, the Westerners hoped they could resuscitate it in the New World according to the models of the "Golden Age of Zen" in the Chinese Tang period (the seventh through ninth centuries). In the Japanese universities, the Western buddhologists-in-training delved into the historical and philological study of that Golden Age, the treasure trove of texts from which Suzuki had drawn so many lively and fascinating paradigms. They were shocked to discover that at the turn of the twentieth century a stash of ancient Chinese Buddhist texts had been uncovered in the caves of Dunhuang, many containing incontrovertible evidence that Zen's traditional history of the Golden Age was concocted in the later Sung period to serve the agenda of a new social and religious elite. Even more disturbing, they learned that Suzuki himself knew those texts even as he continued to repeat the old yarns of events that never occurred.[12] So, the young American scholars concluded, Suzuki was not merely ill informed; he was a con man who had duped them with fool's gold. This naturally led to a new reading of Suzuki.

The 1980s and '90s, and Up to the Present: The Hermeneutics of Resentment

In the 1980s and '90s several American buddhologists wrote scholarly works debunking the traditional history of Zen and its modern proponents such as D. T. Suzuki.[13] Suzuki's writings dropped out of the

12. In fact, Suzuki wrote in his preface to *Essays in Zen Buddhism: Second Series* that he would soon undertake the writing of *Essays in Zen Buddhism: Fourth Series* and that the general topic of that work would be to incorporate new information about the history of Zen as gleaned from the Dunhuang texts. "In the Fourth Series I intend to write a new history of Chinese Zen as can be gathered up from the documents thus made accessible to us." See: Daisetz Teitaro Suzuki, *Essays in Zen Buddhism, Second Series* (Kyoto: Eastern Buddhist Society, 1933) vii. During the years of the Pacific War, when Suzuki wrote almost exclusively in Japanese for a Japanese readership, he did undertake some rewriting of early Zen history. He did not, however, ever write the proposed book in English, and his writings in English after the War did not reflect in any significant way a revised early Zen history.

13. Heinrich Dumoulin, the author of the epochal two-volume *Zen Buddhism: A History* (original edition, New York: Macmillan, 1988–1990; new edition,

canon of English books read in major US Buddhist studies programs and courses. That was not the final blow, however. By the end of the 1990s, Suzuki came under attack as a person, not just a scholar. Brian Victoria's pioneering historical study was persuasive in its accusation that Japan's major Zen masters had colluded in the Japanese militarist wartime ideology. His damning critique focused especially on those masters influential in the establishment of American Zen groups as well as D. T. Suzuki.[14] Dovetailing with the hermeneutics of resentment

Bloomington, IN: World Wisdom, 2005) has been a target of criticism as well for his refusal to sufficiently revise his history in light of the Dunhuang manuscripts. See the introduction by John McRae in the new edition of volume I (India and China) for a review of that criticism.Victor Sōgen Hori's Introduction to the new edition of volume 2 (Japan) addresses that criticism, but contextualizes Dumoulin's work in a much more positive light.

14. Brian Victoria, *Zen at War* (New York: Weatherhill, 1998). Victoria's account is meant to be argumentative rather than merely descriptive, however. That is, his book makes an excellent case for the complicity of leading Zen figures in the wartime ideology and the evidence is, for the most part, selected to support that thesis. This is especially true in the treatment of Suzuki. But, in Suzuki's case at least, there is more evidence. For the other side of the argument, see Kemmyō Taira Satō, "D. T. Suzuki and the Question of War," *The Eastern Buddhist* 39/1 (2008) 61–120. For a balanced and thorough analysis of the Kyōto School and its involvement in the wartime ideology of the state from different perspectives, see the essays collected in James W. Heisig and John C. Maraldo, eds., *Rude Awakenings: Zen, The Kyoto School, and the Question of Nationalism*, Nanzan Studies in Religion and Culture (Honolulu: University of Hawai'i Press, 1995). There are three essays in this collection particularly relevant to interpreting the issue of Suzuki and Japanese nationalism. Christopher Ives, in his "Ethical Pitfalls in Imperial Zen and Nishida Philosophy: Ichikawa Hakugen's Critique" (16–49), focuses on Ichikawa's critique of nationalism, including the way it was supported by Suzuki's "logic of *sokuhi*." Ives also analyzes the nationalistic assumptions inherent in Suzuki's idea of "Japanese spirituality," emphasizing the dualistic (and tendentious) way Suzuki elaborated on the spiritual/philosophical differences between "East" and "West." Ives's critique deftly shows the ethnocentrism lurking in the rhetoric and philosophical assumptions behind Suzuki's general account of Japanese spirituality.

Kirita Kiyohide's contribution, "D. T. Suzuki on Society and the State" (52–74), is a restricted defense of Suzuki based on his published and, importantly, unpublished writings and letters. Kirita's point is that, however nationalistic some of Suzuki's philosophical or cultural assumptions might seem, the evidence is overwhelming that Suzuki did not support Japan's militaristic and imperialistic ventures. Although Suzuki's public criticisms of the government were guarded for fear of retaliation, in his private correspondence, he was outspoken in his disgust for the militarist and imperialist takeover of Japanese politics.

John C. Maraldo's chapter, "Questioning Nationalism Now and Then: A Critical Approach to Zen and the Kyoto School" (333–62), casts a new light and more subtle shading on the issue of Suzuki's nationalism and his idea of Japanese spirituality. Maraldo shows that Suzuki's discourse was, first, primarily aimed at a Japanese, not Western, audience. In the waning years of the war, Suzuki was arguing that Japan's real toward Suzuki already developing among the disillusioned American buddhologists, an opinion spread that Suzuki had all along served a hidden agenda: to support the ideology of Japanese ethnocentrism and imperial expansion. Postmodern critical theory was brought to bear in arguing that Chan/Zen Buddhism in general and modern Japanese Zen specifically (including Suzuki's spin on the tradition) were no more than a rhetorical strategies to establish oppressive authoritarian power relations of master over disciple, samurai over commoner, Japan over the rest of the world. For example, Suzuki had maintained that the "Zen mind" is "beyond good and evil" in its treatment of others, giving the militarists the license to use force without submitting it to the moral evaluation.

How is Suzuki read today? Certainly, his writings are still generally anathema among American buddhologists, but then, Suzuki never claimed he was a Buddhist *scholar.* Indeed, he was primarily self-taught in the field. So, his audience never was the Western Buddhist specialist. How could this be? In his time, there would have been almost none. Indeed, one could argue that the growth of Buddhist studies in the West is a *consequence* of Suzuki's influence. This led some, myself included, to wonder if we are entering a time calling for a new reading of Suzuki's works. Since I have already addressed this issue elsewhere[15] and because it is not relevant to our concerns in this chapter, I will not discuss that issue here. Instead, let us consider the lessons from this case study relevant to understanding the relation between culture and interreligious dialogue.

---

contribution to the world was not military or political, but spiritual and cultural. Further, Maraldo points out the significance that Suzuki chose to distinguish the term he preferred for "spirit," namely, *reisei* 霊性, from the term more commonly used in state ideology: *seishin* 精神. In his way, Maraldo shows, Suzuki was arguing against the state notion of "spirit" while posing an alternative way to appreciate "Japanese spirituality." Nevertheless, because Suzuki was arguing specifically for a *Japanese* spirituality, his analysis still maintained an ethnocentric rhetoric. This is more forgivable when the audience was Japanese and Suzuki was trying to shift the Japanese sense of national identity away from militarism. Yet (as Ives also demonstrates in his chapter) this rhetoric continued in Suzuki's English-language writings in the last fifteen years of his life.

15. See my "Reading D. T. Suzuki Today," *The Eastern Buddhist* 38/1&2 (2007) 41–57.

Buddhism: Religion or Philosophy or Science?

In our account of the reception of Suzuki's writings, we have seen that the US cultural context distilled the Western tension between religion and philosophy into the specific question of whether the goal of Buddhism is a kind of experience or a form of knowledge. Although this issue is not always on the surface, American Buddhists have been split over it for decades. As mentioned already, the Theravāda-derived traditions such as those represented by the Vipassana Centers around the country have emphasized the knowledge side of the distinction. Equally important to that interpretation is Western buddhology's increasing attention to Indo-Tibetan psychological, logical, and epistemological texts. This scholarly approach puts Buddhism more into conversation with neuroscience and cognitive science, a trend supported by the scientific study of meditation techniques and the neurology of different states of consciousness. The scientific study of transformed consciousness dates back to the 1960s with the Transcendental Meditation movement of the Maharishi Mahesh Yogi. Although that tradition was Hindu rather than Buddhist in its inspiration, the idea was soon taken up by Buddhist study centers such as the Natrona Institute, a Tibetan study and meditation center founded in 1974 by Chogyam Trumpa Rinpoche. More recently, the Dalai Lama himself has enthusiastically endorsed the scientific study of Tibetan Buddhism as well as the exchange between Tibetan philosophers and Western scientists. Along parallel lines, the scientific study of Zen meditative states has also been actively pursued not only in the West, but in Japan as well (and more recently in China), probably at least in part inspired by what was happening in the West. [16]

The interface between Western science and Buddhist theory and practice[17] is not, of course, *interreligious* dialogue. In fact, the Maharishi

16. We can see this shift represented in book titles: from Chang Chung-yuan's *Taoism and Creativity* (1963) to Fritjof Capra's *The Tao of Physics* (1975); from Eugen Herrigel's *Zen in the Art of Archery* (1953) to Joanna Macy's *Mutual Causality in Buddhism and General Systems Theory* (1991); from Hisamatsu Shin'ichi's *Zen and the Fine Arts* (1971) to James H. Austin's *Zen and the Brain* (1998). The shift is from the nonscientific to the scientific understanding of experience. It is also a shift from advocating simplicity to delving into complexity itself. If an American Buddhist today seeks explicit "theoretical knowledge" about the world and the mind, the Tibetan tradition has more to offer than Zen in its traditional teachings. In this respect, American Buddhism is shifting back to the idea that Buddhism is a philosophy.

17. For a good overview of the Buddhism-science interface in the West, see Donald

Mahesh Yogi claimed, an assertion that made many experientially oriented American Buddhists uneasy, that Transcendental Meditation was a "science" of how to transform consciousness and not a religion. Many American Buddhists did come around to welcome the scientific studies, however, because the research was scientifically "confirming" what they were personally experiencing. For instance, there is now rather indisputable evidence that long-term Buddhist meditation correlates with neurological change (the latest version of this being that meditation increases what it commonly called "neural plasticity"). As the United States went through the cultural changes of the 1980s and 1990s, going from hippies to yuppies, from focus on personal growth to focus on the acquisition of material gains, from starry-eyed acceptance of Zen to critical rejection of it as a sham, this empirical research gives many American Buddhist practitioners scientific evidence that personal transformation is indeed possible after all. That is, the promise of enlightenment is more than a rhetorical play for power and authority by an elitist class of self-proclaimed "masters." Indeed, the critical theorists who have characterized Zen as a con game have yet to engage seriously the empirical evidence of unmistakable physiological transformation.

The research into the psychophysical benefits of Buddhist meditation has also, incidentally, led to similar research into the practice of Christian prayer, most notably, the original Duke University studies showing that hospital patients who pray also heal faster. And the fascination with Zen paradigms of spirituality has spilled over into an increased interest in the formerly neglected traditions of the simple, contemplative life of Quakers, Mennonites, and Amish. This brings us to the topic of interreligious dialogue, rather than interdisciplinary interplay among philosophy, religion, and science.

Buddhist-Christian Metapractical Dialogue

The specifically *interreligious* dialogue between Buddhism and Christianity originated among Christians and Buddhists who understood the goal of Buddhism as spiritual change achieved through a transformative experience or sequence of experiences. Some of the earliest "dialogue" was more like shared silence than conversation. At least from the early

S. Lopez, *Buddhism & Science: A Guide for the Perplexed*, Buddhism and Modernity (Chicago: University of Chicago Press, 2008).

1960s, Christian and Buddhist (mainly Zen and Theravāda) monastic's meditated together in various collaborative programs in Asia, Europe, and North America. Suzuki's 1957 book, *Mysticism, Christian and Buddhist*, had already pointed out possible areas of comparison.[18] The American fascination with Buddhist meditation led to American Catholicism's rediscovery, or at least re-emphasis, of the contemplative aspect of its own tradition. (A similar transformation occurred in some sectors of American Judaism as well). Thomas Merton and William Johnston were Catholic priests at the intellectual forefront of this movement. The effect went beyond the monastic communities, however. A case in point: with the changes in liturgy encouraged by the ecumenism of Vatican II, the Roman Mass typically includes longer periods of silence for prayer/contemplation.

Of course, interreligious dialogue can be rather restrained in contexts where an exchange of knowing looks is often considered more appropriate than discussing or analyzing what is known. Discussions of comparative mysticism by practicing mystics, rather than by scholars, can often be itself comparatively mystical. When intellectual dialogue does arise in this context, it often centers not on metaphysics, but instead on what I call "metapraxis," the philosophical analysis and justification for why specific practices are efficacious.[19] To cite one example, most religions share an interest in overcoming egocentricity. What techniques are effective in diminishing the ego and why do they work? When taken up in interreligious contexts, the discussion inevitably involves comparisons of philosophical anthropologies and theories of moral education. Because the dialogue focuses more on the meaning and efficacy of praxis rather than the nature of reality, it is more appropriate to think of these philosophical conversations as metapractical rather than metaphysical.

18. D. T. Suzuki, *Mysticism, Christian and Buddhist* (New York: Harper, 1957). In that book Suzuki, following many of the Kyoto School philosophers, focused on Eckhart as the Christian mystic most provocative for Buddhist-Christian dialogue. Earlier Nishitani Keiji had discussed not only Eckhart but also the kenotic theology of Paul in his *Religion and Nothingness*, trans. Jan Van Bragt, Nanzan Studies in Religion and Culture (Berkeley: University of California Press, 1987). The original Japanese text appeared serially in the mid-1950s.

19. For a full explanation of what I mean by metapraxis and its importance to interreligious communication and the comparative philosophy of religion, see my "Philosophy as Metapraxis," in Frank Reynolds and David Tracy, eds., *Discourse and Practice*, SUNY Series toward a Comparative Philosophy of Religions (Albany: SUNY Press, 1992) 169–96.

This sort of dialogue enriches both traditions in that it focuses on common goals, analyses of what hinders progress toward those goals, and techniques for overcoming those obstacles. Such topics in interreligious dialogue reflect the larger secular context of the post-1950s era and its stress on psychotherapy, self-improvement, and body-mind harmony. We already found this phenomenon in the discussion of how Suzuki came to be read in the 1960s. Specifically, we noted the change in goals between the college students of the 1950s versus those of the 1960s: the contrast between going to college to find a career and going to college to find oneself. Another aspect of the 1960s we noted was the student interest in leftist politics. This eventually spurred another area of interreligious dialogue—an interest in social ethics.

Buddhist-Christian Ethical Dialogue

During the 1960s and '70s when the fascination with Zen was at its peak, the analysis of Buddhist ethics primarily centered on Theravāda Buddhism's "loving kindness" (*metta* in Pali) and Mahāyāna Buddhism's "compassion" (*karuna* in Sanskrit). Both stressed nonviolence or, more specifically, nonharm toward any sentient being (a factor correlated with the rise of vegetarianism in the United States). These Buddhist ideals initially appealed to many Americans in part because it was humanistic in its emphasis on *personal* development as contrasted with submission to divine mandates or transcendent authority. This resonated with the counterculture, anti-institutional mood of the day. Moreover, it made ethics more like a mode of *experience*, a cultivated form of responsiveness and sensitivity, rather than s self-conscious or rational adherence to moral principles and mandates. Buddhists generally view loving kindness and compassion as by-products of spiritual transformation, a religious morality without the Judeo-Christian mechanisms of temptation and guilt. For Buddhism, to violate the basic precepts is not sin or transgression, but simply an act counterproductive to one's own spiritual growth. Rather than speaking of "evil" acts, it discusses them as being "unskillful" (*akauśala*).

Yet, many members of the counterculture were also progressives or Marxists who believed the prevailing social, political, and economic institutions were not only wrong, but to be resisted. Looking to the Buddhist tradition for a metapraxis of social change, the American

Buddhists found little detail. Buddhist morality, so deeply entrenched in the personal experience paradigm, seemed inadequate to Americans raised in a culture influenced by Jewish and Christian models of justice and social action. Turning to guidance from their Asian Buddhist brethren, the US Buddhists found little support. Even the Mahāyāna Buddhist monks of Vietnam expressed their moral criticism to the war most spectacularly in individual acts of protest such as self-immolation. At the same time, as we have seen, scholarly research was revealing that Japanese Zen Buddhist leaders during the war years had been morally effete in protesting Japanese militarism and imperialist atrocities, or even worse, had been actively complicit in support of the ideology behind them. Thus, social ethics became a major theme in the development of American Buddhism. About the same time, partly in response to the questions and concerns of their US counterparts, various forms of "engaged Buddhism" arose in Asia, beginning mainly in Southeast Asia and then spreading throughout the Buddhist world. Those movements often involved a class-struggle analysis derived loosely from Marxism in conjunction with traditional religious values. Engaged Buddhism was, in effect, a kind of Buddhist liberation theology and American Buddhists engaged with their Asian counterparts in working out the parameters of a functional Buddhist social ethic. This led to some ethical Buddhist-Christian dialogue within the United States as well.

Buddhist-Christian Metaphysical Dialogue

The most intellectually lofty Buddhist-Christian dialogue occurred through the collaboration of John Cobb and the Japanese Buddhist philosopher, Masao Abe. Abe was a Japanese philosopher who had studied the Kyoto School philosophy of Nishida Kitarō and Nishitani Keiji. He was most influenced personally, however, by Hisamatsu Shin'ichi, a member of the Kyoto School who was less interested in logic and epistemology and more focused on aesthetics. He was a highly regarded Zen teacher and master of tea ceremony. Later in his life, Abe was also influenced by the lectures of D. T. Suzuki (as well as those of Tillich and Niebuhr) at Union Theological Seminary, which Abe attended for a year. Of the Kyoto school philosophers of his generation, Abe was one of the few who could speak English and after retiring from his professorship at Nara Educational University, he subsequently spent the next fourteen years teaching at six different universities in the United States. Cobb assembled a prestigious group of eminent Christian theologians and Buddhist thinkers, including Abe, for the sake of continuing dialogue. Besides Cobb and Abe, the members included such notables as David Tracy, Langdon Gilkey, Gordon Kaufman, Takeda Ryūnsei, Tautest Unno, Joseph Kitagawa, and Francis Cook. This was obviously a high-powered group of intellectuals with personal commitments in one or the other of the traditions. Cobb's idea was to have the Buddhists speak as Buddhists and the Christians as Christians to explore areas of mutual interest and concern in hopes of better mutual understanding and the cross-fertilization of ideas. At around the same time, mainly through the efforts of the Nanzan Institute of Religion and Culture, translations and commentary on the Kyoto School were becoming increasingly available in English. As a consequence, the ideas of Nishitani Keiji (*Religion and Nothingness*) and Tanabe Hajime (*Philosophy as Metanoetics*) became an integral part of the conversations. For example, one prominent topic of discussion was Nishitani's comparison between kenotic theology and the Buddhist notion of emptiness.

After they had met three or four times, I had the opportunity to observe one of the group's meetings. The topic especially intrigued me: suffering. Would it not be fascinating and instructive to hear how these men understood their personal suffering and the suffering of others from the standpoint of their respective religious traditions? That issue never really arose and the discussion quickly moved to the difference between understanding God as being vs. God as emptiness. This strikes me as an example of interreligious dialogue gone wrong. Most importantly, when either Buddhism or Christianity is viewed only philosophically from a doctrinal or metaphysical standpoint, the visceral dimension of concrete personal religious experience can easily disappear. For example, in a time of anguish, how does a Christian draw on the passion of Christ as compared with the way a Buddhist draws on the bodhisattva's compassionate sharing in the suffering of others? Is there a difference between Jesus' suffering *for* us and the bodhisattva's suffering *with* us? Why does so much Christian art depict the suffering of Jesus while there is so little imagery of the suffering bodhisattva in Buddhist art?[20] The discussion

20. An example of the rare exception in Buddhist art are depictions of a story from the *Jataka* narratives concerning the Buddha's previous lifetimes. In the story, the buddha as bodhisattva offers his body to a mother tiger dying of starvation, too weak to

eradicated the one common element in the topic: the *physical* and irreducibly *personal* aspect of suffering. The issue for dialogue should have been how the Buddhists and Christians at the table understand suffering, not how they understand the *idea* of suffering.

I am not here claiming that comparative theological discussions have no value, but only that, unlike dialogues that operate in the practical/metapractical or ethical domains, there is an inherent danger in dialogues that focus on the metaphysical level alone. Namely, they run the risk of losing sight of the personal, incarnate, affective dimension of religious life. It is, by contrast, really quite difficult to omit that dimension when the dialogue focuses on the practical/metapractical or the ethical. Therefore, to be beneficial, comparative metaphysical dialogues in theology must take pains—for both traditions in the dialogue—to anchor the metaphysical in the practical, metapractical, and ethical dimensions of religious life. To compare religious ideas as just ideas is comparative philosophy, not interreligious dialogue.

Conclusions

If it is true that there are no religions, but only religious people, then interreligious dialogue should be interpersonal. As the example of the Suzuki interpretations showed, even when one side of the dialogue is a fixed text, the readings of that text reflect the shifting historical enculturation and religious traditions of its readers. Whereas the history of a religious people's previous interpretations may be a given, tradition is not. A religious tradition is always in-the-making, a people's *present* appropriating of that historical given to address the situation at hand. Tradition decides what in the historical accumulation of interpretations and practices is essential and what is fortuitous, what is central and what is peripheral, what is fixed and what is flexible. That decision process is by people: both as individuals and as members of an ongoing spiritual community. Tradition is another name for *intra*religious dialogue. In this paper, we have glimpsed how Zen Buddhism, incarnated in its English-speaking emissaries, has engaged American culture, incarnated

---

attack and acquire food for herself and her cubs. So, in effect, the bodhisattva suffered *for* the tiger, but interestingly, the usual rationale given is that the tiger, being only an animal, could not understand suffering with the insight the human bodhisattva could. So, the bodhisattva could, as it were, handle the suffering of being eaten better than the tiger could handle the suffering of starvation.

in its American readers and practitioners. Those encounters have led to interreligious and intrareligious dialogues in three domains: praxis/metapraxis, ethics, and metaphysics.

7

Intersections of Buddhism and Secularity

David L. McMahan

Geshe Gang-Up

At a recent conference that brought together scientists, Buddhists, and a handful of Buddhist Studies scholars, an anthropologically significant dustup occurred. A scholar of Buddhism—who himself was a practicing Buddhist in the Tibetan tradition—made an offhanded comment during his presentation about how the Tibetan tradition had mistranslated a term from Sanskrit into Tibetan. He also questioned the efficacy of some forms of Buddhist meditation and asked various other questions common to the academic study of religion. During the question-and-answer period, a Tibetan *geshe* approached the microphone and chastised the professor for his comments, saying that Western professors must be careful not to misrepresent the Dharma to people and that they need to understand the teachings thoroughly and not just toss off uninformed comments. As he continued, another, older *geshe* approached. I thought he would rein in his younger colleague; instead, he piled on, complaining that many in Western academe simply "read a few books" and think they know about Buddhism and that the ones who have thoroughly imbibed the tradition (i.e., he and his colleague) often felt like "second-class citizens" at these conferences, since they were not invited to speak but just to lead meditations. A board member who helped plan the activities of the conference later told me that they were not asked to speak because they tend to just "give Dharma talks" rather than engage in the Buddhism-science dialogue that was the raison d'être of the conference.

This was not a debate between Buddhists and secular humanists. In fact, most of the scientists and scholars at the conference were themselves quite sympathetic to Buddhism and many identified as Buddhists themselves. Yet, the interchange hinted at deep underlying differences in epistemologies, models of authority, and perhaps even ontologies. The *geshes* had completed an arduous curriculum, mastering a complex and cohesive system of doctrine and practice handed down and refined through centuries. In this system, there is room for interpretation, innovation, and nuancing, but the fundamental teachings, they believe, were established long ago by the Buddha and other enlightened beings. They would be unlikely to question, for example, the doctrine of rebirth or the literal truth of miracle-laden stories of ancient Buddhist literary heroes like Milarepa and Padmasambhava.

The scientists and Buddhist studies scholars, however, saw themselves as intrepid explorers of new territory. Many clearly hoped that their studies would confirm the value of their practice, spread the benefits to others, and normalize the study of consciousness, well-being, meditation, and altruism. But most, I'm guessing, were reluctantly open the possibility that this might not work out. Science, after all, while it has its own dogmas and resistance to heresy, is in theory open ended and thrives on continuous self-correction and innovation. Scientists and religious studies scholars are committed to following evidence to wherever it leads, even if it overturns current understanding. Indeed, the overturning of current understanding is highly valued; one wants to be the one who revolutionized the field and overthrew the old paradigm. Scientists must accept the results of their studies even if they go against their own cherished hypotheses and hopes. The narrative of progress—and indeed the empirical fact of tremendous progress in the sciences—is a fundamental aspect of the worldview bequeathed by the European Enlightenment. This feature of the human and physical sciences is one of the particular features of modern secularity. The argument between the scholar and the *geshes* suggests that the scientists and scholars, even those who were committed Buddhists, approached not only their research but their practice of the Dharma out of underlying presuppositions of this secularity. At least with regard to their research, the Buddhist-scientists and scholar-practitioners were first committed to a modern secular understanding of knowledge.

While there have been many efforts to foster Buddhist-Christian dialogue in recent decades, the more pervasive dialogue between Buddhism and Western culture is that between Buddhism and Western secular discourses, by which I mean, very broadly, discourses and disciplines that are, or claim to be, independent of any religious affiliation or influence and operate from a naturalistic standpoint. It is a dialogue that happens at explicit levels, like the conference I mention that brought together neuroscientists with Buddhists, and implicit ones involving the gradual seeping of Buddhist ideas, practices, and images into the broader secular culture and their reconstitution by that culture. The conference is one example of the considerable interest in constructing an area of overlap between the worlds of Buddhism and those of modern Western secularity, and especially its uber-discourse, science. It also hints at some of the fissures between these worlds.

The *geshes* I've mentioned presumably accept a world in which beings are reborn in endless cycles as animals, gods, demigods, hungry ghosts, residents of horrific hells; in which buddhas attain omniscience and supernatural powers; in which teachers are sometimes worshiped as a nearly different order of being. It is far from a secular world. Some Western Buddhists accept this whole "package," yet many adopt selected bits and pieces, combining them with tacit understandings of the world given by their own culture, and especially the background understanding of secular knowledge. Books written for Western Buddhists tend to leave much that challenges implicit secular norms and beliefs aside, concentrating on particular meditation practices, attitudes, ethical orientations, and philosophical concepts. When the Western Buddhists become interested in delving more deeply into the Dharma—often by going to Asia to study—they may well be confronted by a baroque Buddhism altogether unfamiliar and remote from that encountered in the West. Few Buddhists with no ethnic connection to Buddhism practice the "full package," with rituals, cosmology, institutions, supernatural beings, and teachers with considerable authority. This is not just a matter of intellectual belief, although this certainly plays an important role. For example, it is not just that an Englishman who finds himself practicing

Buddhism doesn't believe in rebirth but is attracted to meditation and Mādhyamika philosophy. It is that beneath explicit beliefs—at the level of tacit ways of being in the world—there is a whole network of notions, practices, social relationships, assumptions, associations, power relations, and meanings that constitute the lived world of the (in this case) typical Himalayan Buddhist, and another quite different lived world of the Englishman. This entails profound differences in the way they imagine and experience themselves, others, and the world around them.

This sketch may seem to suggest two separate, static cultures ensconced in their own closed systems—but if this may have been the case two centuries ago, it is no longer. Western secularity and Himalayan Buddhism each have, of course, always been in flux, and now they have begun to intersect with each other and mutually transform each other. What I am interested in here is what happens when two such disparate systems come together and, despite their differences, intertwine, infuse each other, and develop new ideas, practices and ways of being out of that intersection. In the case of Buddhism and Western modernity, different elements of these two complex, nebulaic systems magnetize towards each other and transform each other, creating a zone of novelty and hybridity, as well as contestation. We could see the new forms of Buddhism emerging from this space as "Buddhist modernism," something I have discussed in detail elsewhere.[1] What I want to zero in on here is a bit more specific: forms of Buddhism that explicitly emerge in relation to Western secularity.

The Secular

There is a considerable literature now on secularism and secularity, and I don't have the space to explore it now, but a few points are worth sketching. It is first important to note that when discussing the modern Western secular as a partner in dialogue with Buddhism, I am not referring to secularism as a political theory, but rather to secularity more broadly as a complex of discourses and practices that construe the world and humanity's place in it in nonreligious ways. The secular, however, emerges out of Christianity and the broad, historical and cultural forces of Western modernity. It is not simply an absence of religion

1. David L. McMahan, *The Making of Buddhist Modernism* (Oxford: Oxford University Press, 2008).

or its displacement by a value-neutral science and reason nor sacred kingship by democracy. Rather, the secular has a culture, history, values, worldview, mythology, and unquestioned assumptions. As such, the secular also can function in some respects like a religion itself. People who espouse it have particular social, political, and even cosmic commitments. It is not simply a neutral space of free inquiry unencumbered by tradition, convention, and ideology—though it may often appear to be and, indeed, is empowered through thus appearing. Moreover, the secular is co-constitutive of "religion," as a modern concept; both arise as a modern binary and they are intertwined, not only conceptually but in people's lives.

Although secularity is diverse and multifaceted, one of its features pertinent to my discussion is the naturalistic worldview, in which the world is understood to be governed by impersonal physical laws rather than divine intentions. While illness, storms, and meteorological phenomena once appeared to be the work of conscious agents, most of us now see these as results of natural—that is, impersonal—causes. According to some theorists of the secular, this worldview along with the emergence of capitalism and other aspects of modernity stripped away the gods, spirits, and magic, in Weber's famous phrase, disenchanting the world. Along with naturalism comes a host of decidedly this-worldly values: psychological health, social wellbeing, political goods, work, and consumer culture.

Secularity in the sense to which I am referring, however, does not entail the secularization thesis, i.e., that there has been a gradual displacement of religion in the public sphere, that this occurs inevitably as societies "modernize," and that it will continue until religion is displaced from the public sphere and becomes a private matter. It is not necessary to debate this thesis here; instead I would simply point out that this narrative is in serious doubt today.[2] Different societies modernize in different ways: in some, religion maintains a vibrant role and in some it has become marginalized. Rather than a uniform phenomenon that is spreading throughout the world, secularity can be seen as a differentiated assemblage of ideas, practices, and ways of being that interlace with other values, ideologies, and orientations—including religious orientations. Regarding the last, this might be expected with respect to

2. Peter L. Berger, ed., *The Desecularization of the World: Resurgent Religion and World Politics* (Washington, DC: Ethics and Public Policy Center, 1999).

Christianity's interactions with secularity—again, the latter emerged out of the logic of the former. But what happens when a non-Western tradition like Buddhism begins to become hybridized with Western secularity? If the secular aspects of the broader American and European culture are in actuality still entwined with Christianity, is there now arising a secularity that is similarly entwined with Buddhism? If secularity is a kind of post-Christianity, are there post-Buddhist secularities emerging?

To begin thinking about these issues, I want to first offer a discussion of how the particular interpretation of the role of belief has emerged in this intersection between Buddhism and the Western secular. Then I will discuss a few examples of recent lived forms of Buddhism that claim to be secular. First, though, some brief historical background that might help to contextualize these developments.

The Buddhist Dialogue with Western Secular Discourses

The Buddhist dialogue with secular disciplines—psychology, various physical sciences, modern political thought—and broadly secular ways of thinking has a long history, beginning in the Victorian period. This period is when many of the elements of what we now think of as the secular were emerging as fully formed: modern psychology was developing new views of the mind; Darwin and the geological sciences revolutionized the picture of humanity in relation to other species and placed it in an almost unimaginable scale of time; natural sciences more generally insisted that causality was a closed system of causes and effects, not amenable to the interventions of an external God. Romanticism and Transcendentalism eschewed orthodoxy and developed a new vocabulary of immanent sacrality, seeing the divine as an impersonal force in nature or as welling up within the depths of the soul itself. It was also a time of vigorous scientific positivism when many in Europe and North America were questioning their faith.

It was through apologists' presenting a selective picture of Buddhism as a predominantly secular philosophy in harmony with modern science and other secular disciplines that the tradition initially gained traction in the West. Early Orientalist scholars like Thomas Rhys Davids, for example, promoted an interpretation of the Buddha as an essentially secular philosopher with a compelling ethical and psychological vision.

The first Asian apologists for Buddhism in the West insisted their tradition had no quarrel with the sciences of geology and evolution and claimed causality and karma were in harmony with scientific concepts of causation and natural law. Buddhism, they insisted, did not emphasize the miraculous and supernatural, had no creator deity that interfered with his own natural laws. The Buddha himself was presented as a spiritual psychologist, ethical philosopher, and democratic social reformer. This created a flurry of interest among disaffected Christians during the Victorian period who believed they had found that elusive religion that had no conflict with science. And it put in place a particular way of understanding Buddhism in relation to Western secular discourses that has endured to the present. Moreover, what in the Victorian period was a vague idea that Buddhism is compatible with secularity, or perhaps offered a kind of spiritualized secularity, has over a century later developed into living forms of Buddhism, modes of secularized Buddhism not just in the West but around the globe.

Contemporary Spaces for the Intertwining of Buddhism and Secularity

Belief and the Secular

How contemporary Buddhists often address the issue of *belief* illustrates how secular discourses have influenced the shape Buddhism has taken in American and European cultures. Belief is not the most fashionable thing to discuss in the study of religion today because of the quite valid critiques of past attempts to understand religion in terms of the autonomous subject who freely chooses this or that belief, ignoring the role of culture and history in shaping the horizons of these choices. But I want to touch on the issue precisely because in this particular case it is important to the modern history of Buddhism.

The secular, for Charles Taylor, has to do with the possibility of unbelief in God, where such unbelief becomes one option among others.[3] The secular in this sense is clearly coming out of the matrix of Christianity, where belief holds a privileged place. From the very beginning of its introduction to the West, Buddhism was framed in a particular way that avoided some of the problems Christianity had around the central

3. Charles Taylor, *A Secular Age* (Cambridge, MA: Belknap, 2007).

theme of belief in the modern world. As I've mentioned, in the late nineteenth century, with the rise of positivistic science, many Christians found their beliefs harder to maintain, a phenomenon captured in the historian's term the "Victorian Crisis of Faith."[4] Buddhism was introduced to the West as the religion (or better, philosophy) that avoided the very problems with belief with which the Christian tradition was struggling. This created a particular space for Buddhism as a kind of un-religion, offering a rational, ethical way of life that did not require belief in anything beyond what secular modes of knowledge revealed about the world. German American philosopher Paul Carus, for example, articulated a view common among enthusiasts that Buddhism "is a religion which recognizes no other revelation except the truth that can be proved by science."[5] The image of Buddhism as requiring no belief in supernatural realities or beings and as being in harmony with modern science and other secular discourses has been crucial to its acceptance in the West.

Now let us consider this issue of belief and Buddhism in contemporary times, where the issues have shifted a bit. The current era might be characterized by the *fragility of belief*, not just belief in the supernatural, but belief more generally. This is rooted to some extent in the dominant social and philosophical theories that have undermined Enlightenment epistemology and called attention to the profound role of culture, language, and history in shaping knowledge, introducing an age of uncertainty and relativism in the humanities and social sciences. Scholars since at least the 1950s (and really, since Nietzsche), and now cognitive scientists, have become increasingly suspicious of the power of reason and rational choice in governing human affairs, shifting attention to the irrational, contingent, social, instinctual, material, and political conditions that serve as prime movers of human activities, with reason floating along on top believing that it is in charge.

But one need not crack the books of the leading social and scientific thinkers to feel the effects of epistemic destabilization. It is a larger feature of Western (and increasingly non-Western) societies. A key component of this fragility of belief is a media environment that has

4. Richard J. Helmstadter and Bernard Lightman, eds., *Victorian Faith in Crisis: Essays on Continuity and Change in Nineteenth-Century Religious Belief* (Stanford: Stanford University Press, 1991).

5. Paul Carus, *Buddhism and Its Christian Critics* (Chicago: Open Court, 1897) 114.

exploded in recent decades to include a vast array of contradicting assertions, an environment in which every position has its antithesis, every argument a counterargument. We have an unprecedented number of different religions and worldviews all in close proximity, all offering conflicting truth claims. The mediascape is drenched in contradicting opinions, many funded by powerful institutions. Knowledge of experts, conjecture of dilettantes, and ravings of ideologues all exist side by side on the Internet, and there are few resources for discerning what is of value from what it not. For some this leads to a kind of epistemic anxiety about the possibilities of knowing anything at all (many of us in academia see an increasingly cynical skepticism among our students). Among the possible responses to this anxiety are, first, a fundamentalist retreat into certainty of a particular theology or ideology, second, a vague sense of uncertainty about everything and a sense of looming nihilism.

In what sense does such this situation create conditions conducive to the intervention of Buddhist thought and practice? A good deal of Buddhist philosophy is skeptical about our ability to generate statements of ultimate truth that reflect a self-substantiating reality. Mādhyamika thought is especially suspicious of beliefs or "views" (*dṛṣṭi*), relegating all of them (in some interpretations) to relative or conventional truth (*smvṛti-sātya*). The things that words designate are empty of permanent, independent existence, and the boundaries that language and conceptuality place around them are functional, not absolute. Nothing exists in and of itself; rather all things exist only in relation to the vast array of other things, which are in turn similarly relational. Because the boundaries between things are conventional—constituted by concepts and language—and do not reflect stable, self-existing entities, no philosophical view or statement can provide any final and self-substantiating truth.

Such an orientation may seem congruent with the relativistic skepticism of our age except for the Buddhist assertion that deeply imbibing this truth in meditative practice is positively transformational and releases one from the anxiety, frustration, and suffering entailed in clinging to false reifications. This salvific relativism of Mādhyamika thought rejects the fundamentalist option (clinging to fixed views) and the nihilistic option (that no views are valid in any sense at all) and insists that relative truths are of value as long as they are not confused with truth in the highest sense (*paramārtha-sātya*), which is beyond the sayable and conceivable. This is one way in which Buddhism offers itself to the West, that is, as a philosophy that embraces some of the potentially disruptive, threatening, destabilizing, and disenchanting elements of modern Western thought—in this case the undermining of epistemic certainty—and attempts to rescue them from nihilism. It suggests that the lack of epistemic foundationalism does not necessarily rob the world of all meaning. In fact, this reordering of epistemic claims—the radical relativity of all sayable truth-claims, and the ultimate ineffability of truth in the highest sense—provides a way to embrace what is threatening to the epistemic order of modernity and turn it into something salvific.

This orientation can function in particular ways in the current context, ways that again tend to align Buddhism with secular thought over against the aspects of dominant Western religions that can appear problematic in the modern context. It suggests, for example, that *all* dogma is misguided and is not where "truth" lies (Shunryu Suzuki went so far as to say "believe in nothing"). The underlying binary opposition at work here is that of belief-versus-experience, which recapitulates a tension between Christianity and the secular (and by extension with Buddhism in coalition with the secular). The implication is: Christianity has been reliant upon beliefs, but some of these beliefs can no longer be maintained; moreover, belief in general has become fragile, volatile, dogmatic. Buddhism, according to this picture, relies on experience. The implication here is that experience is more reliable; there is something unassailable about it. It is in some ways parallel to the scientific experiment.

This emphasis on experience may seem to us quintessentially Buddhist, but it in fact draws together elements of Buddhism with those of modern Western culture and its reflexive turn. Romantics and Transcendentalists, for example, saw the divine as revealed in nature and within the interior depths of the individual and so emphasized experience over belief. The psychoanalytic tradition, and later modes of modern psychology, also emphasized the value of turning inward, analyzing and accessing the deep recesses of the mind. Modern fiction explored internal experience in a way unprecedented in literature, revealing the moment-to-moment nuances of thought and feeling, for example in James Joyce and his many successors. Modernist trends in Protestantism deemphasized belief and began to turn toward experience as the locus of the encounter of the individual with God. These and a number of philosophical trends, from Kant to William James, gave a new authority to experience, thus creating a space for Buddhism as a religion of experience rather than belief.

Whether this reading of Buddhism as primarily oriented toward experience adequately reflects the way it has been understood in Asia over the centuries is a matter of controversy.[6] This is not, however, the issue I am addressing here. Rather, I am addressing more the sociological question of why this experiential interpretation of Buddhism becomes compelling in the modern West, and I think it has to do with the hope that "direct experience" can provide what belief has failed to provide: a sense of "alternative certainty," stability, or perhaps comfort with the instability and uncertainty that has, for some, placed a question mark around all beliefs. And so it is quite common in contemporary Buddhist literature to find books and Dharma talks with phrases like "the wisdom of uncertainty" or "the wisdom of not knowing." Stephen Batchelor's secular Buddhist manifesto is titled *Buddhism without Beliefs*,[7] and another recent title reads: *Buddhism Is Not What You Think: Finding Freedom beyond Beliefs*.[8]

The way the issue of belief has been incorporated into discussions of modern Buddhism illustrates a basic pattern that can be applied to other issues in Western articulations of Buddhism. Very generally, that pattern includes: (1) a sense of impasse or crisis; (2) a sense that the West lacks it own resources to address the impasse; (3) a sense that Buddhism both embraces part of what created the impasse (in this case the radical relativity of all truth claims) (4) and yet offers a new way through it.

Note that this adaptation is done from the Western side, as it were: the problems that Buddhism is called upon to address come from the historical logic of Western thought. They are not necessarily the problems as traditionally conceived in Buddhist thought. Buddhist philosophy—as well as Buddhist ethics, meditation, etc.—takes on a certain significance

6. Robert H. Sharf, "Buddhist Modernism and the Rhetoric of Meditative Experience," *Numen* 42 (1995) 228–83; Janet Gyatso, "Healing Burns with Fire: The Facilitations of Experience in Tibetan Buddhism," *Journal of the American Academy of Religion* 67 (1999) 113–47.

7. Stephen Batchelor, *Buddhism without Beliefs: A Contemporary Guide to Awakening* (New York: Riverhead, 1997).

8. Steve Hagen, *Buddhism is Not What You Think: Finding Freedom beyond Beliefs* (New York: HarperOne, 2003).

when examined from the side of Western thought, i.e., when it is taken as an intervention to stem an impasse rising out of the unfolding of Western culture, be it the challenge to Christianity of scientific findings or the encroaching possibilities of nihilistic relativism. The significance and implications of the Buddhist ideas in question might be different when we look at them from the perspective of more traditional Asian Buddhist forms. Western interpretation therefore is always haunted by the possibility of profound misreading or omission: for example, how do the repeated assertions of the omniscience of the Buddha fit with the apparent epistemic modesty of Mādhyamika thought? But there is also the excitement, on the part of both Western enthusiasts and Asian Buddhists, that the modern era evokes undiscovered potentialities in the Dharma as it addresses unprecedented questions and situations.

Secular Buddhism as a Lived Tradition

One significant development in contemporary Buddhism is the attempt not just to have theoretical dialogues on philosophical issues but to develop living traditions integrating selected aspects of Buddhism into the general ethos of Western secular thought and life. The fact that it would occur to anyone to do this says something important about the particular ecological niche that Buddhism has created for itself in the West. It suggests that Buddhism among Westerners—and more and more frequently, Asian Buddhists among the global educated population—is tuned to the frequency of Western secularity.

I take two examples from the Tibetan tradition, since we began with a fissure between Tibetan *geshes* and a Western scholar-practitioner. We might see these examples as attempts to bridge that fissure. They represent what might be called the emergence of a "two-track" Buddhism: one more "religious" and one "secular." The first is a program called Shambhala Training, developed by one of the first Tibetan teachers to attain a wide following in the North America, Chögyam Trungpa (1939–1987). He was an unabashed and controversial innovator, guru to Beat writers and the counterculture, and author of several very successful books in English. His Shambhala training program strips away much of what is typical of most Tibetan Buddhists' practice—rituals for making karmic merit, worship of buddhas, and propitiation of demons, for example—and distills particular elements, especially those related to meditation, presented as a "secular path" of self-development. Shambhala Training incorporates "contemplative workshops, suited for both beginning and experienced meditators. The simple and profound technique of mindfulness and awareness is the basis of a *secular path of meditation*, which can benefit people of any spiritual tradition and way of life. Shambhala Training is the study and practice of Shambhala warriorship—the tradition of human bravery and leadership. This path shows how to take the challenges of daily life in our modern society as opportunities for both contemplative practice and social action."[9] Shambhala, Trungpa insists, is a path of "secular enlightenment" that offers "the possibility of uplifting our personal existence and that of others without the help of any religious outlook."[10]

In addition to the explicit assertion of secularity of the program, notice too the implication that it is a kind of tradition-neutral space in which to practice: "everyone is welcome at our centre regardless of religion, spiritual tradition or teachers, path of practice, opinions, class, nationality, culture, ethnicity, race, language, age, gender, sexual orientation, or physical, perceptual or mental abilities" (http://www.shambhala.org/shambhala-training.php). "Shambhala vision is rooted in the contemplative teachings of Buddhism, yet is a fresh expression of the spiritual journey for our time; it is available to practitioners of any tradition."[11]

What is clear upon reading the literature of Shambhala training is that it is not exactly secular in either the common or scholarly uses of the word, nor is it the orthodox practice of Buddhism. No doubt it makes extensive use of Buddhist concepts and practices: for example, the first stage of the program entails meditation practices that "glimpse unconditional goodness as the ground of our existence."[12] This draws heavily on the concept of Buddha nature, the potential for enlightenment in everyone, but makes no mention of this doctrine per se. The non-Buddhist discourses from which it draws are, however, nearly exclusively secular, especially that of modern psychology. Terminology from both psychology and Buddhism are woven seamlessly together:

9. Online: http://www.shambhala.org/shambhala-training.php/ (italics added).

10. Chögyam Trungpa, *Shambhala: The Sacred Path of the Warrior* (Boston: Shambhala, 1988) 27.

11. Online: http://www.shambhala.org/about_shambhala.php/.

12. Ibid.

the practitioner, for example, is encouraged to "observe how we create a cocoon of habits to mask our fear" (a decidedly modern psychological analysis) and to develop inquisitiveness, awareness, fearlessness and "find the open clear sky of mind" (a familiar metaphor in Tibetan Buddhist literature). The stated goal of the program is not to achieve the transhuman state of nirvana but to "become fully human."[13]

Significantly, Trungpa loosely based Shambhala training on elements of the Kālachakra Tantra, a Vajrayāna text based on the teachings of the Buddha in response to a request by the King of the mythical land of Shambhala. The King, Dawa Sangpo (Sanskrit: *Suchandra*) requested teachings that would allow him to practice the Dharma while still carrying out his worldly responsibilities. Trungpa apparently chose this particular text for its this-worldly orientation, seeing it as appropriate for current Western society. The Shambhala program presents itself as a "secular" path for those who cannot embrace the "religious" elements of Tibetan Buddhism but still might benefit from some of its practices.

Another "two-track" program developed very recently is that of the Tergar Community, founded by Tongey Mingyur Rinpoche, a *tulku* with an avid interest in modern science. The community has two detailed curricula, one entitled "Joy of Living" and the other "Path of Liberation." The latter utilizes identifiably Buddhist doctrines, traditions, and practices—traditionally directed towards monastics and religious specialists—from classic Tibetan texts. They include tantric visualization practices (*sādhanas*), guru yoga (visualizing one's guru as a deity), a series of over one hundred thousand prostrations (*ngundro*), and the six yogas of Nāropa—one of which includes transference (*powa*), developing the ability to transfer one's consciousness through the apex of the head at death.

In contrast to this traditional tantric path, the Joy of Living program's stated goal is to "make the ancient practice of meditation accessible to the modern world." It "provides a comprehensive course of meditation training and study, with programs for Buddhists and non-Buddhists alike." It "emphasizes direct experience and the integration of meditation with everyday life, presenting techniques that can be practiced by anyone, regardless of faith or cultural background."[14] Mingyur's books make frequent reference to scientific studies of meditation, and

13. Ibid.
14. Online: http://tergar.org/meditation/tergar.shtml/.

he often draws on secular, this-worldly rationales to advocate for meditation.[15] He has been actively involved in the current wave of scientific research on contemplative practices and has himself been not only a lay student of neuroscience but a test subject in EEG and MRI studies.

We could also point to other movements of semi-secular forms of Buddhism, such as the Insight Meditation (Vipassana) movement, which derives from Theravāda traditions but takes meditation and certain ethical and attitudinal orientations as central, dispensing with elements of Theravāda that would be construed as more "religious": merit-making, chanting, recitation, devotion, etc. There is also currently an emerging movement that explicitly calls itself "secular Buddhism" or "critical Buddhism." The most famous representative is Stephen Bachelor, who, rather than simply ignoring the "religious" elements of Buddhism difficult to include in a modernist Western image of the cosmos, directly confronts them, asserting that certain elements of Buddhism, for example the doctrine of rebirth, are dispensable and not part of the essential message of the Buddha.

Implications

The Natural and the Supernatural

The reason I characterize these programs and movements as being in dialogue with Western secular discourses is not just that some explicitly say they are "secular." This claim, in fact, illustrates the blurriness of the boundaries between secular and religious, exposing them as codependent and intertwined. Rather, it is that they place themselves explicitly within the frameworks established by secular discourses such as psychology, neuroscience, and the modern physical sciences. For example, they exclude engagement with external agencies like God, gods, or buddhas. They may refer to the Buddha or bodhisattvas as inspiring examples, wise teachers, or ethical mentors but they never suggest that one should pray to them, ask for their assistance, or do rituals to induce them to bring worldly benefits. These new forms of Buddhism are presented as paths of human effort and self-cultivation. Supernatural

15. Yongey Rinpoche Mingyur, *The Joy of Living: Unlocking the Secret and Science of Happiness* (New York: Three Rivers, 2008); and Yongey Rinpoche Mingyur, *Joyful Wisdom: Embracing Change and Finding Freedom* (New York: Three Rivers, 2010).

beings, which pervade much of Asian Buddhist practice, are often reinterpreted as symbols or psychological archetypes. If, as in certain forms
of Vajrayāna or Zen, there is a transhuman ultimate reality presented—
Buddha-nature or *Dharmakāya*—these programs emphasize that it not
a personal external agency but one's fundamental self or the ultimate
reality of the universe, of which everything is a part. This is not to say
that no practitioners of these paths believe in God or spirits or go to
an astrologer. But the essential teachings of these "secular" paths don't
include these and make clear that they are optional or irrelevant.

Of a piece with the rejection of the supernatural is the embracing
of a naturalistic view of the world. I mentioned earlier that modernist articulations of Buddhism emphasized that the world of Buddhism
is a self-contained system without need for a creator God. Buddhism
gained prestige in its early encounters with the West in part through
apologists' insistence on something akin to natural law. The doctrine
that everything arises from a variety of causes and conditions and that
everything is interdependent presented an alternative to the monotheistic view. Today, however, this interdependence has taken on a different
significance, one that repeats the pattern I mentioned above of Buddhism embracing certain potentially destabilizing aspects of Western
modernity and transforming them into positive values. In this case, the
idea of interdependence current among many Buddhists today takes
the Western notion of a thoroughly naturalistic universe and infuses
a sense of sacrality into it. Authors discussing this concept present it
as thoroughly naturalistic and scientific, yet emphasize the wonder of
all things being interconnected, implying an ethic of care for others
and for the natural world. In an individualistic culture, this provides
an alternative vision of individual beings as open, constituted by relationship, fluidly intermingling with other beings and the natural world.
Thus it asserts the naturalistic view, but attempts to rescue it from its
narcissistic and mechanistic-materialistic potentialities. Indeed a great
deal of discussions of Buddhist interdependence today is an attempt to
resacralize a relational world that the sciences have desacralized. Rather
than imagining the world as a vast, random collection of lifeless, purposeless atoms, the contemporary Buddhist imagination of the world
(in some articulations) is of a vast, living interdependent web in which
everything is connected to everything else. Secularized Buddhism then
reenchants the naturalistic view of the world, not by reintroducing gods,

demons, magic, heavens, and hells, but by "spiritualizing" this secular view.

This-Worldly Ethics

Secularized forms of Buddhism tend to have a markedly this-worldly ethic that combines classical ideals of compassion for all living beings and the bodhisattva vow to remain in the world with a distinctively modern affirmation of worldly life. The purpose of meditation in this articulation is not for transcending the ensnaring world of death and suffering in hopes of the ineffable bliss of nirvana but for developing a greater appreciation of the world and living in it more fully and ethically with attentiveness and compassion. While meditative techniques began in India among ascetics whose ultimate goal was to escape the cycle of rebirth and who looked askance at family life, reproduction, political involvement, and sense pleasures, secularized Buddhist meditation fosters a fine-grained appreciation of the minute aspects of life, including family, children, work, and the natural world. There are strains of such appreciation in Buddhist traditions already—the revalorization of lay life in the Mahāyāna, the affirmation of desire in Vajrayāna, and the Daoist-influenced appreciation of nature in East Asian Buddhism—but it is the secular world-affirming ethos of Western modernity that draws these particular elements to the fore and provides them a home.

The this-worldly orientation also entails a degree of social and political involvement probably unprecedented in the history of Buddhism. Socially engaged Buddhism is a global movement of Buddhist social and political engagement that, for example, advocates for human rights, cares for AIDS patients, protests war, and creates rural poverty-relief programs. It adapts the Buddhist recognition of the suffering of all beings and the ethic of universal compassion to modern ideas of social justice and human rights. It addresses not just individual suffering but systemic suffering, mobilizing efforts to alleviate poverty, oppose violence, and advocate for environmental action. Here we see new potentialities in classical Buddhist doctrines that could only be activated in the context of the complex combination of Christianity, Enlightenment Humanism, and their egalitarian concepts of social justice.

Such a this-worldly orientation may appear to betray the soteriological ideals of Buddhism. However, Buddhists have always been concerned with both proximate and distant goals.[16] For many Buddhist laity in Asia (and Asian America), practicing Buddhism involves various ethical commitments as well as an array of rituals for gaining merit, or good karma, that produces the conditions for a better rebirth. Few expect to attain enlightenment in what is largely thought to be an age in which the Dharma has degenerated significantly. Most of the "benefits" that accrue to the individual are "this worldly" in that they do not involve attempts to achieve the ultimate goal of nirvana or Buddhahood, but hope to gain protection from destructive forces, disease, and unfavorable life conditions.

Secular Buddhists often also practice for "this worldly benefits" but differently conceived. Skeptical of spirits and mythical cosmologies and often agnostic about rebirth, practice for them tends to be about decreasing destructive emotions, cultivating compassion for others, and finding internal peace and balance in the often chaotic conditions of modernity. Some secular Buddhists may, in fact, aspire to enlightenment itself, but often not as conceived in orthodox Asian Buddhisms, e.g., transcending embodied life and rebirth altogether in an ineffable state of nirvana, attaining omniscience, or becoming a buddha as classically understood. Enlightenment is more often taken as a this-worldly state of peace within oneself and benevolence towards others.

Disembedding of Meditation

Also important is the assertion that meditation, in many interpretations that tend toward the secular, is open to anyone "regardless of religion [or] spiritual tradition" (see above). The fact that Buddhism is taken to be something a Christian, Jew, Muslim, or Hindu can practice implies that it is not a religion with doctrines, institutions, and priesthoods, but a kind of neutral space in which to practice, i.e., to explore the mind and cultivate certain ethical and attitudinal qualities. Notice the parallel with secularism here, which attempts to create a religion-neutral zone of free inquiry and discussion. Meditation in secularized contexts is also reconstituted as a generic space of internal inquiry, even a kind of scientific exploration, guided by Buddhist ideas but ultimately bound by no tradition and free from dogma and institutional authority.

16. Donald K. Swearer, *The Buddhist World of Southeast Asia*, SUNY Series in Religion (Albany: SUNY Press, 1995; 2nd ed., 2010).

The programs I have mentioned are specific examples of a wider trend of the disembedding of Buddhist meditation from the cosmological, social, ethical, ritual, and institutional contexts of more traditional forms of Buddhism and reembedding them in the contexts of modern secular discourses, practices, and sensibilities. One very concrete consequence of this reembedding brings us back to the Buddhism-and-science conference—meditation, construed as a kind of secular practice of self-cultivation, is suitable for being taught in public schools and studied with public funds. Neuroscientists have enjoyed an avalanche of funding for research on meditation in the past decade or two, some of which would not be possible if the practice were construed as "religious."

The disembedding of meditation has also had the effect of releasing Buddhist contemplative practices into the wider culture, beyond the walls of the monastery and even beyond Buddhist institutions themselves, even the quasi-secular ones. Thus it is now not unusual to find Buddhist-derived meditation at the psychologist's office, the corporate office, or the health club, where it takes on a life of its own beyond the ken of lamas or roshis.

Tensions and Contestations

I don't intend to try to mount an evaluation of these new forms of Buddhism that nestle themselves into secular discourses. I am mainly interested here in pointing out the phenomenon and understanding something of its social significance in a globalizing world. However, mentioning a few possible tensions involving secularized forms of Buddhism will help to elucidate what is at stake for various actors involved. Perhaps the most frequent critique is that this is simply watered-down Buddhism, not the "real" Dharma but merely bits of Buddhism sprinkled over Western culture to season it with exotic flavors.[17] Such critiques might come from more orthodox practitioners, who are concerned that people are taught the "real" Dharma, however that might be conceived in their tradition. Critics tend to level this kind of evaluation not so much at examples like ours—Shambhala, Vipassana, etc.—but rather at forms of secularized Buddhism initiated by Westerners.

The possible loss of elements of Buddhist traditions that some consider essential is another cause of concern for some. These may include

17. Victor Sōgen Hori, "Sweet-and-Sour Buddhism," *Tricycle* 4/1 (1994) 48–52.

doctrines such as rebirth, traditional articulations of enlightenment and cosmology, or ritual practices that many in the West find alien. Secularized Buddhism may be epistemically or ontologically at odds with more orthodox forms of Buddhism, as adherents may not take for granted that the Dharma is "true" but may rather test it against forms of secular knowledge and reject certain elements accordingly. Some have also raised concerns about the this-worldliness of secularized Buddhism: a monk once suggested that Mindfulness-based Stress Reduction—a secularized meditation therapy based on Buddhist contemplative techniques—is just a way to make a person "more comfortable in saṃsāra." More broadly, some have expressed concern that those who embrace secularized forms of Buddhism are unwilling to make radical commitments or take on serious challenges to the received Western worldview. Some scholars raise similar concerns, seeing secularized forms of Buddhism as ad hoc creations involving too much loss of culture or in some cases a kind of cultural appropriation on the part of Western spiritual omnivores.

Institutional and personal authority is another contested issue in secularized versions of Buddhism. One of the most important aspects of secularism is its critical stance toward authority, based largely in Enlightenment philosophy. Buddhism in the West is often presented as a tradition in which the individual is encouraged to decide for him- or herself what to believe and practice. And indeed there are canonical and commentarial passages in Buddhist literature that advocate a critical attitude towards teachers, and these tend to be highlighted in secularized Buddhism. Nevertheless, in most Asian contexts authority has been construed in quite different ways than it has in the modern secularist vision of the autonomous subject. Most schools of Buddhism have strict protocols for authorizing teachers, and devotees often give their teachers a degree of reverence that make some Westerners uncomfortable. With the rise of grassroots "sanghas" that spontaneously emerge among interested Buddhist enthusiasts, many more traditional practitioners may be concerned that people are not learning the Dharma from "authentic" Dharma teachers. This is not an issue with the Tibetan examples I mentioned—Trungpa and Mingyur are both considered authenticated teachers in their traditions—but it is with other, more homegrown teachers of Buddhism in the West who may believe such institutional protocols are unnecessary.

These concerns illustrate some of the tensions underlying the debate between the *geshes* and the Western scholar of Buddhism. They suggest that even adherents of the same tradition may understand that tradition quite differently based on the background picture of the world and its tacit assumptions, sensibilities, and habits of thought and feeling, as well as more obvious differences in explicit beliefs. When these two pictures mingle, a zone of novelty is created in the intersection, with often unpredictable results.

Conclusion

Secularized Buddhism, then, is a loose conglomeration of Buddhisms that situate and articulate themselves largely in the context of modern secular discourses such as psychology, secular philosophies, various sciences (physics, neuroscience), and secular political philosophies. Sometimes there is direct dialogue between Buddhism and these discourses, such as the robust interchange among Buddhists and neuroscientists today. But often the dialogue takes place on a more tacit level, for example, when a writer discusses Buddhist ideas in a way that takes for granted modern scientific cosmology (as opposed to invoking the traditional Buddhist picture of the multi-level cosmos) or discusses the Buddhist analysis of mind in psychoanalytic terms. It is here that we can speak of the cultural shaping of religion, since these Buddhisms emerge out of the complex interface between widely divergent cultures, and out of this interface comes new cultural formations.

The case of dialogue between Buddhism and Western secularism suggests that perhaps the real "action" in dialogue between two different cultural-religious (or secular) formations is often on an implicit rather than explicit level. As James Heisig points out in his essay in this volume, explicit interreligious dialogue between Buddhism and Christianity has often been somewhat contrived, unidirectional, and governed by particular concerns and agendas of liberal Christians. Whatever success they have yielded in interreligious understanding, they have seldom had the power to transform a religious tradition. Historical and cultural circumstances have, however, forced Buddhists into confrontation with Western secularism, initiating a century-old "dialogue" that has emerged organically, out of mutual interest, necessity, and contestation. Perhaps if more explicit interreligious dialogue is to be successful it needs to ride the currents of such organic, broad historical intersections of cultures rather than try to engineer dialogue from the "top down." This is the message of the interface between Buddhism and Western secularism, which has effected not only some degree of mutual understanding between two disparate traditions, but also a mutual transformation.

8

Hindu Identity in a Multicultural World
Hinduism in America

Swami Tyagananda

Hinduism and Change

Confined for centuries to the Indian subcontinent, Hinduism remained more or less isolated and provided Hindus with a relatively stable, undisturbed identity.[1] With the arrival of conquerors from across the borders, India was repeatedly shaken by nearly a thousand years of subjugation under the rule of "foreigners." The challenges that Hindus faced were enormous. Every significant response to these challenges brought about subtle changes in how Hindus saw themselves and others, and how they saw their own religion and culture in relation to other religions and cultures. These changes transformed, in however subtle a manner, some of the Hindu practices and beliefs. A few of these changes were voluntary and conscious, while the rest were either forced or simply the inevitable result of the meeting with strangers. The description of the incremental changes that Hinduism underwent can now be found in most books on Indian history. Not surprisingly, the change worked in both directions:

1. There were of course identity issues within the Hindu social structure, such as those related to caste, but the religious identity was never in question in the old India, before its population became diverse through the arrival of conquerors from across the border and, later, the arrival of missionaries and their aggressive proselytization activities.

158

even as Hinduism evolved, as it tried to absorb and assimilate the new situation, the non-Hindu elements also evolved and became modified in the Indian cultural setting.

While military conquests, political subjugation and administrative control were decisive factors in modifying Hindu practice and self-identity, they were by no means the only factors. Every living tradition is continually changing. Change or "modification" (Sanskrit, *vikā ra*) is in the very nature of every living entity. Hinduism traditionally lists six characteristics of change: existence, birth, growth, transformation, decline, and decay. That is why the word *neo-Hinduism* (a term popularized by the German Indologist Paul Hacker) makes little sense to practicing Hindus, because it seems to imply the existence of a "Hinduism" frozen in time at some arbitrarily chosen point in history, so any subsequent change can be viewed as a departure from the "original" entity. But evolutionary transformation in living entities is a sign of life, not deviation from some imagined original state.[2] This is not to deny the utility of a label such as *neo-Hinduism* to mark off an era, provided it is not meant to indicate a deviation from some pure, supposedly "original" Hinduism.

The changes that occurred when India was mostly under the control of non-Hindu rulers were certainly significant. Changes in the perception and practice of Hinduism are continuing to occur even in present-day India, with its still predominantly Hindu population under a democratic government and a secular administration. Nevertheless, compared to the changes that Hinduism has undergone and is undergoing in India, the corresponding changes in the West are even more significant. This is not surprising, given that the Hindus in the West are a minority and the challenges and difficulties of surviving, learning, working and teaching in a radically different culture are more complex and complicated.

The complication arises, at least partly, due to questions related to the identity of Hinduism, since it has become a matter of debate in some circles. Is Hinduism a religion or "a sociocultural unit or civilization

---

2. The same is true of other living religious traditions as well, such as Buddhism, Judaism, Christianity, and Islam. For a listing of differences between a so-called traditional Hinduism and Neo-Hinduism, see Lola Williamson, *Transcendent in America: Hindu-Inspired Meditation Movements as New Religion*, The New and Alternative Religions Series (New York: New York University Press, 2010) 18–20.

which contains a plurality of distinct religions"?[3] Such problematizing of Hinduism's identity is largely confined to academic study and is not a major issue for most Hindu practitioners, whether born and raised as Hindus or those who later embrace the faith as their primary religious affiliation. At the personal level, for most of them, what matters is that their faith invests their lives with a deeper meaning and purpose and brings them fulfillment at various levels. At the social level, their identity as Hindus is certainly important to them, especially outside India. As members of a minority religion, some Hindus in the West manage to compartmentalize their lives by being religious inside their homes and secular outside. Others focus on the mystical and intellectual aspects of their tradition and try to downplay its social and ritualistic aspects. Some among these, mostly ethnic Indians, celebrate Hindu festivals in religious groups that have been formed in major cities with sizable Hindu populations. Such groups also promote Indian classical dances, music and food. Indian culture and Hindu religion are inextricably intertwined in the minds of most Hindus.

The differing perceptions of Hinduism result from the academic/practitioner, secular/religious, outsider/insider or the East/West divide, although these divisions are blurry and the categories are far from rigid. Since what changes are noticed and how they are interpreted depend on the lens of the observer, I should point out here that my observations are filtered through the lens of a Hindu monk, born and raised in India, and currently residing in America. Though my knowledge of Hinduism has been acquired in a traditional, nonacademic setting, I try to be sensitive to academic concerns and, though I am viewed as an "insider," I respect and value "outsider" viewpoints.

Hinduism's spread outside India, specifically in the Western world—and, more specifically, in America—occurred in at least three major ways: first, through its books and the ideas they contained; second, through its teachers that dared to cross the seas, a rebellious and transgressive activity in the eyes of the orthodox at one time but now so common that it's not even noticed; third, through Hindu immigrants to the West. Chronologically, the texts appeared first, followed by Hindu teachers and, later, by Hindu immigrants. The texts, the teachers, and the immigrants were like waves on the religious waters that lashed against

---

3. Heinrich Von Stietencron, "Hinduism: On the Proper Use of a Deceptive Term," in *Hinduism Reconsidered*, Günther-Dietz Sontheimer and Hermann Kulke, eds., South Asian Studies 24 (New Delhi: Manohar, 2001) 33.

America's shores in succession. The forces they generated, the influence they exerted, and the changes they underwent make for a fascinating study.

Hinduism in the West: Through the Early Texts

The Upanishads, which are the philosophical portions of the Vedas, traveled to the West through a circuitous path. In 1657, Dara Shikoh wrote a Persian translation of several of the Upanishads, which was then translated into Latin by the French Orientalist Abraham Hyacinthe Anquetil-Duperron. Upon reading this text, Schopenhauer wrote: "How entirely does the Oupnekhat breathe throughout the holy spirit of the Vedas! How is every one who by a diligent study of its Persian Latin has become familiar with that incomparable book, stirred by that spirit to the very depth of his soul! . . . In the whole world there is no study, except that of the originals, so beneficial and so elevating as that of the Oupnekhat. It has been the solace of my life, it will be the solace of my death!"[4] Among the earliest English translations of the Bhagavad Gita was the one written by Sir Charles Wilkins, which inspired both Ralph Waldo Emerson and Henry David Thoreau, the foremost lights of the Transcendentalist movement in New England. Sir Edwin Arnold's translation of the Gita in verse (1885) was also greatly admired. Max Müller's monumental fifty-volume series, The Sacred Books of the East, made Hinduism and other Eastern traditions accessible to the Western world. It was a time when scholars had begun studying language development in relation to cultural development. India's Vedic culture was believed to be the ancestor of European Classical cultures, and Sanskrit was thought to be the oldest of the Indo-European languages. Müller's volumes contributed to an increased interest in Indian culture, which also set Indo-European ("Aryan") traditions in tension with Semitic religions.

Not all of the early books on Hinduism were appreciative of Indian culture. A few were positively antagonistic, caricaturing Hindu beliefs and replete with misinformation. Written mostly by Christian missionaries, these books were intended to evoke maximum outrage and sympathy from their Western readers, who were expected to fund the

---

4. From the first edition (1819) of his *Welt als Wille und Vorstellung* ("The World as Will and Representation"), translator unknown. Oupnekhat is very likely a version of one of the Upanishads or a compilation of extracts from various Upanishads.

missionary efforts to bring true religion and good culture to the ignorant, superstitious, savage people of India. A characteristic example of
such books was Caleb Wright's *India and Its Inhabitants*, first published
in 1858. Filled with information which was predominantly false, ca-
lumnious and sensational, the book had a phenomenal success among
the intelligentsia. Its preface cited "testimonials from the presidents of
twenty American colleges who gave unstinting praise."[5]

A more appreciative knowledge of Hinduism at the time could be
found among Transcendentalists. In much of the Midwest and southern
states of the country, it was missionary propaganda that seems to have
had great influence in shaping people's conception of Hinduism. What
was needed in order to have a better and more tangible idea about Hinduism and its followers was a group of living representatives of Hinduism, people who lived and practiced the Hindu way of life. This became
available in America when indigenous Hindu teachers appeared on the
scene.

Hinduism in America: Through Teachers

Swami Vivekananda and Vedanta

By all accounts, Swami Vivekananda (1863–1902) was the first genuine
teacher of Hinduism who came to the West. The first truly representative
interfaith event in recent history—interestingly named the "Parliament
of Religions"—was held in 1893 in conjunction with the Columbian
Exposition in Chicago. It brought to America for the first time many
indigenous teachers of Eastern traditions, Vivekananda among them.
The sheer novelty of the ideas that he taught, not to speak of his own intellectual and spiritual brilliance, caught the imagination of his Western
audiences. Notwithstanding the translations of the Upanishads and the
Bhagavad Gita that were circulating in some circles and the marginal
presence of Hindu ideas among the Transcendentalists, it was Vivekananda's physical presence on the American soil and the enthusiastic
reception and exposure in the newspapers that his ideas received which
made Hinduism more visible and in some sense signaled its arrival in
North America.

5. Marie Louise Burke, *Swami Vivekananda in the West: New Discoveries*, 6 vols.
(Calcutta: Advaita Ashrama, 1983) 1:223.

Although his early lectures were devoted to clarifying the "manners and customs of India" and explaining the basic tenets of his Hindu tradition, Vivekananda shifted the discourse to the principles that guided Hindu thinking. This instinctive and adroit shift from particulars to the general, or from "manners and customs" to philosophy, put the focus not on Hinduism but on what Vivekananda preferred to call Vedanta. He employed the word "Vedanta" in three different ways. First, it was used as a more accurate term to denote "Hinduism" or the wisdom that guides the Hindu way of life. The word *Hindu* originally referred merely to the people living on the other side of the river Sindhu, and that—in Vivekananda's time in the late nineteenth century—would include Christians, Muslims, Jains, and others as well. So the word, according to Vivekananda, had "lost its significance." He asked in 1897: "What word should we use then? The other words which alone we can use are either the Vaidikas, followers of the Vedas, or better still, the Vedantists, followers of the Vedanta."[6] Vivekananda was aware of the mind-boggling diversity in what passes under the name of "Hinduism" and explained his rationale for using the word "Vedanta" thus:

> It is very hard, therefore, to find any common name for our religion, seeing that this religion is a collection, so to speak, of various religions, of various ideas, of various ceremonials and forms, all gathered together almost without a name, and without a church, and without an organization. The only point where, perhaps, all our sects agree is that we all believe in the scriptures—the Vedas. This perhaps is certain that no man can have a right to be called a Hindu who does not admit the supreme authority of the Vedas . . . Whatever be his philosophy or sect, every one in India has to find his authority in the Upanishads. If he cannot, his sect would be heterodox. Therefore, perhaps the one name in modern times which would designate every Hindu throughout the land would be "Vedantist" or "Vaidika," as you may put it; and in that sense I always use the words "Vedantism" and "Vedanta."[7]

This is important to keep in mind, for Vivekananda's use of the term *Vedanta* often gets mistakenly and narrowly identified with Vedanta (or Uttara-Mimamsa) as one of the six orthodox systems of Hindu

6. *The Complete Works of Swami Vivekananda*, 9 vols. (Calcutta: Advaita Ashrama, 1976) 3:118, hereafter cited as *CW*.

7. *CW* 3:228–29.

philosophy. Vivekananda also made it clear that it was wrong to identify Vedanta exclusively with the nondualistic (advaita) school of thought. The other schools of qualified nondualism (visishtadvaita) and dualism (dvaita) have "as much reverence for the Upanishads" and "claim as much authority for Vedanta" as the nondualists.[8]

The second way in which Vivekananda used the term Vedanta was as a text, referring to the Upanishads which are said to contain the essence of Vedic wisdom (Veda + anta, essence). But the evolution in the meaning of Vedanta goes even further in Vivekananda's exposition. Going to the basic meaning of the term *Veda*, in the sense of "knowledge" (Sanskrit *vid*, to know), the word "Vedanta" acquires a universal connotation, meaning the "essence of knowledge." In this sense, it becomes transcultural, crossing religious boundaries, and embracing the truth in its entirety, no matter in what cultural, religious, linguistic, and philosophical form it is clothed. In this highest generalization of the term, it breaks free from even the limitation of the term *Hinduism* and becomes identified with truth itself. It is this truth that Vivekananda taught under the name *Vedanta*, albeit clothed in Hindu terminology and conceptual framework. Vivekananda made it clear that any other terminology and any other framework would be equally effective and powerful, so long as they yielded what every human heart instinctively longs for: purity and perfection, fulfillment and freedom.

Vivekananda's teaching found a permanent home through a string of Vedanta societies that were founded in America, two of these by him in New York (1894) and San Francisco (1900). Today there are twenty Vedanta societies with resident monastics, and several more groups organized informally in other cities under the guidance of Vedanta monks and nuns. Besides a full roster of programs at the Vedanta societies, Vivekananda's successors are active on college campuses and work with interfaith groups in major cities of America. The Vedanta societies don't proselytize and the "Hinduism" that is taught and practiced there, although still a work in progress, is a good example of how a religion transplanted from one culture to another can evolve through assimilation and absorption of the strong elements in the two cultures.

The Vedanta societies in America are branches of the Ramakrishna Order, named after Sri Ramakrishna (1836–1886), a much-revered Hindu saint who was Vivekananda's guru. The Order's branches in India

8. *CW* 3:229.

and other Asian countries are generally known as Ramakrishna Math or Ramakrishna Mission. They not only serve as centers for religious study and practice but also do enormous work in the fields of health, education, and rehabilitation during natural calamities.

Paramahansa Yogananda and SRF

In the early decades of the twentieth century, "Vedanta" became the Western face of Hinduism and evolved along the lines initiated by Vivekananda. The Hindu teachers that came after him generally downplayed Hindu mythology, ritual, and personalities, and focused on principles and practice. Paramahansa Yogananda (1893–1952) arrived in 1920 to speak at the International Congress of Religious Liberals in Boston and made America the focus of his work. Presenting his teachings in lay and scientific terms while avoiding Sanskrit terms from Hindu scriptures and frequently invoking the Bible, Yogananda won the hearts of his listeners for the next three decades. He soon set up the Self-Realization Fellowship (SRF). His book, *The Autobiography of a Yogi*, first published in 1946, became a bestseller and has remained a perennial favorite of those interested in Eastern, more specifically Hindu, wisdom.

Moving to the West Coast, Yogananda built his movement's headquarters in California. The spiritual practice he taught was Kriya Yoga. He and his organization understood the pulse of the people well, as is evident from his teaching in a manner with which Westerners could relate. The titles of some of his lectures makes that obvious: "Everlasting Youth," "Science of Healing," and "The Science of Success and the Art of Getting What You Want."[9] Yogananda quickly developed a large following and also reached out to more people by making his lessons available via mail order. Today SRF has more than five hundred temples and centers spread in more than fifty countries.

Maharishi Mahesh Yogi and TM

The next Hindu teacher who created waves in the West was Maharishi Mahesh Yogi (1914–2008). Such was the power of his personality and

9. Philip Goldberb, *American Veda: From Emerson and the Beatles to Yoga and Meditation: How Indian Spirituality Changed the West* (New York: Harmony, 2010) 116.

teaching that among his early followers were celebrities such as the Beatles and Mia Farrow, whose association with the Maharishi propelled his own popularity to great heights. Like Vivekananda and Yogananda before him, he was the product of a Western-style education and was fluent in English. Following their lead, he stressed the "scientific" nature of his teaching, almost dissociating it from popular religion. For instance, he preferred the use of the term "deep rest" to samadhi and made meditation fashionable, telling his followers that it was so simple and natural that anyone could do it. His teaching on meditation was called "Transcendental Meditation" and became popularly known as TM.

TM opened the door to the scientific study of meditation. Its popularity had less to do with its being a religious practice and more to do with it being presented as a secular and scientific exercise that produced tangible, this-worldly results such as stress-reduction and a peaceful life free from anxieties and traumas. The promise that meditation had the power to remove emotional wounds and other karmic disturbances attracted thousands to its practice. By the mid-'60s TM centers had opened in many world capitals and had attracted people of all ages, especially college students. The numbers of those practicing TM swelled to several hundred thousand when teachers in large numbers were systematically trained to initiate newcomers in the art of meditation.

Maharishi gave Vedanta a secularized name: "Science of Creative Intelligence," and it became the focus of Maharishi's International University, which opened in 1973 outside Santa Barbara in California, and moved a year later to Fairfield, Iowa, under the name of Maharishi University of Management. The organization was incorporated as an educational nonprofit, not as a church. The Maharishi's method of work and his approach were markedly different from those adopted earlier by Vivekananda and Yogananda. The Maharishi, his family, and close associates created charitable organizations and for-profit businesses in the West that include nearly one thousand TM centers, schools, universities, clinics, health supplements, and organic farms.

Srila Prabhupada and ISKCON

A. C. Bhaktivedanta Swami (1896–1977)—Srila Prabhupada to his followers—appeared on the scene a few years after Maharishi. Prabhupada primarily taught the path of devotion (bhakti) to Krishna and spread the teachings of Gaudiya Vaishnavism. In an environment that was ripe for alternative forms of spirituality, he encouraged his audiences, which consisted of hippies, folksingers and protesters, to chant the name of God, specifically, the name of Krishna. He established the International Society for Krishna Consciousness, or ISKCON, more popularly known as simply the "Hare Krishnas." It needed extraordinary courage and conviction to start a movement that required its followers to be celibate, vegetarian, and drug-free. Not all followers submitted to these requirements fully, but many made a valiant effort and some succeeded. Prabhupada was convinced that their waywardness and frivolities would be abandoned when they experienced "Krishna consciousness," or the bliss of love for Krishna. The ISKCON movement also achieved prominence by the committed support of George Harrison, one of the Beatles, who remained a staunch supporter until his death.

Besides Vivekananda, Yogananda, Maharishi, and Prabhupada, whose impact in America was profound and lasting, there were several other Hindu teachers, including Swami Muktananda of the Siddha Yoga lineage, who were the focus of great interest for some time. Some of the teachers and the movements they initiated became mired in controversies and scandals, and a few others seemingly vanished after a blitz of media exposure. Among the contemporary Hindu teachers with considerable influence in the West is Mata Amritanandamayi Devi (b. 1953), popularly known as "The Hugging Saint" or "The Hugging Mother." While her teachings comprise the traditional Hindu elements, the distinguishing feature of her mission is the hug that everyone receives from her when they approach her with their spiritual questions or worldly afflictions. With her hug she offers both consolation and guidance, and her followers have reported finding joy and peace as a result of practicing her teachings. While normally stationed in India, she undertakes regular world tours and has thousands of admirers and devotees in America and other Western countries.

Most of the Hindu teachers in America, past and present, emphasize the universality of their teachings. This makes sense, considering the fact that the majority of their listeners in the first half of the twentieth century were neither Hindus nor India-born. The early Hindu teachers presented their teachings in a logical manner, showing how "scientific" their approach was, and this was clearly a major reason their ideas were warmly received. Whether the rationalism and cosmopolitanism were inherent in their Hindu upbringing or whether they were acquired as students in their British-run schools in India is the question. According to Lola Williamson, it is the latter. Speaking of "natural religion" based on rationality, she writes, "It begins with Enlightenment ideas in Europe and America, travels to India through the British, becomes part of the Hindu Renaissance, and then returns to America in the nineteenth and twentieth centuries with the teachings of Hindu gurus."[10] The influence of Western-style education and the early Orientalists on some of these teachers is unquestionable, and it stands to reason that, equipped with that education, they were able to closely examine their own tradition and easily find the characteristics that would appeal to Western audiences. This also explains the reluctance of the early teachers to speak about aspects of Hinduism that were specifically India-centric, namely, the beliefs, rituals, and mythologies that were meaningful only to those born and raised in that culture. Vivekananda, for instance, taught that principles were universal, not persons. He wrote in Bengali from New York in 1896 in a letter to a fellow monk: "The masses will always have the person, the higher ones the principle; we want both. But principles are universal, not persons. Therefore stick to the principles he [Ramakrishna] taught, let people think whatever they like of his person."[11] Vivekananda focused on principles of Hinduism—the word *Vedanta* became more closely associated with his teaching—recognizing that these principles could be adapted by anyone and incorporated, wholly or partially, into their own cultural and religious worldview.

Hinduism in the Post-1960s

The 1960s brought about great changes in America. There was greater openness to what was new, almost a demand for something radically different, such was the atmosphere of disillusionment and the dislike toward social and religious conformity. In such an environment, it was possible to present culture-specific icons and practices, which is precisely what Prabhupada did through ISKCON, encouraging the worship of Krishna and introducing Gaudiya Vaishnava ritual, mythology, and belief-system. In those years of free exploration, Muktananda's Siddha Yoga also thrived with its promise of shaktipat, the awakening of the

10. Williamson, *Transcendent in America*, 23.
11. *CW* 6:362.

kundalini. All of this proves, yet again, the need for practices, rites, images, etc., as abstract philosophy can be intellectually stimulating but is seldom enough for deeper and lasting fulfillment. A large number of Americans embraced alternative forms of spirituality in the 1960s, and Hindu teachers found eager and sincere followers, mostly young people, who were hungry to learn and experience something new.

The Vedanta societies in America, whose activities had until then revolved around lectures and scripture classes by swamis of the Ramakrishna Order, began to be more open about their worship (*puja*) practices. Before the '60s, the shrine in the Vedanta societies often remained a private area, where the swamis prayed, worshiped and meditated. The shrine was accessible only to a few close members. After the '60s, newcomers found easier access to the shrines and the *pujas* became more public. Durga Puja and Kali Puja, the ritualistic worship of God as Mother, are now celebrated in most of the Vedanta societies and draw record crowds every year. This has attracted a greater number of people of Indian origin, whose presence has altered the demographic of the Vedanta societies. The influx of Indian immigrants in America since the mid-sixties has radically changed the face of Hinduism in the country.

Hinduism in America: Through Immigrants

The Immigration and Nationality Act of 1965 was a watershed moment in Asian American history. Reversing decades of exclusion and restrictive immigration policies, the Act resulted in large numbers of immigrants from non-Western nations entering the United States. These new arrivals, which included a significant number of Hindus from India, have transformed the demographic, economic, and cultural characteristics of many urban areas. According to a 2007 estimate, Hindus constitute about 0.4 percent of the total population.[12] The number is small, but it still is a great leap from the almost nonexistent presence of Hindus before the immigration law was relaxed.

The arrival of hundreds of thousands of Hindus born and raised in India succeeded in changing how Hinduism was viewed and how it was presented. Almost all of the early Hindu entrants in America were either students or trained engineers and doctors. They came to the New

12. Pew Forum on Religion & Public Life's US Religious Landscape Survey 2007. Online: http://www.pewforum.org/.

World for higher studies, better research facilities, and more lucrative jobs. Many who came as students remained after graduation, found jobs, raised families, and made America their home. While the excitement of finding one's bearing in a new place and new culture lasted for a few years, it was not long before they began to experience pangs of separation from the land of their birth, which had been their cultural, social, and religious home. The memory of their Indian childhood and upbringing became even more intense when they faced the responsibility of raising their own children in their adopted land.

The emphasis on principles that Vedanta represents, and that was highlighted by early Hindu teachers in the West, was replaced in Indian immigrant communities by the emphasis on tradition, which usually meant "doing things the way they are done in India." Beginning with small weekly gatherings and family shrines, there were soon large temples in major cities. Hindu ritual hadn't received much prominence in the early decades of the twentieth century, but now it became important. There are currently more than one hundred temples in the United States, spread across forty-two states.[13] Trained staff is often imported from India for the daily services in the temples. Visits to these temples by students and interfaith groups are common in order to get a firsthand acquaintance with Hinduism. A new wave of Hindu teachers, whose teaching is directed primarily to ethnic Indians, have made their way to America to supply the need for the kind of Hinduism that most immigrants long for.

Not surprisingly, the kinds of tensions common within all new immigrant communities have surfaced between the generation that arrived from India and their children (and grandchildren) who are born and raised in America. The issues at stake are not simply their cultural and national identities but also their religious identities, and what kind of religion they belong to. Parents often raise their children with Indian-style Hinduism at home, complete with a list of *dos* and *don't*s, but they don't—often because they cannot—explain to them why things are done in a specific way. This creates problems for the children in a public space, such as when they go to school and are not able to articulate what their religion stands for or why its specific practices are done. There is an intense desire to belong and to have a strong religious identity, but not enough authentic resources available to help the new generation of

13. For a complete listing, see online: http://hindutemples.us/.

Hindus growing in the country. Although a few colleges and universities have Hindu chaplains on their campuses, their numbers is considerably smaller than the need.

Another source of tension is the way Hinduism is presented in classrooms and the way it is practiced at home. In India religion is learned at home or in places of worship, in nonacademic settings. In most Indian schools and colleges, religious study enters haphazardly and hesitatingly through courses on history, culture, philosophy and "moral science." The academic study of religion has not become a part of Indian education system in a significant way. By contrast, Hinduism has been studied in America long before Hindu immigrants arrived in large numbers. The early wave of Hindus were—and most of them even today are—primarily engaged in the fields of medicine and technology. Very few, if any, are interested in humanities, religion in particular, since it isn't considered a worthy academic pursuit on which to build a financially strong career. For all these reasons, the number of Hindu practitioners teaching Hinduism in academia is still considerably smaller than Hinduism scholars who are not themselves religiously Hindu.

Although most scholars of Hinduism and those who write books on Hinduism are respectful of the tradition and make a sincere effort to be fair and objective, their findings, interpretations and conclusions are sometimes at odds with the kind of Hinduism the immigrants learned and practiced in India. Nor is it the Hinduism that they have taught their children and that is practiced at home. This disconnect between Hinduism as presented in the public domain and as practiced in the privacy of home has understandably generated tension, particularly since those teaching and writing books are generally not Hindus. It has either dismayed and confused the hapless Hindu students and appalled their elders, or produced vocal protests at what they perceived as a willful maligning or belittling of what was sacred to them. In response to this disconnect, several advocacy groups have sprung up to represent and defend Hindu interests. With the growth of such groups, Hindus have begun to assert themselves more visibly and vocally in social, cultural and political affairs of the country.

The State of Hinduism in America

The three Hindu waves—the texts, the teachers, and the immigrants—on the religious waters of America have continued to renew themselves, their mutual interactions and their engagement with American culture have continued the process of assimilation and absorption. In due course we may see a form of Hinduism, still recognizable with its Indian roots, but which will have become American in every other way. That day is still far off, but the process is already under way.

While it is difficult to make a definitive statement about where Hinduism stands today in America, a few critical reflections might contribute to the topic which must be viewed from different angles and at different levels. Needless to say this is clearly an enterprise that is beyond the scope of a single observer.

Hinduism and Education

Hindu children continue to learn the basics of their religious beliefs and practices at home but they also have the opportunity to study them in the classroom. America is now the most religiously diverse nation on the planet and most of its schools offer courses and opportunities to study different faiths. How these faiths are represented in textbooks has justifiably become a sensitive issue, since a biased or prejudiced view can do immense harm when it is thrust upon impressionable young minds. In 2005 a controversy erupted in California over what was seen as an unfair portrayal of Hinduism and Indian history in sixth-grade history textbooks, generating much anger and frustration. In response, a few textbook publishers quickly moved to have sections on Hinduism edited and revised by Hindu scholars and practitioners to make sure that there were no gross factual errors or prejudiced interpretations.

The gulf separating academic and nonacademic study of Hinduism needs to be bridged, and it must be done without diminishing the value of either. This is not easy, considering that such a gulf continues to exist in the study of other religions as well. But it would do a world of good to Religious Studies as a whole if ways could be found to share the insights across the insider/outsider, practitioner/scholar divides. It might help the world's increasingly secular societies to recognize the value of studying religion even if many may not subscribe to it—and this can be done without compromising their declared allegiance to the basic values of secularism.

Hinduism and Universality

The relationship between religion and culture is a complicated subject, for the terms "religion" and "culture" are defined in diverse ways. Nevertheless, it cannot be denied that religion and culture provide strong support to each other, and the two can be so powerfully intertwined in so many different ways that they might seem inseparable. This can be challenging when a religion lays claim to being universal. That is the difficulty Hinduism in the West faces: even when it emphasizes how universal its principles are, Hinduism's identification with Indian culture makes it seem not so universal, after all, and raises interesting questions. There are no easy answers to these questions. No world religion with a substantial following speaks with one voice, certainly not Hinduism which historically has been as decentralized and as unorganized as any religion can ever be.

If Hinduism's claim to universality is to be taken seriously, then it should be possible to de-link its principles from Indian culture. In other words, even a person from a different culture should be able learn, practice, and benefit from Hindu wisdom without having to sacrifice his or her native culture—and, more importantly, be accepted as a genuine Hindu. This is possible and has happened in a few cases,[14] but the connection between Hinduism and Indian culture is too strong at present to make this a common occurrence.

Media can play a major role in shaping opinion, establishing connections and leading others toward a desired conclusion. The existing books, both fiction and nonfiction, theater, television and movies still play to stereotypes of Hinduism as an ethnic Indian religion. The early books on Hinduism were primarily translations of Hindu scriptures. The majority of books today deal with a host of other subjects related to Hinduism. Some of the books are found shelved in the New Age section in bookstores, which is ironic, considering that if any religion can lay claim to being really Old Age, it would be Hinduism. Many fine and

14. See, for instance, Jeffery D. Long, *A Vision for Hinduism: Beyond Hindu Nationalism* (London: Tauris, 2007) 5–20.

thought-provoking books on Hinduism have been published by some scholars in recent years.[15]

Hinduism and Interfaith Dialogue

Hindus have historically not been enthusiastic participators in interfaith dialogue. This may have something to do with India's unpleasant experience with aggressive Muslim invaders and proselytizing Christian missionaries in past centuries. The suspicion that the "dialogue" is meant to only establish a connection which will later be exploited to the other's advantage may have held back many Hindus from even offers that were genuine and well-meaning. The other reason for the lack of enthusiasm may also be the self-serving and delusional perception of Hindus that they are far superior to others and have nothing to learn from them. After all, some ancient Hindu texts had a word for those not a part of Hindu society: *mleccha*, and it is derogatory in every sense of the term. There are innumerable studies of Hinduism by other religionists but hardly any of other religions by Hindus.

Thankfully these attitudes are on the decline and Hindus in America today seem genuinely interested in interfaith dialogue. On campuses across the country, Hindu students actively participate in interfaith activities, often taking leading roles in such programs. For interfaith dialogues to be raised to the next level, it is necessary that every participant be taken seriously in order to make genuine sharing possible. Being still a minority and their faith still little understood, Hindu participants often find themselves on the back foot, explaining popular misconceptions regarding their faith rather than, as equal partners, sharing the wisdom of their tradition. This will no doubt change in the years ahead and the quality of the interfaith dialogue and programs will improve.

It is useful to recognize a "dialogue" that has already taken place in America for decades now, silently and unobtrusively and often unconsciously. It can be seen at the individual level, when Hindus in America interact with their neighbors, friends, co-workers, and converse on diverse topics including religion. It occurs also through letters and emails that are exchanged between them. The essays and books on Hinduism, followed by responses and counterresponses to them, can be viewed as

15. Among these are the books of Francis X. Clooney, Anantanand Rambachan, Jefferey D. Long, and Gavin D. Flood.

a form of literary dialogue. Thus it is possible for a dialogue to occur in real time as well as spread over days, years, even centuries. It is the exchange of ideas that is central to a dialogue, not when and in what form that exchange occurs.

"We Are All Hindus Now"—Really?

Lisa Miller created a minisensation with her provocative column titled "We Are All Hindus Now," in *Newsweek* (August 31, 2009). Among the staggering statistics she provided from a 2008 Pew Forum survey and a 2008 Harris poll were these: 65 percent of Americans (including 37 percent of white evangelicals) believe that "many religions can lead to eternal life," and 24 percent believe in reincarnation. According to the Cremation Association of North America, more than 33 percent of Americans now choose cremation, up from 6 percent in 1975.[16] Add to this the phenomenal growth of yoga studios around the country and the entry into mainstream language of words such as karma, yoga, guru, pundit, and kundalini, and one may begin to wonder at the extent of Hinduism's influence in America. While Hindus have generally been proud of these changes and cite these as evidence of Hinduism's influence on American culture, questions have been raised about how much of this can really be credited to the influence of Hinduism and how much of it is due to a combined influence of many other factors.

A more interesting response to the phenomenon may be: so what? Just how much does any religion really own an idea or a concept or even a practice? At a deeper level, aren't we all simply human beings trying to figure out our place in this life, its meaning and purpose and goal, and using whatever historical, cultural, intellectual, and religious resources are available to us? Just as the meaning, need, and utility of national boundaries can be questioned in today's world filled with multinational corporations and international trade agreements, the meaning, need and utility of religious boundaries can also be questioned. For, when we begin to reflect deeply on the basic questions of human existence, we become earnest students of life finding our way in the darkness of ignorance and willing to welcome the light of knowledge, no matter from which direction it comes.

16. Lisa Miller, "We Are All Hindus Now," *Newsweek*, August 14, 2009. The complete text of Miller's essay can be found online: http://www.newsweek.com/id/212155/.

Desperately clinging to one's religious identity may one day become as incongruous as clinging to one's identity as a child. After all, we do outgrow the various stages of life, so it should be no big deal to one day outgrow all identities that somehow cut us off and separate us from others. Can we discover our identity which is absolute and independent of everything? That, at any rate, is the Hindu ideal, which even the Vedas become non-Vedas.[17] At that point, all concepts break down to reveal the truth which is not the monopoly of any single religion: it is the truth that belongs to all, it is the truth that is all.

This thesis naturally raises two questions: what *really* constitutes Hindu identity and how important is it?

Hindu Identity

Because of Hinduism's historical connection with India and its culture, there is still a strong ethnic element associated with Hindu identity. Thus merely being born into a Hindu family establishes one's Hindu identity unless she or he publicly disowns it. Even people who don't observe any Hindu festival or practice can identify themselves as Hindus, but this serves simply as their identity marker and nothing beyond that. Hindu identity becomes meaningful and religiously significant only when a person professing it studies Hindu scriptures; observes Hindu rituals and festivals; or practices prayer, worship, and meditation as taught in the Hindu tradition. While those who are born Hindus may or may not do any of this, those who adopt Hinduism as their primary religious identity most certainly do. It is also possible to do all of these things and yet not formally identify oneself as a Hindu. Considerable fluidity thus exists in questions related to Hindu identity.

Even though Maharishi and his TM movement studiously avoided using religious terms, going to the extent of incorporating their organization as an educational nonprofit, not as a church, it still was seen as "Hindu." The word "Hindu" is rarely invoked in the discourses of Yogananda's successors at SRF, as also at the Vedanta societies, and yet they are viewed as Hindu. How we identify ourselves and how others identify us may not always be same. It cannot be denied that, whether publicly acknowledged or not, Hindu identity provides the person with a worldview and a framework through which to understand life's purpose and

17. *Brihadaranyaka Upanishad* 4.3.22.

meaning. It is also undeniable that Hindu identity becomes vital in the observation of Hindu sacraments, as it determines how the key elements of life-cycle events such birth, marriage and death are observed.

Implicit in the Hindu worldview is a view of the truth *beyond* the world. The truth that Hinduism points to is beyond birth and death, beyond time and space, and beyond all duality. The Hindu way of life is designed to prepare a person to travel on this pathless path that is beyond all concepts and ideas, including the idea of "Hinduism." This is illustrated in the Hindu tradition by the example of a tiny plant that needs to be hedged and protected when it is young, but which eventually outgrows the need for protection when it is strong and mature. From this perspective, all religious faiths provide the necessary protection and care to a soul when it is weak, but it must eventually become strong and break free from the need to be confined within concepts and ideas. For the truth is not only different from but also infinitely greater than any idea of it. The truth that is pointed out in the Hindu tradition is not a Hindu truth any more than it is a Christian truth or an Islamic truth. No one has a monopoly over that truth. It is the truth that stands on its own merit, without any name and without any form. To put it into words is to distort it. It is meant only to be experienced in the depths of one's being. When that ineffable experience occurs, all identities are discarded, including Hindu identity.

9

Converts to Islam as Culture Brokers
Classical and Contemporary Examples

Marcia Hermansen

In the following paper I intend to explore the conference theme "Inter-religious Dialogue and the Cultural Shaping of Religions" through the topic of conversion to Islam. Conversions take place both at the historical centers and on the expanding frontiers of religions, sites where cultural shaping is most evident in the lives of individuals and the tradition as a whole. I will use the cases of recent Western converts to Islam to argue that contemporary developments such as globalization and mobility may have shifted attitudes to cultural brokerage while allowing more conscious articulations of what is either essential or "cultural" about religious identity and practice. Before I do so, I will lay out several instances of premodern conversion to Islam in order to set the stage for considering elements of continuity and change in the roles played by converts in the cultural shaping of religion.

It is not my intent to claim that "conversion" is either theologically or phenomenologically the same across disparate religions. At the same time, although my examples are drawn from Islamic contexts, I suggest that they raise theoretical questions of general interest and applicability. The figure of the convert in interreligious dialogue is itself provocative. Are converts evidence of the success or the failure of this enterprise?

Converts are, on the whole, on the front lines of borrowing, bricolage, and acculturation and therefore need to be considered within any discussion of the cultural shaping of religion.

Let's start with a very broad look at conversions and the concept of the "origins" of Islam. Islamic theology is supersessionist with regard to previous religions and cultures and yet has mechanisms for a strategic acceptance of continuity. Islam views itself as the final and complete revelation in a series of prophetic missions that go back, at the cosmic or mythic level, to the prototypical human, Adam, who is also incorporated as a Prophet, into Islam. Islam is further conceived of as the natural (*fitri*) religion.[1] This motif has further theological backing in the Qur'anic motif (7:172) of the Primordial Covenant in which all souls who will ever come into existence stand before Allah in a time before time (pre-eternity) and respond to the question, "Am I not your Lord" with the attestation, "Yes, indeed you are." This covenant establishes the Islamic theological framework that humanity must recognize or remember the truth (believe in God) that is already innate. While Islam as a specific historical religion and practice emerged in seventh-century Arabia, for Muslims the essence of generic "islam" is the eternal and existential relation of the universe and humanity to the Creator God.[2]

That having been said, in historical terms, even on the basis of the corpus of Muslim insider sources such as the Qur'an, hadith, and the early biographies (siyar) of the Prophet Muhammad and his Companions, it is clear that there were preexisting religious and cultural currents in Arabia, and that individuals around the Prophet shifted their allegiances,[3] practices, and world views from these to the new Islamic

1. As in the hadith report that all humans are created according to an inherent nature (*fitra*). The general interpretation is that this sound inherent nature is "Islam." There are a number of hadith on this theme reported in Muslim's collection under "qadr" (destiny). #6425 Abu Huraira reported Allah's Messenger (may peace be upon him) as saying: "Every child is born but according to Fitra. He then said. Recite: The nature made by Allah in which He created man, there is no altering of Allah's nature; that is the right religion" (30:33). #6426 Abu Huraira reported Allah's Messenger (may peace be upon him) as saying: "No babe is born but upon *Fitra*. It is his parents who make him a Jew or a Christian or a Polytheist."

2. On the contrast of "Islam" vs. "islam" see Sachiko Murata and William C. Chittick, *The Vision of Islam* (New York: Paragon, 1994) 45–47.

3. The question of the religion of the Prophet Muhammad, and even his parents, before Islam, can be somewhat delicate. They are not considered to have practiced pre-Islamic paganism but rather are placed in a category of "hanifs"—pre-Islamic instinctive monotheists.

religious and social order through processes of *baya* (swearing allegiance to the Prophet Muhammad), *Islam* (practicing particular ritual actions), and *iman* (espousing specific theological doctrines).[4] In fact these three elements, that could represent identity, practice, and beliefs, may serve as guidelines in this paper for subsequent discussions of the negotiation of religion and culture in the Islamic tradition.

In addition to its supersessionist outlook, Islam is also inclusivist in terms of its relationship to Judaism and Christianity. The purpose of the new religious dispensation is said to be correcting errors and distortions in practice and belief that had crept into those previous revelations, either through historical slippage or deliberate human manipulation. At the same time there is an acknowledgement of elements of continuity in many religious practices and central tenets, allowing Jews and Christians to be characterized as fellow "Peoples of the Book." Pre-Islamic tribal religion is more directly rejected and replaced, yet even in this case there exists the view that in the past the Arabs had been following soundly revealed practices that had decayed over time, thus allowing some continuities to be maintained, for example, in the pilgrimage rites surrounding the Ka'ba.

Early Muslim negative valuations of non-Islamic Arabian culture are represented by the term *Jahiliyya*, meaning "the Age of Ignorance." The culture of the Jahiliyya Arab tribes before the coming of the Islamic revelation was considered to be rough, quarrelsome, and ignorant. In the mid-twentieth century the term *jahiliyya* reemerged in the writings of Islamists such as Sayyid Qutb (d. 1966) and Abu'l Ala' Maududi (d. 1978) who condemned what they perceived to be a new "ignorant age," defined by the West or by modernity conceived in secular terms that were challenging and changing the face and tastes of Muslim societies and therefore needed to be resisted by a return to faith and an Islamization of social and political institutions. According to this model, Islam and its corresponding social and political sphere were portrayed as an ideal total system or a complete way of life set off against negative non-Islamic alternatives. This modern characterization of *jahiliyya* often has ramifications for rejecting cultural elements, not only modern Western ones, but many practices developed in many regions of the Muslim world over the long history of Islamic expansion and the acculturation

---

4. On this see W. C. Smith's writings on faith and belief in Islam, including *Faith and Belief* (Princeton: Princeton University Press, 1979).

of diverse populations that cannot find textual justification or precedent in the Qur'an or the recorded practice of Muhammad and his
Companions.

Muslim Converts as Culture Brokers: Historical Examples

I will summarize three historical moments or examples of conversion as
background for this discussion:

1) The first is the phenomenon of early converts from Judaism and
Christianity becoming cultural brokers in the formation of Islamic tradition. This example illustrates the early challenge of defining legitimate
vs. illegitimate continuities or borrowings from previous religions and
cultures.

The trope is of Jewish rabbis in Medina testing the knowledge of
Muhammad against their own heritage appears on several occasions in
the Qur'an. In each case Muhammad has knowledge of shared religious
history or elements that surpasses that of the rabbis, or alternatively he
receives revelation that corrects their views, or simply states that the
matter is not one within the scope of human knowledge. For example
the verse: "They will ask you about the Spirit, Say (O Muhammad) the
Spirit is at the Command of my Lord and you have been given but little
knowledge" (Q 17:85).

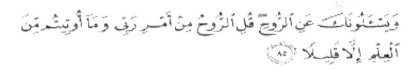

This verse is said to have been revealed at a time when rabbis in Medina
queried Muhammad about the "Spirit." Yet the Qur'an is elliptical in
many of its accounts of previous Prophets and events of sacred history
that were familiar in Biblical tradition and exegesis. The emergence in
early Islamic history of a group of raconteurs known as the *Qussas*, who
enthralled the new Muslim community by elaborating on the Qur'anic
material is thought by some to have been a response to a thirst for more
detailed accounts at the popular level.[5] This burgeoning extra-Qur'anic

5. Jonathan P. Berkey, *Popular Preaching and Religious Authority in the Medieval
Islamic Near East* (Seattle: University of Washington Press, 2001).

corpus spawned several genres of literature that are broadly defined part of Islamic religious tradition, such as the "tales of the Prophets" (*Qisas al-Anbiya*).[6] Much of this material ultimately found its way into Qur'anic exegesis (*tafsir*), and the hadith collections that were, after all, only compiled in the ninth century and later. Materials that were suspected to have been drawn from the Jewish tradition are somewhat pejoratively termed, the *Isra'iliyyat* (tales from the Israelites).[7] Attitudes to these materials in Muslim scholarship vary, but are often suspicious if not downright condemnatory. At the same time, the Prophet himself seems to have permitted and even encouraged such cross over.

The case of a particular convert from Judaism to Islam, Muhammad ibn Ka'b al-Qurazi (d. ca 118 AH), is illustrative in that he is regarded both as a valuable narrator of hadith information and a source of interpretive material drawn from Jewish tradition that was acceptable as long as it embellished, rather than contradicted, aspects of Islamic tradition.[8]

Here we have one example of conversion that illustrates ambivalence regarding the incorporation of previous cultures and traditions. We may conclude that the earlier religious tradition with historical and cultural overlap needs to be integrated and learned from, and yet distinguished and distanced during the initial phases of the emergence of a "new" dispensation. This distinction is crucial in the process of establishing and maintaining discrete identity in practice and belief.

2) The second historical example is taken from a crucial period in the formation of Islamic tradition, the ninth century (third Islamic century), a time of scholars' setting the parameters of hadith collection and evaluation, and establishing the roots of the shari'a and applied jurisprudence. With the expansion of Islam as a religion of empire, new populations, in many cases of non-Arab background, were incorporated

---

6. A translation of such tales in literary form is *'Ara'is al-Majalis fi Qisas al-Anbiya or Lives of the Prophets as recounted by Abu IshaqAhmad ibn Muhammad ibn Ibrahim al-Tha'labi*, translated and annotated by William M. Brinner, Studies in Arabic Literature 24 (Leiden: Brill, 2002).

7. Isra'iliyyat traditions are discussed in Brannon M. Wheeler, *Prophets in the Quran: An Introduction to the Quran and Muslim Exegesis* (New York: Continuum, 2002).

8 "Al-Qurazi, Mohammad ibn Ka'b," in *Encyclopaedic Historiography of the Muslim World*, ed. N. K. Singh and A. Samiuddin (New Delhi: Global Vision Publishing House, 2004), 809 ff.

through a process of gradual "Islamization." At a certain point individuals concretely assumed Muslim identity, evidenced in many cases by their changing their names and adopting other aspects of concrete and visible identity. In groundbreaking research, historian Richard Bullied analyzed data found in biographical dictionaries to statistically map the decades when the largest segments of the new populations were going through this transition on the expanding frontiers of the Muslim empire in Iran, Spain, and North Africa.[9]

The results of mapping the highest number of converts corresponded to the precise decades in which the greatest efforts were being made by Muslims in these regions in the articulation of intellectual and procedural strategies to codify and apply traditional materials, in particular, the hadith, in order to derive Islamic practice and belief. It is well known that many of the intellectual giants in this enterprise were, in fact, individuals from Central Asia and Iran, if not converts themselves, then children or grandchildren of the first generation of converted Muslims in their areas. In a historical leap of imagination, I would like to invoke this case as yet another instance of the process of cultural borrowing.

In these cases the converts, coming from distinct (non-Arab) linguistic and cultural spheres, embrace the new religion expanding into their area of the world and with great zeal and enthusiasm, master the prestige language, Arabic. They also appropriate the transmitted religious sources, striving to make sense of them and to make them useful—a sort of routinization of the charisma of the religion and its founder—in a way that struggles to be both traditionally authentic and applicable to its new context. They are thereby inculcating the new outside tradition into their own lives and cultural environment, and through the mastery of its sacred language and sources, they take their own place at its subsequent intellectual center. A prominent example of this is al-Bukhara (d. 870), compiler of the most prestigious hadith collection among Sunni Muslims.

A further dimension of the interplay of Islam and culture both in this period and subsequently, is embodied through the phenomenon of "cultural" Islamization—the gradual assimilation of largely non-Arab pre-Islamic cultural practices, institutions, and tastes to be more in

---

9. Richard Bulliet, *Conversion to Islam in the Medieval Period: An Essay in Quantitative History* (Cambridge: Harvard University Press, 1979). An accessible summary is available online: http://www.fathom.com/feature/2199/index.html/.

conformity with the teachings and practices of the Islamic religion, including bringing them under the purview of Islamic law (shari'a). Muslim intellectuals and legal experts from the time of the classical Muslim empires until today have continued to discuss the relationship between Islam and culture, both in reflecting on the acculturation of diverse regional, cultural, and religious elements and in responding to processes of social and cultural change, especially with the onset of modernity.

Many Muslim thinkers, among them Shah Wali Allah of Delhi, an eighteenth-century figure, have struggled with the conceptual tension between the universal claims of Islam as the final and complete revelation and the legitimacy and persistence of particular historical and cultural articulations of previous religions.[10] As previously noted, the Islamic theology of progressive revelation or supersessionism places Adam as the first Prophet to receive divine guidance. Therefore symbolically or theologically Islam may accord a recognition and acceptance to all human cultural expressions that were deemed neutral or compatible with Islamic norms.

Islam, or more properly, Muslim practices and cultures—the cumulative tradition—were not considered immune to processes of decay and slippage over time. Hence, terms drawn from the earliest Muslims scriptures were applied to characterize corrective movements and processes such as *islah* (reform or correction), *tided* (renewal)[11] and *ihya* (revival). In these cases it was not Islam itself that was conceived of as having been compromised but rather deviant or corrupted practices or beliefs found among the *umma* (the Muslim community).

Particularly in the realm of legal theory, Muslim scholars have debated the extent to which apparently sound or neutral preexisting cultural institutions and practices should be continued or adapted in Islamic societies. In the realm of law, Muslim jurists use the terms *'ada* (custom) and *'urf* (good and acknowledged practice) to indicate how culture, and specifically non-Muslim cultural practices, could be compatible with Islamic norms, even if they were not directly mandated by

10. On this tension see Marcia K. Hermansen, "Shah Wali Allah of Delhi's *Hujjat Allah al-Baligha*: Tension Between the Universal and the Particular in an Eighteenth Century Islamic Theory of Religion," *Studia Islamica* 63 (1986) 143–57.

11. Historian John Voll discussed the concepts of *tajdid* and *islah* in a seminal book chapter, "Renewal and Reform in Islamic History: *Tajdid* and *Islah*," in *Voices of Resurgent Islam*, John L. Esposito, ed. (New York: Oxford University Press, 1983) 32–47.

its codes. Their Qur'anic proof text for this was taken from verse 7:199: "Accept [from people] what comes naturally [for them]. Command what is customarily [good]. And turn away from the ignorant [without responding in kind]."[12]

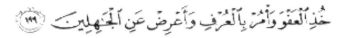

Muslim scholars of the classical period coined the legal maxim that "cultural usage shall have the weight of law" and followed the principle that fair judgments must take into account the particular cultural realities under which diverse Muslims lived.

The early Hanafi scholar Abu Yusuf (d. 798) and the Medieval Maliki jurist al-Qarafi (d. 1285) are examples of Muslim scholars who recognized good, local cultural norms as falling under the rubric of the *sunna*, broadening the concept from the specific precedents established by the Prophet Muhammad.[13] Such Islamic jurists were generally positive toward culture while allocating a transcendent and shaping role to religion.

3) My third premodern example of converts and acculturation involves debates over cultural products and expressions such as music and popular celebrations and how these were sometimes justified as instruments for conversion. We find among some classical Muslim thinkers attitudes that sought to more strictly delimit the bounds of the culturally acceptable. The incorporation or invention of undesirable or even heretical elements was denoted by the term *bid'a*. *Bid'a* conveys the idea of innovation in a negative sense, a heretical innovation in doctrine or practice that attempts to interpolate something that is either culturally alien or newly concocted into Islamic belief or practice. The famous hadith that defines *bid'a* is: "Every new matter is an innovation (*bid'a*), every innovation is misguidance, and every misguidance is in the Fire

12. Ibid., Qur'an 7:199. Muhammad Asad translates this verse as: "Make due allowance for man's nature, and enjoin the doing of what is right; and leave alone all those who choose to remain ignorant."

13. Certain of these legal maxims and concepts are discussed in Umar Faruq Abd-Allah, "The Cultural Imperative"; online: www.nawawi.org/downloads/article3.pdf viewed Sept. 9, 2011. For the maxims see also http://www.uga.edu/islam/law_maxims. html. Sherman Jackson incorporates similar argumentation in his work, *Islam and the Blackamerican: Looking Toward a Third Resurrection* (Oxford: Oxford University Press, 2005).

(of Hell)." [14] On this ground a number of cultural practices and even arts and music, were totally or in part, deemed to be innovative and beyond the pale of Islamic legitimacy and therefore were outlawed and condemned by certain scholars.

A case illustrating this tension might be the use of religious music known as Qawwali by an Indian Sufi Order, the Chishtis, during certain of their rituals. Sufism is the mystical interpretation of the Islamic religion and historically its practices and institutions were very widespread and influential, particularly in areas of the world such as South Asia and Africa where they interfaced well with preexisting local cultures and religious attitudes and practices. In fact, some credit Sufism with enabling the spread of Islam due to its friendliness to local languages and practices, and its colorful and embodied nature that engaged and absorbed local and folk traditions. [15] The Sufis themselves on occasion employed culture-specific explanations to explain why particular practices deemed inappropriate in some contexts might be Islamically and spiritually desirable among new populations. An example is the recommendation of loud and physically robust practices of the *hadra* or *dhikr* for the Turks—who in a culturally essentialist argument, were described as having "rougher" natures. [16] Still I cite this example of a naturist rather than a culturally nativist argument as a premodern attempt to grapple with adjustments in religious tradition at the frontiers of cultural encounter. Later Turkish and European scholars would look at this same phenomenon of culturally distinctive robust practices among Sufi orders in the Turkic cultural sphere, and explain them as the persistence of elements of pre-Islamic shamanic ritual.

Many Muslim religious scholars, classical and contemporary, condemn Sufism as un-Islamic and certain practices such as listening to devotional music as *bid'a*. Recently Wahhabism and its global manifestations have been particularly hostile to Sufism and to cultural artifacts

14. Hadith included in al-Nawawi's, *'Arba'in* as reported from Abu Dawud and al-Tirmidhi.

15. This perception is extremely common at both popular and scholarly levels. See for example, Muzaffar Alam, *The Languages of Political Islam: India 1200–1800* (London: Hurst, 2004) 82ff.

16. *Hadra* is the term in parts of the Arab world for a communal Sufi ritual and *dhikr* (remembrance of God) is individually or communally ritualized in most Sufi communities. For example, Shah Wali Allah in his book on Sufi practices, *Hama'at* (Hyderabad, Pakistan: Shah Wali Allah Academy, 1964) 68ff.

and expressions generally. In fact, debates about the permissibility of forms and genres of music and art mark Islamic religious discussions about the role of culture from very early times until the present. Thus, according to more puritanical interpretations of the religion, not only is the culture previous to Islam, or the cultures into which Islam spread, negatively marked—but certain aspects of human cultural performance are construed in themselves to be frivolous, hostile, or seductive.

Twentieth-century examples of tensions between the religious realm and the cultural one abound, perhaps more prominently in the case of Muslims who were confronted not only by modernity, but by a modernity often defined in culturally alien terms. In the aftermath of the Islamic revolution in Iran of 1979, all music was initially banned. Later, then some revolutionary marches were permitted, and eventually Persian classical music was deemed acceptable, and even promoted by the government.

For contemporary American and global Muslims populations, cultural practices on the front line of *bid'a* debates could include celebrating birthdays, local holidays such as Halloween, Valentine's Day and Thanksgiving, or greeting neighbors and co-workers at the time of their religious festivals.

Contemporary Converts to Islam

Now let us move forward to consider cases of contemporary converts to Islam in the West in terms of the themes of identity, practice, and belief across cultures. As noted in some of the other papers in this volume, many cultural encounters today, including conversions, are no longer exclusively or even primarily construed in terms of Jews or Christians encountering other traditions or vice versa, but rather secular modernity has become the primary cultural and even conceptual partner.

One factor that I have observed to be distinctive about recent conversions to Islam as opposed to premodern cases is the rapidly shifting ground of American culture, in which each decade is popularly perceived to have a dominant theme or ethos.[17] Furthermore, the acculturation of Islam has been profoundly affected by the political relations between the

17. Marcia Hermansen, "Two-Way Acculturation: Muslim Women in America," in *Muslims of America*, ed. Yvonne Y. Haddad (New York: Oxford University Press, 1991) 188–201.

United States and the Muslim world and the global mood about "Islam," Islamic resurgence and revivalism. In a previous paper, I described generational styles or tropes among American women converting to Islam in the late twentieth century, broadly characterized as the social activists of the 1960s, spiritual seekers of the '70s, and the structure-oriented Islamists of the 80s and 90s.[18] My point is that "cultural shaping" across religions is not an exchange across stable or static regional or civilizational wholes but rather consists of groups and individuals negotiating their "crossings" based on elective affinities to what is salient or attractive. These negotiations and perceived affinities are themselves situated within particular, and increasingly changing, Zeitgeists.

Western Converts to Islam: From Colonial to Postcolonial

A further way that I have investigated these historical shifts was by comparing the narratives of Westerners converting to Islam during the colonial period to postcolonial convert narratives.[19] Conversions of Westerners, usually Europeans, to Islam that occurred during the colonial period were often among privileged Europeans who were stationed in the Muslim world or traveled there. Among the motifs that I found in the accounts of these colonial converts that suggest processes of acculturation were their decision to join the Muslims after becoming disaffected by the colonial rule over Muslim societies,[20] and their sentiments that as Europeans or Americans they could somehow influence the direction of Muslim dealings with Western colonial powers more effectively—for the benefit of Muslims.

For example, notable convert intellectual and translator of the Qur'an, Muhammad Asad (d. 1992), noted the perplexity of other Westerners when they realized that "my activities at the United Nations made it obvious that I identified myself not merely 'functionally' but also emotionally and intellectually with the political and cultural

---

18. Hermansen, "Two-Way Acculturation."

19. Marcia Hermansen, "Roads to Mecca Conversion Narratives of European and Euro-American Muslims," *Muslim World* 89 (Jan 1999) 56–89.

20. There is a sense of this in the autobiographical statements of French intellectual convert Roger Garaudy, for example in *Min al-ilhad ila al-Iman: Liqa'at wa muhawarat.* ed. Rami Kallawi (Damascus: Dar Qutayba, 1990) 127–48.

aims of the Muslim world in general."[21] There was also a sense that this would help the Muslims even in the later writings of American convert, Maryam Jameelah, who as a child in the 1940's wrote to her father, "I am saving the pictures and books which Daddy gave me on my birthday so I can go to Egypt or Palestine and keep the Arabs like they are instead of copying us."[22]

The colonial period converts to Islam were unabashed about bringing their previous cultural skills to bear on solving Muslim issues. In some cases they were also drawn to be spokespersons for Islam in Western cultures and to participate in interfaith dialogues—a notable example being the American, Muhammad Russell Webb.[23]

During the colonial period contact with Muslims occurred because Europeans went there and writers conveyed the sense of passing and even surpassing their new Muslim community due to their access to Western power and knowledge. More recent accounts Western conversions to Islam result from shifts in immigration laws and patterns in Europe and the United States.

The means of encounter across traditions likewise is in flux. In twentieth-century conversion accounts much emphasis is given to the importance of reading Islamic literature that had increasingly become available in translation. Now, with the spread of the internet, virtual experiences of Islam and Muslims occur to such an extent that individuals take *shahada* (become Muslim) or join Sufi orders through online communities and virtual practices. The question raised by some of these virtual environments is the extent to which these new forms of practice retain cultural relevance? Do they represent a stage along the way to physical proximity, engagement with Muslims, and acculturation, or have the grounds and spaces of intercultural and interreligious dialogue shifted due to technology?

21. Muhammad Asad, *Road to Mecca* (New York: Simon & Schuster, 1954) 1. Asad was an Austrian Jew who became Muslim in Arabia during the 1920s. He subsequently served as a representative of the new Islamic state, Pakistan, at the United Nations in the late 1940s.

22. Maryam Jameelah, *Memoirs of Childhood and Youth in America (1945–1962): The Story of One Western Convert's Quest for Truth* (Lahore: Muhammad Yusuf Khan & Sons, 1989) 9. Jameelah's autobiographical writings have recently been treated in novel form by Deborah Baker in *The Convert: A Tale of Exile and Extremism* (Minneapolis: Graywolf, 2011).

23. Umar Faruq Abdullah, *A Muslim in Victorian America: The Life of Alexander Russell Webb* (Oxford: Oxford Univesrity Press, 2008).

Returning to the discussion of converts as culture brokers, it is clear that in terms of class analysis the majority of early twentieth-century converts to Islam were privileged European males.[24] Although they may have been considered eccentric for "turning Turk"[25] by their class equals back home, they still had a voice that would be listened to. Postcolonial conversions, in contrast, reflect a new world system of middle class mobility, spreading disenchantment, and personal quest for religious experience, spiritual enlightenment and a sense of communitas. Whether abroad in Muslim societies or in the company of others in the West these new cohorts of converted Muslims seek genuine contact and intimacy. They look into people's eyes and they are impressed by a kind of recognition on the part of the Other which is able to include them in a new sacred community. In doing so they aim to transcend the degradation and alienation of the modern world.

Their conversion accounts also reflect the new mobility of the Western middle classes in terms of resources and travel to exotic locations. Such converts are therefore less prone to exoticize their experience. It is presented not for titillation but as a report of something that others might be considering as well. These accounts are guidebooks, rather than travelogues. In short, the emergence of a "how to" genre of convert literature to Islam suggests a more explicit awareness and expectation of individual converts negotiating the crossing of both religious and cultural worlds.[26]

The impact of globalization on interreligious encounter could profitably be elaborated in terms of literary theorist Ali Behdad's discussion of the nineteenth-century shift from travelogue to guide book

24. At present, female converts are greater in number, which makes sense since more recent conversions are often relational, and it is much more common for male Muslims to have contact with non-Muslim females, given gender expectations and practices.

25. For this expression and the early history of European conversions to Islam, see N. I. Matar, "The Renegade in English Seventeenth-Century Imagination," *Studies in English Literature 1500–1900* 33 (1993) 489–505; and Matar, "Turning Turk: Conversion to Islam in English Renaissance Thought," *Durham University Journal* 86 (1994) 33–41.

26. Examples are the works of Jeffrey Lang, an American professor of mathematics, *Even Angels Ask: A Journey to Islam in America* (Beltsville, MD: Amana, 1997); Lang, *Struggling to Surrender: Some Impressions of an American Convert to Islam* (Beltsville, MD: Amana, 2000); Lang, *Losing My Religion: A Call for Help* (Beltsville, MD: Amana, 2004); and L. Lynn Jones, *Believing as Ourselves* (Beltsville, MD: Amana, 2002).

production in Europe as symptomatic of "belatedness" in travel. Behdad characterizes nineteenth-century travel "as an extension of cultural domination"[27] related to an increase in bourgeois voyaging to the Orient and the economic rationale of making the journey conceivable by making the sites familiar and knowable. There is a resonance between our study of conversion accounts to Islam and the "belated traveler's quest for elsewhere as a response to the onset of modernity in Europe."[28]

Earlier narratives written by converts to Islam tended to implicate Mecca as the "last Orient," the final "elsewhere," and more than one account is identified as being "the first" by a "real" European Muslim to go on the Hajj. In late twentieth-century conversion accounts we still find a certain nostalgia for the authentic, traditional, Orient, and an identification with returning to this original state of authentic spirituality through traditional Islamic practice.[29] However, there is no longer an external "elsewhere" for the Western Muslim converts in the new millennium. They find themselves in a world that is culturally hybridized, yet colonized by monocultural consumer products and media, newly populated by Muslims neighbors and co-workers, yet increasingly politicized along West vs. Islam lines.

At the same time, the Muslims being encountered have changed. In contemporary Muslim societies, and now among Muslim communities settled in the West, the return to piety and the extent of religious revival is quite remarkable. Vast social mobilizations of individuals to support organizations or parties, or simply to enact changes in their own daily lives in the name of religion, are apparent almost everywhere among Muslims. Some of these changes of heart involve attraction to Sufism,[30] some lead to participation in pietistic movements such as the Tablighi Jamaat, and others engender support for Islamist movements and parties.[31]

27. Ali Behdad, *Belated Travelers* (Durham: Duke University Press, 1994) 37.

28. Ibid., 16.

29 I might note some interesting counterexamples of oppositional discourse—a kind of de-orientalized Sufi discourse in some of the followers of Idries Shah, and a kind of popular anti-Islamic writing that celebrates the predilection of "Orientals" for Coca-Cola, blue jeans, and rap music.

30. Fedwa Malti-Douglas, *Medicines of the Soul: Female Bodies and Sacred Geographies in a Transnational Islam* (Berkeley: University of California Press, 2001).

31. As treated by Saba Mahmood, *The Politics of Piety: The Islamic Revival and the Feminist Subject* (Princeton: Princeton University Press, 2005; 2nd ed., 2012).

The modernization theorists of the 1950s and 1960s who argued for an inevitable trajectory of secularism in developing Muslim societies were left behind in the wake of the Iranian revolution of 1978. The continued emergence of successful political Islamization movements in the 1980s, some top-down and some popular, indicates the vitality of internal forces toward conversion in today's Muslim societies.

Evidence of internal conversion processes includes how Muslim women in large numbers—many educated and upwardly mobile—have adopted forms of a global Islamic (shar'i) dress.[32] The cultural capital for today's young Muslims is likely to include manifestations of piety and mastery of the intricacies of Islamic jurisprudence (fiqh) and other discourses of "authentic" Islamic knowledge that were marginalized or neglected in their parents' and grandparents' cohorts. Explanations for these changes include responses to modernity and postmodernity, resistance to Western neo-imperialism, and the impact of access to mass literacy and university education.[33] Can we also consider such developments in terms of cultural and religious borrowings, for example, a global "Protestantization" of religion in which individual interpretation of scripture trumps cultural practices and traditions? Or are forces of modernization and globalization culturally and religiously neutral, arising only from historical and material factors rather than symbolic and ideational change?

Global currents that put "Islam first" may be erosive of distinct cultural expressions of Islam so that the "cultural" in cultural shaping is called into question. Among Islamist Muslims we may observe hostility to culture and an attempt to "correct" or "sift" it. For example, we find this in what Arab American Anthropologist, Nadine Naber, calls the "Islam first" attitude currently prevalent among American Muslim youth.[34] "Islam First" is characterized by an individual's defining identity in terms of "true or pure Islamic practice" which allows a critique or rejection of culture at large as well as of particular Muslim ethnic cultures such as those of immigrant Muslim parents, whose practices may be grounded in specific ethnic or local interpretations rather than Islamic

32. On this development see Leila Ahmed, *A Quiet Revolution: The Veil's Resurgence, from the Middle East to America* (New Haven: Yale University Press, 2011).

33. Dale F. Eickelman, "Mass Higher Education and the Religious Imagination in Contemporary Arab Societies," *American Ethnologist* 19 (1992) 643–55.

34. Nadine Naber, "Muslim First, Arab Second," *Muslim World* 95 (2005) 479.

shari'a norms.[35] I see such trends as running counter to the thesis of an increase in openness to interreligious learning. Just as cultural diversity is flattened in such movements, interreligious learning is likely to be irrelevant or rejected.

Converts to Islam and Interreligious Dialogue: Bridges and Culture Brokers?

As I move to summarize some of the ways in which today's Muslim converts illuminate our theoretical concerns with interreligious dialogue and the mutual shaping of religions and cultures, I think it is clear from my examples and the other case studies presented in this volume that internal variation within a given tradition as well as shifts in historical context present an almost bewildering complexity in considering how these shaping processes occur.

In the case of American Muslims, let me initially set out two special concerns that make their situation especially salient. The first is their minority status in the broader American population, either in terms of their race/ethnicity, their religion as Muslims, or both. The second is a prevailing sense of needing to "resist" some elements of a "dominant" culture, whether that of white Anglo-Saxons or postreligious Americans. In the case of African American Muslims, we also find since the 1980s a need to resist some aspects of the culture of immigrant Muslims who seek to impose their version of Islam on black Americans.[36]

Interreligious learning, then, plays out differently among immigrant Muslim communities than among white or African American converts to Islam. While converts are not always culture brokers, those in that role may be called upon to balance their greater familiarity with the nuances of Christianity or Judaism, not to speak of American secularism, with their choice in rejecting elements of the previous religious and/or secular perspectives in favor of Islamic belief and practice. In order to attempt to give some conceptual order to my observations, I

---

35. A further nuance to this observation is that in some cases "true Islam" may consist of the elements I like, while "parents' culture" is associated with the aspects or practices that I don't like. Since what I like and don't like are to some extent functions of the culture in which I grew up, therefore in some instances "true Islam" may actually represent adjustment to a new local culture.

36. This is discussed by Sherman Jackson, *Islam and the Blackamerican: Looking toward a Third Resurrection* (Oxford: Oxford University Press, 2005).

will highlight four broad categories within which to consider particular Muslim converts and their roles in dialogue and mutual cultural shaping in contemporary America.

The Role of the "Traditionalists" among Western Converts to Islam

Here I refer to a group of individuals known by several designations including, Traditionalists or Perennialists.[37] Earlier Traditionalists such as Rene Guenon (d. 1951) and Frithjof Schuon (d. 1997) were European intellectuals who studied comparative religions and ultimately converted to Sufi or mystical Islam. Each had strong comparative interests and took an approach to traditional religion as having a mystical inner core such that all religions were regarded as paths up the same mountain the pinnacle of which is enlightenment or mystical experience of the divine.

However, there is a variation within Traditionalism in terms of how practical and experiential learning across religious traditions can occur. One Traditionalist position might be characterized as being that all authentic traditions are legitimate paths, but an individual must follow a particular one among them.[38] This seems also to be the position held by Seyyed Hossein Nasr, known to have been a follower of Schuon,[39] and recognized as his main successor among the Islamic wing of Schuon's

37. On the usage of the term "Traditionalist" with a capital "T" to refer to those influenced by Guenon's thought, see Mark Sedgwick, *Against the Modern World: Traditionalism and the Secret Intellectual History of the Twentieth Century* (Oxford: Oxford University Press, 2004) 21. As Sedgwick points out, being traditionalist may simply mean a person's general appreciation of past cultural or religious currents. Perennialism refers to the position that all religions spring from a common perennial or primordial source that subsequently took on diverse forms. This position, while it characterizes many Traditionalists, is older and more diffuse than that of this particular group.

38. Nasr discusses the topic of religious pluralism in his *Religion and Religions: The Challenge of Living in the Multireligious World* (Charlotte: University of North Carolina Press, 1985); "Islam and the Encounter of Religions," in *Sufi Essays*, 2nd ed. (Albany: SUNY Press, 1991) 123–51; and "Religion and Religions," Ch. 1 of *Religion & the Order of Nature* (New York: Oxford University Press, 1996) 9–28. For a critique of Nasr's pluralism see Muhammad Legenhausen, "Misgivings about the Religious Pluralisms of Seyyed Hossein Nasr and John Hick," *al-Tawhid* 14/4 (n.d.). Online at http://www.al-islam.org/al-tawhid/pluralism2.htm/.

39. Mark Sedgwick, *Against the Modern World: Traditionalism and the Secret Intellectual History of the Twentieth Century* (Oxford: Oxford University Press, 2004) 154.

followers in the United States. In terms of interfaith dialogue, the idea that all traditions have validity provides a common ground. Schuon himself was involved in native American religion, which demonstrates that among some Traditionalists converts learning from and even participating in rituals from other religions is acceptable.[40] This said, the distinction between interreligious learning from and appropriation of "native" rituals is critical, and this brings us to the delicate issue of power relations in processes of acculturation. Furthermore, for convert Traditionalists,[41] conversion is not externally dramatic in most cases but rather consists of subtle adjustments in the inner daily lives of elites that would probably not negatively impact reception in their previous networks. For most of these converts, Islam seems to represent mostly a form of nostalgia for the authentic and a quest for a reenchantment of the world emerging from post-Christian Western contexts.

Consider the case of "retraditionalized" Muslims who come to understand Islam in a way that recovers some elements of Sufi thought, especially that of Ibn 'Arabi (d. 1240), and then attempt a revival of "traditional architecture" etc. in their own homelands. This raises several questions: can one speak of mutual shaping? Who are the partners in this? Is the case of Traditionalist converts to Islam or Sufi Islam partnered with Western romanticism or esotericism and then joined in opposing secular, "fallen" modernity?

A case that is in my opinion a related yet distinct expression of traditionalism is that of Hamza Yusuf Hanson, an American convert who represents a way to embody Islamic "traditionalism" in a manner that has proven attractive and compelling to a broader Muslim audience in the West.[42] Hanson and others who espouse this sort of Muslim

40. Not without some degree of controversy, the discussion of which is beyond the scope of my argument at this time. Traditionalists have been among the most active in Muslim-Buddhist dialogue: for example, *Common Ground between Islam and Buddhism: Spiritual and Ethical Affinities*, ed. Reza Kazemi (Louisville: Fons Vitae, 2010).

41. Mark Sedgwick pointed out a theoretical challenge with formulating a concept of "convert perennialists." (personal communication) Since from this perspective the source of all religion is one—is perennialism itself what is being converted to rather than a specific faith tradition, or alongside of a faith tradition. In this regard it could be observed that, for example, Guenon was identified as a Muslim during the latter part of his life, which was spent in Cairo in a Muslim environment.

42. Many works in the Muslim West mention Hanson as an important figure and his articulation of "authentic, traditional" Islam is lauded as a potential counter to Salafism, especially among youth. Some more critical and academic work on Hanson

traditionalism are not associated with the Guenonian or Schuonian Traditionalists, but do embody some similar characteristics such as suspicion of and distaste for secular modernity and return to the specifics of religious tradition, in this case Islam, as a response. The hunger for individual religious experience and spirituality, especially on the part of younger Muslims in the West, is here fused with the quest for authenticity, embodied in mastery of classical sources of the Islamic religion. While initially Hanson stressed the threat of modern, secular culture in areas such as humanistic education that could destroy Muslims' faith and confidence in their religion, post 9/11 Hanson became an advocate for the "indigenization of Islam in America" such that it would no longer be an 'imported' religion. For example, according to Hanson, indigenous or indigenized American Muslims could watch the Super Bowl, participate in the Thanksgiving Holiday, and so on.[43] Such examples of acculturation are, however, calls to embrace civil religion, not invitations to absorb or reflect on interreligious borrowings. Still, traditionalists, including Hanson, are often on the forefront of interreligious dialogue, especially with representatives of interfaith spirituality such as the Dalai Lama

A further example of traditionalist convert brokerage or negotiation of culture is exemplified by Dr. Umar Faruq Abdullah of Chicago's Nawawi Foundation, a Euro-American Muslim and scholar of Islamic law, who works with other American Muslim scholars to refine an interpretation of Islam that is both authentic and able to be rooted in the American experience. In a long position paper, "The Cultural Imperative" available on the Nawawi Foundation's website, Abdullah writes: "In history, Islam showed itself to be culturally friendly and, in that regard, has been likened to a crystal clear river. Its waters (Islam) are pure, sweet, and life-giving but—having no color of their own—reflect the bedrock (indigenous culture) over which they flow." In China, Islam looked Chinese; in Mali, it looked African."[44] The metaphor of the

---

and his discourses exists, at this point in dissertation form only. For example, Timur Yuskaev, "The Qur'an Come to America: Pedagogies of Muslim Collective Memory," PhD diss. (Chapel Hill: University of North Carolina, 2010) 137–97.

43. Council on Foreign Relations. Transcript of "Conference Call with Hamza Yusuf Hanson, Sept. 11, 2007"; http://www.cfr.org/publication/14289/religion_and_foreign_policy_conference_call_with_hamza_yusuf.html?breadcrumb=%2Fbios%2Fbio%3Fid%3D25%26page%3D2/.

44. Umar Faruq Abd-Allah, "The Cultural Imperative."

water flowing over the bedrock epitomizes a model of "Islam above culture" (in the Niebuhrian sense).[45] I note, however, that this process is not entirely trickle down or one of Islam shaping culture from above, but rather is framed along the line of local Muslim practice being able to incorporate positive content from what already exists in a culture. Theologically, everything is already under the purview of Islam. Muslim thinkers are able to embrace the inherent goodness in the world and its cultures along with the potential of good universal human nature as in the Qur'anic: "Indeed We created the human being in the best stature" (95:4).

These strands within Traditionalism in the Schuonian articulation and other forms of "Islamic" traditionalism or even "neotraditonalism," then, provide a theological framework for integrating, learning from, and even welcoming elements from preexisting cultures and (to an extent) their religious heritage, provided that they are not incompatible with Islamic ethos and practice.

Progressive Muslims and Converts

Another movement that included American convert Muslims who aspire to transform culture are the Progressive Muslims who emerged post-9/11, especially in the United States and South Africa.[46] Progressive Muslims advocate an activism that would go beyond the liberal attitudes and secularizing values espoused by certain Muslim elites, and call for a recovery and implementation of the mandate for social justice inherent in the Qur'anic injunctions and the example of the Prophet. Their advocacy of gender justice and mosque state separation, however, would not appeal to more traditional or conservative Muslim groups whose positions are more reflective of the Niebuhrian "above culture" or "against culture" categories. Many progressive Muslims also embrace "cultural" expressions such as art and music produced under Islamic inspiration, rather than restricting themselves to legally circumscribed

45. H. Richard Niebuhr elaborates on the model of "Christ" (or Christianity) above culture in *Christ and Culture* (New York: HarperCollins, 2001) 166ff.

46. After an initial burst of energy and production epitomized by the volume edited by Omid Safi, *Progressive Muslims: On Gender, Justice, and Pluralism* (Oxford: Oneworld, 2002), the progressives fragmented as a movement. On issues facing progressives, see Omid Safi, "The Progressive Movement in North America and Beyond," *Muslim Public Affairs Journal* (Jan 2006) 76–81.

forms of religious expression. Naturally, the category of progressively identified Muslims is much broader than that of converts to Islam, but the role of converts to Islam among progressives is worth considering.

Like Traditionalists, in general progressive converts make few visible changes to their previous lifestyle on becoming Muslim.[47] They play an ambivalent role as culture brokers because they run the risk of being perceived by other Muslims as "Westernizing" Islam through advocating liberal progressive norms such as feminism, LGBT rights, and so on, while for Christians or secular Muslims they are not "different" enough to be interesting as dialogue partners, unless, of course they qualify for the role of "native informer."[48]

Progressive interventions may also destabilize traditional Muslim expectations of the docile/zealous convert. A prominent example would be Muslim feminist scholar Amina Wadud leading the mixed congregational prayer in New York City in 2005. As an African American Muslim female, Wadud further performed an act of public de-veiling as a critique of the elision of race and culture through the imposition of the standard hijab to cover a woman's hair. To encourage her listeners to move beyond their assumptions about modest dress, Wadud recites what she calls her "hijab mantra" in public appearances: "If you think that the difference between heaven and hell is 45 inches of material, boy will you be surprised." And with theatrical flair, she often removes her own hijab and drapes it on her shoulders.[49]

47. This observation does not hold for the "Islamic" traditionalists or neo-traditionalist cohort of converts whose adoption of identifiably Muslim dress and gendered practices may be more visible.

48. This is beyond the scope of my discussion in this paper, but the term "native informer" was coined by cultural theorist Hamid Dabashi for cases such as Ayan Hirsi Ali and Azar Nafisi "comprador intellectuals who have moved to North America and Western Europe and are acting as native informers in the manufacturing of a sort of useful knowledge that facilitates the imperial domination of the countries from which they have immigrated" (online: http://weekly.ahram.org.eg/2006/797/special. htm/). Hamid Dabashi, "Native Informers and the Making of the American Empire," *Al-Ahram Weekly* 797 (June 2006) 1–7.

49. Raquel Ukeles, "Modest Dress in Judaism and Islam." Online: http://www. myjewishlearning.com/practices/Ethics/Our_Bodies/Clothing/Hats_and_Head_ Coverings/head-coverings/Modest_Dress_in_Contemporary_Judaism_and_Islam. shtml/.

African American Converts

African American Muslims, many but not all of whom are converts, have distinct and important perceptions concerning the relation of Islam to culture. This community is said to represent as much as 40 percent of American Muslims. The revival of African American Islam in the early twentieth century by black identity movements signals the role of Islam in American blacks' placement of religion "against" the oppressive majority culture in which they lived. While some aspects of preexisting Christian practice and identity were rejected, many were integrated as part of a stream of "black religion," along with the embrace of currents in metaphysical religious teachings[50] that permeate American religious history.

As African American Muslim movements developed, the Islamic teachings of Elijah Muhammad enabled his community to articulate and implement a new set of values that also inculcated many norms of success already embodied in white middle class American culture.[51] At the same time, the distinctive experience of African American Muslims requires that they remain able to resist and critique Islam represented exclusively in the ethnic cultural terms of immigrant Muslims, as Sherman Abd al-Hakim Jackson assesses:

> They [Blackamericans] are both repelled by the American experience, by virtue of their history as a marginalized minority, and attracted to it, by the virtue of their connection to a uniquely rich Afro-American historical and cultural tradition. Their search for a bona fide Muslim identity is still in its exploratory stage. To this point, however, the record of successive turns and turnabouts has proved one thing if nothing else: Whatever this Afro-American-Muslim identity turns out to be as a final product, if it is to be life-affirming as opposed to a paralyzing agent, it will have to embrace, however discriminately, rather than ignore the reality and history of African-Americans, just as effectively as it fortifies for them the boundaries between Islam and non-Islam.[52]

50. On American metaphysical religion see Catherine L. Albanese, *A Republic of Mind and Spirit: A Cultural History of American Metaphysical Religion* (New Haven: Yale University Press, 2006).

51. Sherman Jackson, *Islam and the Blackamerican: Looking toward a Third Resurrection* (Oxford: Oxford University Press, 2005). These include abstinence from drugs and alcohol, the Protestant work ethic, and the like.

52. Sherman Abd al-Hakim Jackson, "Muslims, Islamic Law and Public Policy in

I further cite Jackson, a preeminent Blackamerican Muslim scholar and theologian, in a passage that echoes my earlier historical example[53] of Muslim converts' negotiation of preexisting cultures.

> Do you know what that means?—listen to me! Abu Hanifa died in the year 150 AH (767 CE); Malik died in 179 AH (795 CE); al-Shafiʻi died in 204 AH (819 CE);[54] that means that all these men lived, made their contributions and died when Muslims were still a numerical minority! But they had the fortitude and the vision to understand the difference between "non-Muslim" and "un-Islamic." Many of the institutions that came to be identified as Islamic institutions did not start out as Islamic institutions. There were institutions that Muslims in their numerical-minority status found in these societies, which they then appropriated in ways that could serve the interests of the community. This is the tradition to which we need to return, especially here in America.[55]

Feminist Convert Theology

In a forthcoming article on "Muslim[56] theology and Interreligious Dialogue" American Muslim convert Jerusha Lamptey employs insights from feminist and womanist Christian theologies to suggest pluralist approaches to interreligious dialogue among Muslims. In order to make this case she draws on conceptions of "difference" in the work of female Muslim interpreters of the Qurʾan, in particular Amina Wadud, Asma Barlas, and Riffat Hassan, who have themselves been influenced by contemporary Christian feminist approaches. Invoking contemporary feminist theory, Lamptey notes that female Muslim theologians constitute an essential interpretive resource for two central reasons: "First, women—whether silent, silenced or unheard—have generally suffered from interpretative 'voicelessness' within Islamic history; the Islamic interpretative tradition has historically been dominated and controlled

---

the United States"; online: http://www.ispi-usa.org/policy/policy4.html.

53. See fn. 26.

54. [Ed.] These are all famous early Muslim legal scholars.

55. Sherman Abd al-Hakim Jackson, "Imagining the Future of Islam in America" in *Islam and Muslims in America* ed. Marcia Hermansen (Chicago: American Islamic College, 2011) 78.

56. *Muslima* is the feminine form of *Muslim*.

by men. Thus, the mere inclusion of a largely excluded voice has the potential to proffer new insights. Second, the central interpretative task of these scholars is the elucidation of a Qur'anic conception of human difference, specifically sexual/biological difference. Elements of this specific conception of difference can be generalized and utilized as a guide in articulating other conceptions of human difference."[57] The respect for and attentiveness to "human difference" advocated in this passage therefore extends from gender to faith tradition. Lamptey's efforts to formulate a new Muslima theology for interfaith engagement represent a further case of the role of American converts to Islam in interreligious learning. This highlights the voices of Muslim feminists and womanists who join women from various religious traditions facing the terror of patriarchal texts and seeking collaborative strategies to combat essentialist interpretations of scripture. Certainly not all feminist Muslim theologians are converts, nor are all female converts to Islam feminists. This example does, however, suggest that one site of interreligious dialogue and learning today is among those groups oppressed by religion tradition who bond due to their common exclusion or marginalization.

Conclusion

Examples of acculturation among converts to Islam, both classical and contemporary, disclose elements of both continuity and change in processes and concerns. In premodern cases, Muslim responses to conversion and acculturation were far from uniform and debates on the role of previous cultures and religions practices disclose the lack of consensus in this regard. Responses to these processes and manifestations of acculturation indicate both instances of Muslim resistance to incorporating elements of indigenous culture and practice and Muslim embrace of intercultural learning.

As a religion that makes a universal claim and that historically expanded rapidly across diverse regions exhibiting a range of cultures and religions, Islamic theology and practice provided a range of intellectual and pragmatic resources that enabled acculturation. Are mass

57. Jerusha Lamptey, "From Sexual Difference to Religious Difference: Toward a *Muslima* Theology of Religious Pluralism," forthcoming in *Muslima Theology: The Voices of Muslim Women Theologians*, ed. Marcia Hermansen, Ednan Aslan, and Elif Medeni.

conversions that entail the adoption of practices from other religious traditions on a mass scale, a thing of the past, no longer to be expected in the modern world?

The contemporary examples cited here of converts to Islam from Traditionalist and progressive persuasions as well as among African Americans and feminists suggest that conversion and some degree of acculturation are more readily accepted by those groups within a faith community who are advocating interpretive flexibility. In the case of more recent Western converts to Islam, let us note that modernity and the assumption or dominance in the West of a secular setting has made conversion across religions, even conversion to Islam, less controversial. I would argue that one reason for this is the loosening of religious identity markers, another is the fact that the tradition left behind is no longer by default Christianity or Judaism. Thus the contemporary American Muslim convert, in many of my examples, could become a comfortable interlocutor in interreligious dialogue with Jews, Christians, or others; or could find employment as an instructor of religious studies, not only at public educational institutions but also at many private denominational ones. Such converts are in the current context less likely to be perceived as a threat or affront to the faith commitments of those who adhere to their previous religious identity.

Of course, this contrasts with the social and in some cases legal and financial costs of conversion out of Islam that exist in certain Muslim societies. One may wonder whether this difference is due to the fact that Islamic theology is supersessionist, because classical Islamic law specifically penalized apostasy (*irtadd*), or whether it is due to the fact that Muslim societies still view religion as a primary and public marker of identity.

Finally, are American converts to Islam ultimately "hybrids"? Is their primary impact in the sphere of acculturation as individual culture brokers or bridges through helping Muslims from immigrant background negotiate Western culture, either in practice or symbolically? And, like hybrids in the animal kingdom, are such individual converts ultimately sterile[58] in the sense of being a phenomenon of a particular moment in history where they may play an ephemeral role as Muslims in interfaith dialogue and academic contexts, to be replaced, as soon as possible, by Muslims who are more "representative" through being more comfortably distinctive in ethnicity, race, dress, and so on?

58. The discussion in postcolonial theory of the fact that hybrids are, in biological terms, often sterile, occurs in Jonathan Friedman, "Global Crises, the Struggle for Cultural Identity, and Intellectual Pork-Barrelling: Cosmopolitans versus Locals, Ethnics and Nationals in an Era of De-hegemonisation," in *Debating Cultural Hybridity: Multi-Cultural Identities and the Politics of Anti-Racism*, ed. Pnina Werbner and Tariq Modood, Postcolonial Encounters (London: Zed, 1997) 70–89.

10

Changing Faces of African American Islam

Identity and Cultural Adaptation in an
American Muslim Tradition

James W. Morris

JESUS IS COMING!
(read the Qur'an)
— bumper sticker encountered
recently in inner-city Philadelphia[1]

Any American with even a vague acquaintance with African American churches and the wider cultural life of their surrounding urban

1. The messianic return of Jesus in the last days (either as or closely associated with
the triumphant eschatological figure of the Mahdi or "Rightly-Guided One") primarily
based on details included in later hadith—and typically associated with certain highly
ambiguous Qur'anic verses—is a central element of Sunni eschatological tradition,
inspiring over the centuries multiple messianic movements throughout the Muslim
world, but perhaps most frequently in the broad belt of "Sudan" lands between the Sa-
hara and tropical Africa from which many slaves were brought to North America. This
role of Jesus is particularly highlighted in the "Ahmadi" religious movement whose
missionaries were active in African-American communities as early as the 1920s.
See background in R. B. Turner's book in n. 2 below, as well as Yohanan Friedmann's
study of the wider messianic background in *Prophecy Continuous: Aspects of Ahmadi
Religious Thought and Its Medieval Background* (New Delhi: Oxford University Press,
2003).

communities would have little difficulty in deciphering the multiple possible meanings, audiences, and assumptions suggested by this intriguing public proclamation, whether we take it to be a proud acknowledgement of someone's own personal cultural identity, a provocative challenge to discover and explore the deep messianic dimensions of Sunni tradition and hadith (particularly visible throughout the history of North and West African Islam), or a more irenic reminder of the profound spiritual similarities and cultural premises shared by African American forms of both Islam and Protestant Christianity. In fact, probably each of those meanings were intended. As such, it is a poignant reminder of the maturity and self-confident "acculturation" of a multifaceted and profoundly American dimension of Islam that has survived and gone through many transformations over the three or more centuries separating us from the first Muslim slaves brought from West Africa to North America.[2]

At the same time, given this volume's topic of interreligious dimensions of cultural identity and acculturation, it is surely worth noting that these sociocultural processes always work both ways, whatever the apparently "dominant" or "host" culture in question. Thus historians and social scientists have only recently begun to appreciate the manifold ways in which so many particularities of the distinctive "slave religion" of African Americans—to name only a few, the central ritual role of ecstatic communal music and dance, of rhythmic group chant (or call-and-response), the charismatic preacher, spiritual and psychic healing, the messianic eschatology of liberation and justice associated with the "Mahdi" (and Jesus), or the integration of so many other cultural aspects of popular West African beliefs and practices—correspond profoundly to the distinctive forms of Islam brought over by so many early Muslim slaves, who understandably included the most literate and learned of those captives. These characteristic features of African American Christianity were not simply taken over from the Anglo-Protestant slaveholders: taken together, they help us to appreciate both the depth and the

---

2. There is now an immense and rapidly expanding literature devoted to all dimensions of this question, on both the American and preceding African-Muslim sides. For an initial historical overview, see Albert J. Raboteau's pioneering *Slave Religion: The "Invisible Institution" in the Antebellum South*, 2nd ed. (Oxford: Oxford University Press, 2004); and Richard Brent Turner, *Islam in the African-American Experience* (Bloomington: Indiana University Press, 2003), and especially the bibliographies in both volumes.

actual historical sources of the African Muslim cultural antecedents in question.[3]

Or to put this cross-cultural connection in the memorable words of my wife and fellow explorer, an insightful natural anthropologist frustrated with attending yet another session of hours of ecstatic *dhikr* (unforgettable spiritual music, group chanting and rhythmic meditation) somewhere in the wilds of Iranian Kurdistan, Khorasan, or western Afghanistan: "Why didn't you just join a black church back home, rather than come all this way to do the same thing!" It has taken me almost four decades now, and the help of hundreds of students and colleagues all over the world, to begin to appreciate the full ramifications of that wry observation. So here—in historical sequence and with briefly anecdotal setting and coloring—are a few stages of that process of discovery, hopefully offering some useful insights into just the most recent decades of this ongoing American tale of acculturation and shifting cultural identities.[4] Of course we can take it for granted that most Americans, at least of a certain age and historical literacy, can fill in all the wider sociological and historical developments that form the backdrop for these transformations—a backdrop that is particularly intriguing because (as we shall return to at the end of this essay) so many regions

3. While the scholarly awareness of the inseparability of Muslim identity (in West Africa as everywhere else) from distinctive local cultural identities often far more important in religious life and practice than elite Arabic scriptural or learned traditions is now widely familiar to scholars (including Africanists and other students of the wider slave diaspora) in many pertinent fields, this was not the case even a few decades ago. I can still remember my initial surprise, in showing an anthropological film on Sudanese camel traders, at discovering that their daily *dhikr* and work song during their migrations turned out to be one of the most common Mississippi/Chicago blues riffs; or in encountering the reactions of my African-American Oberlin students to another film on Sudanese Qadiri shrine rituals and singers at *'Id al-Adhā*, when they suddenly recognized in the highly stylized circumambulation processions of these far-off dervishes some of the most distinctive and familiar forms of dance from their neighborhoods—or in another case, from the initiatic rituals of another student's African-American Ivy League fraternity.

4. The period covered in this essay is from 1967 to roughly 2000, when a professorship at a British university limited my ongoing contact with African-American Muslim students and colleagues. Those same decades witnessed even more diverse and multi-faceted developments regarding the implantation and acculturation of dozens of American Sufi orders and the arrival of new waves of Muslim immigrants, in both the United States and Canada, from virtually every region of the traditionally Muslim world. Those related forms of American Muslim acculturation and their distinctive challenges are only briefly introduced at the end of this essay.

of the wider Islamic world have subsequently gone through very similar and even more rapid transformations in more recent years.

South Chicago in the Late 1960s and Early 1970s: The Nation of Islam and Malcolm X

My first direct personal contact with African American Muslims, as an undergraduate living on the south side of Chicago, was with the Nation of Islam and the distinctively white-robed street-corner vendors of their newspaper, *Muhammad Speaks* (referring to their charismatic leader, Elijah Muhammad, d. 1975). While much of the earlier history and internal divisions of that movement are now widely familiar through the frequent school reading assignment of Alex Haley's *Autobiography of Malcolm X* (published in 1965, the year of his assassination), at that time this group was widely portrayed by the public media not as a religious movement, but as a highly dangerous, violent and separatist political cult, with a bizarre "reverse racist" ideology and incomprehensible theological teachings. The familiar historical and social circumstances underlying its insistence on building a separate and self-sufficient African American community, of course, were already reflected in many influential earlier movements for an African American cultural homeland (whether in Africa or inside the U.S.)—of which the most influential "Muslim" form only a few decades earlier was no doubt the Moorish Science Temple and its self-styled Prophet, Noble Drew Ali. At that time, in a Chicago torn by massive riots, burning whole neighborhoods and requiring the help of an entire airborne division for their pacification, together with endemic, often bloody racial tensions, it was perhaps understandable that these unfamiliar and suddenly visible expressions of Islam would be viewed by outsiders in terms of the publicly visible, loudly "revolutionary" ideologies of Black nationalism, pan-Africanism, and anti-imperialism, together with their wider global counterparts in a profusion of national or ethnic liberation movements. In retrospect, of course, the clamorous rhetorical presence of those competing ideologies seemed to completely obscure the lasting constructive engagement of this and other African American Muslim groups with the wider Islamic tradition (a point so evident in the unforgettable concluding chapters of Malcolm's book, regarding his Hajj and its transforming aftermath), along with the other cultural pathways—personal names, dress, music, etc.—through which more visible elements of African Islam were to more lastingly color the broader African American culture, and the even wider popular culture of sports and entertainment. The profound contrast between the actual lives of African American Muslims (religious and otherwise)—soon to be reflected in the dramatic transformations of the Nation of Islam to more standard and ecumenical Islamic practices and teaching soon after the death of Elijah Muhammad—and the uniformly negative public images relating to that group at the time is a healthy reminder of the long tradition of demonizing media illusions and projections regarding various unfamiliar minority religious groups (by no means restricted to Islam: see the nineteenth-century Mormons, for example) continuing on down to our own time.

Brooklyn in the Late 1970s and Early 1980s: Storefront Islam and Immigrant Encounters

Returning from the tumult of revolutionary Iran and the solitude of dissertation writing to international banking and the vibrant street life of Atlantic Avenue (a formerly Lebanese neighborhood by then replaced by Yemenis and other Hispanic immigrant groups),[5] what immediately struck me at this time was not the Arab churches and mosques I had been expecting in that Brooklyn neighborhood, but the mushrooming profusion of tiny storefront Imams, *shaykhs*, and *masjids*, each with their brochures and pamphlets—interspersed with equally self-styled (and often feminine) "archbishops," "deacons," and other evangelical and Pentecostal preachers: a vigorously entrepreneurial religious world competing for the spiritual guidance and communion of their primarily African American local Brooklyn audience. But meeting and talking with these would-be religious founders—a few of whom have since become the Imams of thriving multiethnic mosques in Brooklyn with hundreds or even thousands of active adherents—quickly revealed a relatively new and creative dimension in the long unfolding of African-American Islam. For many of these teachers and preachers had themselves recently gone off on their own religious and spiritual quests to various regions of Africa, the Caribbean, or the Arab world, and had returned from those journeys inspired with a sense of mission to both

5. This time and place is the setting of Wayne Wang (and Paul Auster's) remarkable film *Smoke,* for those unfamiliar with Brooklyn.

imitate and creatively transform and communicate, for these Brooklyn audiences, the many different forms of Islam they had encountered during their journeys and studies abroad. (With minor adjustments in the audiences involved, this also mirrors the history of the dozens of disparate Sufi groups and spiritual lineages that were rapidly develop- ing among white middle-class audiences throughout the United States at the same time.) In retrospect, it is difficult to imagine the host of cultural and theological complexities encountered by these practical religious entrepreneurs in creatively negotiating their way between this spectrum of different, often originally foreign versions of "Islam" and the distinctive forms of (largely Protestant) Christianity familiar to their local audiences and hoped-for adherents. Again, the side-by-side coex- istence up and down Atlantic Avenue of so many nascent Christian and Muslim African American groups and aspiring spiritual guides was a remarkably vivid reminder of the shared (if usually unsuspected) his- torical and cultural roots of their competing religious visions.

The other highly visible Islamic dimension of New York in this period (if in Queens more than Brooklyn at that time) was the succes- sive waves of immigrant refugees from the wars and civil turmoil in Iran and Afghanistan, precursors of a host of subsequent immigrant groups (whether economic or political refugees) arriving from so many different regions of the Muslim world over the following decades, from Bosnia to Central Asia, and from all over Africa. This was the period when African American Muslims, whatever their formal group or back- ground or depth of involvement with Islam, first began to unavoidably encounter the (unsolicited and often hostile) comments and judgments of Muslim immigrants from all these other countries, each nationality naturally promulgating their own native culture and religious traditions (or revolutionary anticolonial political visions) as the "real" Islam— thereby leading to an ongoing process of multidimensional accultura- tion and difficult adaptation that has only intensified down to our own day.

Temple and Inner City Philadelphia in the Late 1980s: Cultural Integration and New Islamist Ideologies

Returning to Temple University and the inner city of Philadelphia in 1989, after a decade of illuminating work as a "court theologian" (as

Fazlur Rahman insightfully called it) working on the construction of new international higher-educational and social institutions for one major transnational Muslim community—with the hope of eventually creating the first international Islamic university—I found myself in what at first glance looked like the impoverished neighborhoods of south Chicago familiar from my undergraduate days. But the larger situation of African American Muslims in the meanwhile had been transformed in very different ways. In short, African American Islam had been transformed from the "new religion" or cult and apparently radical choice of a few scattered urban individuals and their families, into a multifaceted community of many different groups, integrating a very wide range of understandings and practices, and into a genuine tradition passing down from the founding generation to younger generations, with all the creative institutional challenges that development always entails. And both those new developments inevitably required an educated, religiously literate community leadership able to interact knowledgeably and constructively with other Muslim groups (primarily recent immigrants), as well as with their considerably more familiar African American Christian neighbors and family members.[6]

Thus the American Muslim scholars I helped train for their doctorates at that formative period (1989–1995) included some of the first African American Muslim PhDs working on Islam in the relatively new discipline of religious studies.[7] Together we organized in 1993 (at DePaul University in Chicago) the first nationwide conference on "Islam in the Americas", bringing together academic scholars and Muslim activists, intellectuals and leaders from all parts of the U.S. and Canada. Not surprisingly, these students and their subsequent academic careers have often been devoted to explaining, defending and clarifying the "Islamic"

6. Reflecting the concomitant historical movement of many African-Americans beyond isolated urban neighborhoods, this period was also marked by an increased engagement with certain Sufi groups (previously largely white, educated, and middle class), such as the unusually active group in Philadelphia at that time surrounding the influential Sri Lankan Sufi teacher Bawa Mohaiyaddin, whose early community there has been the subject of an ongoing series of studies by another of my Temple PhD students, Prof. Gisela Webb of Seton Hall University.

7. Most academic scholars of Islamic religion prior to that period had been formed in text-centered departments of Semitic studies, Near Eastern languages, history, and the like, rather than in the nascent field of religious studies (where teachers of Islam were only slowly entering undergraduate departments in the later 1980s) or in the other related social sciences.

character of their own Muslim communities and perspectives (primarily in theological encounters with other cultural versions of Islam drawn from different foreign historical settings), together with responding to the less academically visible challenges of making an effective and permanent place for Islam in public schools, prisons, community-based health and social service organizations, the military, and all the other practical institutions closest to the everyday lives of the mass of African American Muslims today.

The other new development emerging at that time was the development of a broader and clearer consciousness of being African American *Muslims* (i.e., as part of a much wider global religious community and tradition), integrating a wide range of local mosques—now often centered on individual local activists and Imams, rather than wider umbrella groups like the Nation of Islam—and increasingly engaged at various levels with other immigrant Muslim ethnic groups, although often still working as individuals rather than in the more institutional or official contexts (that have been often dominated by a single ethnic or political group). Interestingly, this period was also marked by a strong sense of activist engagement with local African American Christian groups (and related political organizations) centered around practical and political issues of shared community interest. This latter development was dramatically mirrored in the very different roles and varied perceptions of a figure like Louis Farrakhan, who eventual became a widely respected and influential national *political* figure among African Americans of all backgrounds,[8] while remaining the religious leader of a theologically quite peculiar remnant of the original "Nation of Islam," whose communities await the imminent eschatological "return"—in a vivid echo of classical Shiite messianic conceptions—of their prophet, Elijah Muhammad.

A third development I also encountered for the first time at Temple, primarily among my many foreign PhD students hailing from countries stretching from Malaysia and Thailand to the Sudan and Nigeria, was that many of them had received full doctoral scholarships from Saudi-funded charitable organizations dedicated to the peculiar new project of the "Islamization" of various countries and institutions, in ways that clearly mirrored the familiar rhetoric and widely appealing mythical worldviews of earlier totalitarian movements in both Europe and Latin

8. See especially his major role in the Million Man March (1995).

America. While these foreign doctoral students themselves were from traditional learned Muslim family backgrounds, and almost all interested in procuring solid academic credentials in their chosen traditional fields of Islamic studies (where as professors they have often gone on to positions of national and international influence), this was for all of us a first alarming encounter with the dramatic influences of massive oil-based funding for this intoxicating new blend of international, highly politicized forms of militant "anti-imperialism," whose ambitions were now repackaged and conveyed in widely appealing new slogans drawn from earlier extreme Hanbali (Wahhabi) and reformist, Salafi theological movements. In response to the contemporary events in Afghanistan and Iran, this recently constructed religiopolitical ideology was actually supported by our own government at that time as a powerful "anticommunist tool," which was soon to have such catastrophic repercussions in so many parts of the world. Of course the 1980's also witnessed a host of virtually identical attempts at formulating and promulgating a new "revolutionary (Shiite) Islam"[9] by the new Iranian regime, but which were less well financed and whose appeal eventually turned out to be lastingly effective primarily among a few preexisting Miami Shiite communities outside Iran.

Oberlin, Toledo, and Cleveland in the 1990s: Building Institutions and Wider Connections

In the 1990s, moving to an area of the U.S., from Detroit to Cleveland, long marked by the largest waves of Lebanese ("Syrian") Arab Christian and Muslim immigration earlier in the twentieth century, I found the transformed and clearly more established social position of African American Muslims was dramatically represented by the presence of two large competing mosques. They were set among the monumental Protestant church buildings (and central synagogue) of the earlier Rockefeller era that line Cleveland's lakefront Euclid Avenue, almost all of them by then transformed into diverse African American congregations,

9. At one stage in this period, the annual religious (lunar) calendars distributed by the revolutionary heirs of the Pahlavi Foundation in New York, listing primarily the death days of each of the Imami Shiite Imams, were marked by the striking inclusion of Malcolm X's death day as the only archetypal martyrdom listed there from the past twelve centuries. Religious "enculturation," whether successful or not, often begins as just such an unfamiliar gamble.

representing a highly visible reflection of Cleveland's deeper social transformations over the postwar period. (The various more recent immigrant Muslim communities then largely frequented their own *salafi*, strictly Sunni, and Pakistani-dominated mosque in a nearby Cleveland suburb.)

This familiar American pattern of ethnic and residential religious segregation, however, was not the only possibility. Indeed in this period (1990's) it was already becoming increasingly difficult to separate the story of many African American Muslims in that region from the history of more recent, often highly prosperous Muslim immigrants and of a few American Sufi groups (such as the earlier, often longstanding followers of Chishti Sufi branches of the Inayat Khan lineage) already present in the Cleveland area for some decades. Whether through links of marriage, education, or other social encounters and shared religious interests, middle-class Muslims from all these different backgrounds began very tentatively at this time to discover (or at least to seek out) areas of shared interests and commitment. While their respective motives and the major obstacles to cooperation were understandably very different for each group, they each increasingly recognized a common need for an educated elite and broadminded future leaders able to build the effective new educational and other social institutions necessary to maintain an ongoing cultural identity—an identity whose nature was of course perceived quite differently by people from each of these three broad groups—within a wider society where the transmission of that Muslim religiocultural identity across generations could by no means be taken for granted.[10]

10. By this period, the perceived challenge had little to do with competing Christian identities or "assimilation" into a wider Christian culture—concerns that do not seem to have been particularly significant for American Muslims in recent decades— but rather with the rapid spread of prevalent forms of the shared mass consumer-based culture with no particular religious dimensions at all. Here it may be helpful to emphasize that different immigrant ethnic Muslim groups in the United States (for historical reasons particular to each ethno-national situation) have often had sharply contrasting typical approaches to participation in local mosques and other externally visible markers of an Islamic identity.

The nuanced explanation of this critical point, generally ignored by the media and outside observers in general, would require a much longer paper. What is indispensable is to be aware of the multitude of different ways of being profoundly "Muslim"— or perhaps more importantly, *mu'min* and *muhsin* (a person of true faith, and someone with a beautiful and deep positive impact in the world)—and of the corresponding severe limitations of the handful of media-stereotyped "markers" (usually associated

One memorable illustration of the new challenges marking this period took place during a visit with a group of my religious studies students to the long-established, impressive central mosque of Toledo, where our group was escorted by the remarkable Egyptian Imam who was responsible for leading a community of several thousand Muslims (at that time still primarily first- and second-generation immigrants) from more than sixty-five countries. (Only the local Shiites and African Americans apparently had their own separate meeting places at that stage.) As the Imam was detailing the extraordinary challenges of somehow integrating the religiocultural expectations of immigrant Muslims from so many countries and cultures with the very different ambient American cultural norms, and particularly the problems of ensuring the lasting interest and participation of their children, often dazed by the now-alien cultural expectations of their parents, one of my more conservatively raised Jewish students (now herself a feminist rabbi) remarked that she felt like she was back home in her own family's synagogue, wrestling with the same underlying dilemmas of maintaining one's religious identity without capitulating to what were seen as outmoded (or even more troubling) inherited cultural traditions. Her observation brilliantly encapsulated the particular ongoing challenges now flowing from the combination of (1) the new mixing of previously more separate strains of *American* Islam (African American, Sufi, etc.) with a host of very different immigrant ethnically Muslim cultures and traditions; and (2) the necessity of creating appropriate educational resources and related cultural institutions (from schools at all levels to family support systems and senior care facilities) capable of establishing and maintaining a broader group identity, while at the same time ensuring the creative and effective adaptation of these many competing imported versions of "Islam" to the changed (and constantly changing)

---

in the U.S. or Canada with a narrow outward set of recent Arab or Pakistani signs of religious identity) that determine which American Muslims are socially visible or invisible to their fellow citizens. Travelers will quickly discover that these stereotyped hostile public "religious" cultural markers of Muslims are also dramatically different—although at least equally distorting—when one moves from one European country to another. For example, Muslims are typically perceived as Sunni "Turks" (though perhaps half of them are Kurds or Alevis) in Germany; as North African "Arabs" (ignoring the majority of Berbers, West African Muslims, Kurds, and others) in France; or as "Pakistanis" (a popular notion somehow including Bengalis, while excluding Arabs, Turks, native British-born Muslims, and seventy-odd other Muslim immigrant groups) in the United Kingdom.

circumstances of newer generations who were often not particularly identified with those earlier alien cultural identities and traditions. [11]

At that time, all of this seemed a peculiarly American immigrant situation and a rather familiar challenge, given the ongoing repetitive dramas of immigration and religioethnic identity in American history. Besides the more visible challenges of religious educational institution building, this period was marked by the sudden emergence in the lives and moral engagements of my young Muslim students (whether American, recent immigrant, or foreign in origin) of a series of newer religiotheological preoccupations which suddenly tended to supplant the highly politicized "revolutionary," liberationist slogans and struggles (whether couched in recent Islamist or older Leninist vocabularies) that had preoccupied Muslims of my own generation for several decades, and which have until very recently dominated public religious discourse in many new Muslim nation-states. These new central theologoumena—which students today may well take for granted, but which have only recently been adopted so visibly and actively by the youngest generation in many Muslim countries—would surely include the following: our duties and stewardship with regard to preserving pristine nature, natural resources and the wider environment; the inherent rights and expanded social roles of women; the creation and protection of effective nongovernmental activist organizations ("civil society"); the just treatment and acknowledgement of all minority groups and cultures; and effective, universal access to higher education. Here we must emphasize one intrinsic quality of each of these global political and ethical challenges of our time, whose implications have become clearer in the following decade: any effective response to each of these issues necessarily must involve participants and motivating "theologies" drawn from all the major groups and sects within each of the major religious traditions, Islam included. We shall return to this observation in the final, contemporary section below.

The building of inclusive local Muslim institutions designed to meet the real, ongoing needs of families from all backgrounds, while at the same time responding creatively to the necessary transition from

---

11. See our millennium conference paper, "The Unique Opportunities and Challenges Facing American Muslims in the New Century," *The American Muslim* 12 (2002) 17–26, to be included in our forthcoming *Openings: From the Qur'an to the Islamic Humanities.*

traditional cultural settings (which include not only immigrants' diverse homelands, but also the ongoing inner-city poverty and segregation that faced most earlier African American Muslims) to the actual situations of second and third generations, is a matter requiring considerable economic resources and community leadership. But it also presupposes the type of education that will encourage practical, social and religious innovation at the highest level: and that is certainly not the sort of approach usually associated with traditional Muslim religious educational systems, which typically have been rooted for centuries, at the popular level, in forms of rote imitation (*taqlīd*).

In retrospect, what was so remarkable about this period (and what was so visible in the extraordinary set of young Muslim students I was fortunate to work with then, from so many American and foreign backgrounds) was the way that they all intuitively understood the central role of a solid grasp of the scriptural roots and historical evolution of the wider Islamic tradition, in *all* its manifestations, as an indispensable ground for creative innovation in ways that would remain coherent with that inclusive tradition. Not surprisingly, several of them have now moved on to become themselves professors and teachers of Islamic Studies, deeply engaged at the same time in the concerns of their own ethnic communities of origin. The other, more unexpected outcome, is the way that so many of those students (and their peers from similar elite colleges, primarily women in the cases that immediately come to mind) have so personally responded to the challenges of institution building at the level of their own families and surrounding Muslim communities. To take only a couple of striking examples from this period, there is the then-new Muslim country-music singer and NPR journalist from North Carolina who, as her family grew, brought together other Muslims from many different backgrounds in the Chapel Hill area to create their own Montessori schools, then grade school, and who are now developing high school classes. Or another who now works with a Sufi-based foundation in the Bay Area that seeks out and makes more widely available on the internet the filmed teachings and insights of traditional spiritual teachers from endangered aboriginal cultures around the world. In ways closely mirroring the unexpectedly broad and lasting results of the educational and nuclear family focus of the original "Nation of Islam" in earlier generations, the cumulative effects of such individual creative "bottom-up" efforts and institution-building stand in striking contrast to the often futile and directionless attempts at highly politicized, governmentally sponsored (and constrained!) Muslim institution building that I have witnessed (and been intermittently involved with) throughout my decades of teaching in both France and the UK.

One final observation here involves what has turned out to be a profoundly influential—if largely unexpected and unintended—global development whose roots were established during this same period of the 1990s. The gradual emergence of religious studies programs as a core element of liberal arts education during this period, prompted departments around the country to slowly hire specialists in Islam who were asked to deal with the wider Islamic tradition in all its dimensions and manifold historical expressions. This, in turn, led to the necessity of translating and effectively communicating the shared foundational elements of that tradition (sacred texts, key spiritual practices, and the central role of the Islamic Humanities in all their pregnant diversity of cultural expressions and adaptations) in ways that were originally intended simply to reach American undergraduate students from Christian or Jewish backgrounds, with no knowledge of Islam at all. No one then could have imagined the ways in which the resulting cumulative body of sound and effective English translations, broader interpretive perspectives, and more balanced historical and contextual understanding (i.e., not identified exclusively with the agendas and perspectives of any particular Muslim ethnic group, sect, culture or historical period) would eventually match up so providentially with the religious intellectual, social and educational needs and challenges now facing the most recent generation of young Muslims pursuing their university studies in English no longer just in Canada and the U.S., but increasingly across all the now digitally connected regions of the much wider Muslim (and non-Muslim) world.

A New Millennium: Postimmigrant Identities, Hispanic Muslims, and English as a Global Islamic Language

Since it is difficult, in observing and reflecting on recent events, to separate lasting and substantial changes from the sound and fury of politics and media imagery, we will mention only a few more recent developments here, whose lasting influence remains to be determined. By far the most obvious and important development, of course, is the ongoing creation of local, community-based Muslim educational and welfare organizations, adapted to the particular needs of second and third generations of integrated American Muslims (and also visible in much of Western Europe). Not surprisingly, that process—quite visible around Boston, as in every major American urban area—has unfolded in ways that have often tended to follow, at least at this more local level, a rapid institutional evolution quite familiar in the earlier history of American Judaism[12] To remain for a moment with this essay's guiding interest in the evolution of African American Islam, one striking phenomenon only gradually attracting wider attention is the increasing numbers of young Hispanic Americans (especially of Mexican background) who are identifying themselves as Muslim, for a spectrum of reasons that mirror somewhat the motives of earlier African American Muslims, but also with some key particularities.[13] Thus the primary alternative religious reference point here, within the families of these first-generation Muslims, is a very different Hispanic Catholic tradition. And the deeper cultural and historical links with Islamic civilization and identity in this case hearken back to the older Hispanic Arabic and Morisco culture, preserved across North Africa, which still so profoundly permeates so many facets of Latin American culture (from food to architecture and social structures) across the centuries, just as with West African Muslim culture in the case of the first American slaves and their descendants.

12. This evolution—familiar in the American context from the earlier experiences of both Jewish and Catholic immigrants of multiple ethnic origins—has rapidly moved, over the few decades covered by this paper, from initial family and small informal, often neighborhood and single-ethnic associations to larger, more inclusive and publicly visible formal institutions in at least four main areas: (a) the adaptation and construction of ever-larger dedicated places of worship, soon followed by (b) the gradual creation of Muslim pre-schools, elementary education (whether in separate schools, or more commonly through evening and weekend programs), and eventually regional academies or private schools at higher levels (including by now several nascent universities), as well as other community-welfare institutions (homes for the aged, charitable societies, etc.); (c) the creation of initially spontaneous and then more formal representative associations at local, state, and eventually national levels; and (d) the gradual shift in staffing of all the above institutions from primarily foreign (and foreign-educated) imams to locally born and educated professionals from diverse Muslim family backgrounds.

13. See the revealing field research and ICS [Islamic Civilization and Societies] senior thesis drawing on individual case studies of young Hispanic Muslims in Chicago and Boston by our Boston College student Ambar Flores, "En el Nombre de Allah: A Study of Latino Muslims in Boston and Chicago" (Spring 2011; Boston College archives).

Compared with all earlier generations of American Muslims, what is surely most striking in this new millennium—at least for American Muslim intellectuals and many younger people, since this observation may not apply to other groups less concerned with international issues—is that the pressures and challenges of acculturation (theological and otherwise) are increasingly framed in relation to prominent wider *international* Muslim groups and ideologies. It is very difficult to judge at this point the lasting impacts of this momentary public fascination, given the prominent recent historical events that have given rise to it. But one cannot help noting the ways in which the pervasive ideological slogans and political preoccupations of those earlier generations we have just passed in review likewise often seem rather superficial in retrospect. One concrete indication of this new pressure of "international acculturation" is the way that a number of Muslim scholars and young people in the U.S. and Canada who come from "minority" Muslim groups (primarily Shiite ones, but also certain Sufi *tariqas*) now go to great efforts to identify with the local majority forms of Islam, in ways that would earlier have been unimaginable in their families' countries of origin. But this recent "Muslim ecumenicism" may also reflect more simply the clear professional need to avoid being identified with any particular partial or sectarian point of view.

One final cultural adaptation of at least momentary importance is the sudden recent emergence of English (and of classical Islamic literatures now written or translated into English) as an increasingly important pedagogical vehicle for Islamic thought and teaching across much of the Islamic world. The wide-ranging literature and contextual explanations in question, of course, were largely translated and produced by a handful of religious studies scholars (and some Sufi teachers), primarily in North America, for the particular local needs of their teaching. But these resources have providentially been brought together, through newly accessible digital resources, with a new generation of ambitious Muslim students, in many different countries, whose primary language of university instruction at the moment happens to be English. The combination of these factors have not at all replaced Arabic and Persian, as the two key civilizational languages of the wider tradition, for those relatively small groups of specialized students still able to dedicate the years of study required to master the primary religious sources in those original sacred languages (where they are usually embedded within longstanding pedagogies strongly resistant to change or original, creative and more ecumenical thinking). But this suddenly near-universal availability of primary sources and related interpretive contextualization in English translations has given rise to an unimaginably rapid "democratization" of Islamic religious study and learning for many of the most privileged and active groups of students from rapidly globalizing societies, often combined with the spontaneous formation of new, informal social settings for religious study and teaching using these web-based resources.[14]

To clarify the point, this wider phenomenon of the sudden globalized networking (often in English) of Islamic education has no relation to the familiar older patterns of elite "prestige study," based on building an academic career by pursuing a rare diploma at the specialized metropolitan universities of some former colonial power. And this networking is in fact becoming at least equally pervasive in regard to the forms of teaching, guidance and communication by Sufi shaykhs and teachers (now including women) based in many nations: influential religious figures who were likewise normally restricted, until very recently, to the small, intimate *majlis* of a teacher and his or her handful of chosen local disciples. Other papers in this volume can no doubt add their own dramatic examples of the ways that such near-instantaneous transnational intellectual networking is rapidly reconfiguring the long-established foundations of Islamic education and intellectual life in ways that are as yet unpredictable in their consequences, but which were until recently quite literally unimaginable.

Conclusion

It should be obvious that the historical developments outlined in this paper have gradually forced many American Muslims, from all backgrounds and ways of life, to take on in an ongoing and constantly

14. As a concrete illustration of this development (paralleled in the experience of many colleagues at American universities), within a few days of agreeing rather reluctantly to do a private Arabic/Persian reading course this past semester for one Harvard doctoral student in Ottoman history, who was quickly joined in this seminar by five other students from three different departments there, I suddenly received e-mails from other graduate students studying in Indonesia, Iran, Malaysia and Canada, all asking just when and how they could access the "i-cloud" recordings and readings for this seminar, which they had immediately heard about from their friends in Boston.

challenging way the practical theological task of differentiating more clearly between the "accidental" cultural and traditional norms associated with their locally inherited religious tradition and the more universal metaphysical perspectives and spiritual and ethical principles that are so central to the Qur'anic conception of *Dīn* (primordial "Religion" with a capital "R"), as a metaphysically and concretely universal covenant and reality engaging all creatures. That difficult lifelong task of discernment and creativity, once historically relegated to small groups of philosophically adept thinkers and teachers (*muhaqqiqūn*) or spiritually illuminated "true knowers" (*'urafā'*) today tends to fall unavoidably on Muslims all over the world, not so much from cultural contact with non-Muslim religions, as from their own unavoidable cultural contact with shared global conditions of life that are in fact new to everyone (even if they are often still popularly referred to in many nations as somehow "Western").

The recent history of African American Islam is particularly intriguing and revealing in that regard. As I was constantly reminding my Temple students (both foreign and African American), at a point in time when Muslims from elsewhere tended reflexively to view American Muslims as a strange and possibly unwelcome "innovation" (one thinks of the earliest Jewish followers of Jesus regarding the strange spectacle of gentile adherents and teachers), what at first glance might appear as "new" in African American settings is really as old as the earliest messianic period of the charismatic proto-Islamic monotheistic "faith-movement" (*mu'minūn*).[15] In fact, the unfolding of this recent portion of American religious history actually constitutes an endlessly fascinating living laboratory for witnessing firsthand the largely unrecorded processes underlying the transhemispheric spread of Islam throughout most of Asia and much of southeastern Europe in the post-Mongol period, into those areas where the vast majority of Muslims live today and have lived for the past five centuries, practicing their faith in so many diverse and creatively adapted local forms.

In a strange historical irony, since I first recognized those deeper dimensions of the African American Muslim experience, many of the earlier African American challenges of cultural adaptation and

---

15. See the accessible recent summary of modern scholarship on this mysterious formative period in Fred Donner's *Muhammad and the Believers: At the Origins of Islam* (Cambridge, MA: Belknap, 2010).

enculturation have suddenly been closely mirrored throughout the wider Muslim world, for at least two generations, due to (1) the widespread loss (without effective replacement) of traditional forms of religious teaching and authority (including especially the supplanting of many of the traditional local Islamic humanities, in music, poetry, and other arts); (2) the constant challenges of new and completely unfamiliar cultural choices (especially regarding extended family structures and women's proper roles) within the new socioeconomic imperatives of predominantly urban life ; and (3) the necessity of creating or choosing coherent new forms of Islam in light of those unavoidable new existential choices and demands.[16] Or to put it in more traditional Islamic terms, most Muslims a few decades ago often conceived of other Muslims living in these recent and unfamiliar foreign settings as being somehow *muhājirun*: this evocative term (used in Arabic for the "exodus" as well) refers—in a poignant allusion to early Islamic sacred history—to those who have been forced by necessity to leave their accustomed native land and seek refuge in unfamiliar territory. But today, with the rapid social, economic, cultural and political changes flowing from the loss of smaller moral communities that adapted over long periods to little-changing conditions of life —combined with the unfamiliar new exigencies of life that we familiarly call "globalization"—everyone who safely stayed at home has likewise been forced through a profound inner estrangement or loss, one often at least as devastating as the challenges of mere physical immigration. Or even worse, because this Kafka-esque mass exile *in situ* is so commonly experienced as something forced, unchosen, and irredeemably permanent.

Even more importantly, though, this new globalized world is typically neither alien nor strange to their own children: it is simply their home. But as yet, we can only speculate about the more lasting features, and possible civilization, of that world-to-come.

---

16. Of course the recent Islamist political ideologies adapted to the novel framework of the new (post–World War II) nation-state are one of the most visible of those contemporary transformations, often concealing behind superficially familiar religious rhetoric the radical nature of the historical transformations that they actually ratify and often encourage. But even more dramatic changes can be found at all the deeper levels of social, intellectual, and cultural—and hence spiritual—life. In most cases, those underlying shifts do parallel similar earlier adaptations in civilizations in other parts of the world, albeit changes that have occurred elsewhere in very different historical circumstances and paces.

11

Speaking with Sufis

Dialogue with Whom and about What?

Frank J. Korom

Opening Remarks

I wish to ask two interrelated questions that seem to me to be relevant to discussions of interreligious dialogue and, by extension, to the cultural shaping of religions. The first is quite straightforward: Is interreligious dialogue even possible? The second is somewhat slipperier: If it is possible, then with whom are we speaking and about what? Both questions might seem simplistic and rather naïve when talking about the well-established, so-called world religions, which have been in contact with one another for most of written history, but are not so easily dismissed when discussing newly formed religious communities, what many sociologists refer to as NRMs, new religious movements.[1] By nature, such movements are caught up in the complicated processes involved in self-definition, which are part and parcel of the birthing pains associated with the establishment, sustenance, maturation, and growth of a

1. Notoriously difficult to define, yet ubiquitous in their presence, they certainly need some broad classification. See, for example, Dewey D. Wallace Jr., "Sects, Cults and Mainstream Religion: A Cultural Interpretation of New Religious Movements in America," *American Studies* 26/2 (1985) 5–16. He defines them as "small groups that are generally perceived as being outside the mainstreams of the religious life of a community and that holds views which the larger society finds unusual" (5).

legitimate (i.e., socially acceptable) religious organization. This process forces NRMs reflexively to make conscious choices about how to portray themselves vis-à-vis other more established religious communities, a point to which I intend to return below.

To explore the two questions raised above, I will focus on a small religious community based in North America but with roots in Sri Lanka, formerly known as Ceylon.[2] The group goes by the name of the Bawa Muhaiyaddeen Fellowship, and it is based on the teachings of a departed saint informally called Guru Bawa or Sheikh Bawa, depending upon whom you ask.[3] Before getting into the theoretical discussion in the concluding section, some background on the roots and establishment of the group will be useful for providing the appropriate context necessary to understand the complexity of the theoretical issues involved.

2. Sirimavo Bandaranaike changed the name of the country to Sri Lanka only in 1972 after the Marxist insurrections that erupted there in 1971, so it was called Ceylon when the figure at the center of my discussion here first achieved public prominence. For consistency's sake, however, I shall use the contemporary term throughout.

3. The term *guru* was officially dropped in the United States in 1978 due to the so-called guru invasion of the late sixties. Hence, in the editor's note to one publication printed by the organization Bawa founded, we read the following: "He became disturbed by the behavior of some of these individuals and by the money-making organizations they had built, and he did not wish to be associated with them. So in 1978 Bawa Muhaiyaddeen had the title guru officially removed from his name and from the Fellowships that had grown around him" (M. R. Bawa Muhaiyaddeen, *Truth and Light: Brief Explanations* [Philadelphia: Fellowship Press, 1974] 10). However, the term continues to be used in northern Sri Lanka among his Tamil Hindu followers. Before coming to the U.S., Bawa seemed to be indifferent to what he was called, which raises the question about whose decision it was to drop the Hindu title in favor of a Muslim one. Some of the senior Sri Lankans living at the Fellowship house in Philadelphia are of the opinion that it was the Americans who decided to make this change, not Bawa himself. Bawa did, however, mention false swamis and gurus many years prior to his arrival in the United States. See, for example, M. R. Bawa Muhaiyaddeen, *The Pearl of Wisdom* (Philadelphia: Fellowship Press, 2000) 121–22, where he says that there are millions of false teachers who will suffer thirty-five million rebirths for their treachery, while the true one is "kicked and chased away." The Tamil term *bawa* is used for holy father-like figures in general, especially among Sufis of the Rifai order. It is also a surname among Muslims in Sri Lanka and Sikhs in the Punjab of India. For classifications of Muslim holy men on the island, see M. M. M. Mahroof, "The Faqirs of Islam," *Islamic Culture* 41 (1967) 99–109; M. M. M. Mahroof, "Mendicants and Troubadors: Towards a Historical Taxonomy of the Faqirs of Sri Lanka," *Islamic Studies* 30 (1991) 501–16.

On an Island Sacred to Many Faiths

Between 1940 and 1942, dates that remain very tentative, a holy man emerged from the jungles of southeastern Sri Lanka, near the pilgrimage site of Kataragama, sacred to Hindus, Muslims, and Buddhists, after some decades meditating in various secluded locations throughout the island.[4] He was a nonliterate Tamil-speaking sage whose religious affiliation was rather vague, at first, as were the place of his birth and the date of his arrival on the island. Very little is known about this individual prior to his emergence from the wilds, and all we really know about him prior to his "discovery" is what he himself chose to tell us in short vignettes interspersed here and there in the massive oral corpus of his formal and informal discourses. Indeed, a quest for the historical persona behind the liturgical one later motivated his disciples to compile an esoteric autobiography culled from hundreds, if not thousands, of hours of taped sermons.[5]

At the invitation of two Tamil Hindu brothers who met him in the jungle during a walking pilgrimage (*pada yatra*) to Kataragama, he eventually settled in Jaffna, the predominantly Tamil-speaking north, circa 1942, where he ministered to whomever required his services from the home of the two brothers.[6] His clientele consisted mostly of Hindu

4. According to his own reckoning, he lived in solitude on the island for forty-five and a half years prior to the start of his public ministry. See Frank J. Korom, "Charisma and Community: A Brief History of the Bawa Muhaiyaddeen Fellowship," *Sri Lankan Journal of the Humanities* 37 (2012) 19–33. On the significance of Kataragama as a sacred place of pilgrimage, see Gananath Obeyesekere, "Social Change and the Deities: The Rise of the Kataragama Cult in Modern Sri Lanka," *Man* 12 (1977) 377–96; Gananath Obeyesekere, "The Fire-walkers of Kataragama: The Rise of Bhakti Religiosity in Buddhist Sri Lanka," *Journal of Asian Studies* 37 (1978) 457–76.

5. It is titled *The Tree That Fell to the West* (Philadelphia: Fellowship Press, 2003), but it reads more like a self-fashioned hagiography unhindered by time and space than a historical account of his life. Nonetheless, pilgrims traveling from the U.S. to Sri Lanka often use it as a guide for visiting places Bawa used to frequent. In July of 2011, for example, thirty-three pilgrims from the Toronto branch of his Fellowship visited Sri Lanka to tour the sites mentioned in the book.

6. Bawa claimed that he needed to go north anyway to rid Jaffna of sorcerers who were using black magic to corrupt and ruin the region. Hence, the coincidental meeting in the jungle with the two brothers was not by chance but rather predetermined, a catalyst for his departure to do battle with evil forces in the north. The motif of a Sufi arriving in an area to rid it of some sort of pestilence is a common one throughout the Muslim world, but especially in South Asia. See Riazul Islam, *Sufism in South Asia: Impact on Fourteenth-Century Muslim Society* (Karachi: Oxford University Press, 2002) 11.

peasants who were drawn to him purportedly because of his powerful gaze, which was said to be able to destroy or financially ruin a person when the saint was angered.[7] He had also demonstrated his mastery of bilocation, levitation, and other superhuman feats, such as not eating, attributed to Sufi saints over the ages, which further attracted people to him. In about 1952, according to some sources, he had acquired a former Dutch warehouse dating from the colonial period where he opened a spiritual commune (*ashram*), at which he litigated local land disputes much in the manner of a judge; healed the sick using herbal medicines and his own saliva; exorcized demonic forces from possessed individuals with a staff; and taught perennial truths to the philosophically inclined on a daily basis, after which he would fall into mystical trances in the evening when he would perform astral travel to continue "God's work," as he called it, throughout the many universes in his cosmology.[8]

Shortly after founding his commune, the sage acquired land south of Jaffna in the nearby region of Puliyankulam, which he cleared and farmed to feed the multitude of people who now sought him out on a regular basis.[9] Advocating vegetarianism, he grew rice, coconuts, and

---

7. Many people therefore avoided looking directly at him. According to numerous oral sources, Bawa himself joked that he had to learn to control his anger over the years, so as not to take the life of another unjustifiably. But according to an octogenarian follower of his in Colombo, Bawa's wrath was, at times, used against his enemies, those who wished to do him harm, as he relates in a story told in chapter 35 of his first transcribed book of teachings, in which he actually shows anger. At one point in the story, he acts with impatience and annoyance, when he pulls out a *kris* (curved dagger) and sword and threatens to kill the husband of one of the girls for which he used to care, at which a bridge keeper who denies him crossing says he has to develop *sabr* (patience). The moral of the story is that even *bawas* can lose their composure on occasion. See M. R. Bawa Muhaiyaddeen, *The Pearl of Wisdom* (Battarmulla, Sri Lanka: Printer Private Limited, 2000).

8. One source indicates that the year was 1944, after which he lived in the village of Kokuvil for seven years followed by seven more years in Kondavil before founding his *ashram* in Jaffna town. See Chloë Le Pichon, *et al.*, eds, *The Mirror: Photographs and Reflections on Life with M. R. Bawa Muhaiyaddeen* (Philadelphia: Published Privately by the Author, 2010) 4. This would have made it 1958. However, as one historian has pointed out, Sufis are notoriously cavalier when it comes to chronology. See Islam *Sufism in South Asia* (Karachi: Oxford University Press, 2002) 31. This is why the dates of Bawa's career up until his period in Colombo must remain tentative. For parallels of Sufi saints as curers and healers elsewhere in South Asia, see Katherine P. Ewing "The Sufi as Saint, Curer, and Exorcist in Modern Pakistan," *Contributions to Asian Studies* 18 (1984) 106–14.

9. The farm has been reclaimed and refurbished recently after the end of civil hostilities between the Tamil Eelam and the government of Sri Lanka. However, it is not

vegetables, but also kept two pet deer named after the Hindu deity Murugan's wives and a dog named Tiger (*puli*) at both the commune and farm respectively. By that time, he was already being called reverentially Guru Bawa or Swami Bawa, the former referring to him in the role of teacher, the latter in his capacity as spiritual father and lord among his Hindu followers.[10] Moreover, this father figure image of him was further equated with lack of ego, mind, and creed, what his Muslim admirers would later refer to as the perfect man (*insan kamil*), a technical term referring to a primordial consciousness inherent in all human beings, but manifestly embodied in the Prophet of Islam.[11] In Bawa's case, however, it was one of a number of associations used to connect him to the Muslim "saint of Baghdad" Abdul Qadir Jilani in this context, the ascribed founder of the Qadiri order, with whom he had symbolic ties, despite very vague lineal connections.[12] In fact, in some ways, his praxis was more in line with the Chishti order based in Ajmer, India. But this lack of concrete affiliation lent to his aura of mystique that allowed people to perceive him as a timeless, otherworldly being not bound by space.[13]

yet at the level of production where it can produce food in any significant quantity.

10. It is important to note here that Bawa was not identified as a Sufi at this early stage in his career, a point that he himself made repeatedly, even though he did teach an esoteric understanding of Islam and the Qur'an, albeit by drawing extensively on the vocabulary of Hinduism to do so, especially terms used regularly in *tantra*. More will be said about this below.

11. Ibn Arabi (1165–1240), arguably the foremost Sufi thinker throughout the centuries, was the first to expound fully on the concept. See John Little, "Al-Insan al-Kamil: The Perfect Man, according to Ibn al-Arabi," *Muslim World* 77 (1987) 43–54.

12. Jilani (1088–1166), whose foot legendarily rests on the neck of every saint, was appointed chief of saints by God, and was *al-ghawth al-azam* (the succor to the world), also shared with Bawa the title *muhyiddin* (reviver of religion) and enjoyed the lofty status of *qutb* (spiritual axis), the latter of which only appears singularly in each generation. These and other associations link the two. This is why Bawa spent a significant number of years meditating in a cave in central Sri Lanka known as Dafthar Jailani, the office of Jilani. For a description of the site, see Dennis B. McGilvray, "Jailani: A Sufi Shrine in Sri Lanka," in *Lived Islam in South Asia: Adaptation, Accommodation, and Conflict*, ed. Imtiaz Ahmad and Heinz Reifeld (Delhi: Social Science, 2004) 273–89. For other places where he resided prior to his public career, see Korom, "Charisma and Community: A Brief History of the Bawa Muhaiyaddeen Fellowship," *Sri Lankan Journal of the Humanities*, 2012. One thing Jilani did not share with Bawa, however, was celibacy, since he married four wives and fathered forty-nine sons after the age of fifty!

13. Bawa would eventually link the two orders by declaring Jilani as well as Moinuddin Chishti (b. 1141), the founders of each, to be *qutb*s, cosmic axes, a term that his own followers would come to apply to him in 2007, eleven years after his death.

Bawa's fame as a counselor, exorcist, and healer spread quickly throughout the villages of the northern Tamil country, which prompted urban Muslim intellectuals and Theosophists residing in Colombo to seek him out and eventually bring him to the capital. At first, he purportedly refused, stating that he was a tree upon which too many people would perch.[14] But as pressure mounted on him, he gradually gave in and moved to the city part time to establish the Serendib Sufi Study Circle (SSSC) in 1962. The SSSC, although using the Islamic term *Sufism* in a generic way to refer to mysticism more broadly construed, was originally a nonsectarian spiritual organization officially incorporated by the parliament of Sri Lanka in November of 1974,[15] by which time Bawa was already ensconced in a rented row home in a collegiate neighborhood of West Philadelphia. To understand how this great leap across oceans and continents took place, we must travel to the City of Brotherly Love as it was in the transformative era of the late sixties, when a large number of young people were experimenting with alternative

---

See Qutb M. R. Bawa Muhaiyaddeen, *Faith* (Philadelphia: Fellowship Press, 2007). The aforementioned Chishti, also known as Gharib Nawaz (helper of the poor), is the first of the six recognized *awliyas* (friends of God) of the order who brought it to India. Aspects of his teachings that pertain to Bawa are obedience to the sheikh, renunciation of the material world, distance from worldly powers, supporting the poor, service to humanity, respect for other devotional traditions, dependence on the Creator, not the created, and disapproval of showing off miraculous deeds. Because of their respect for other devotional traditions, the Chishtiyya do not demand formal conversion to Islam. In addition, they also recognized Jilani as a Chishti sheikh, which made linking the two orders unproblematic for Bawa. The logic here is that just as one could belong to two Sufi orders, one could also, by extension, belong to two religions, even if not formally abandoning one to embrace the other.

14. See Le Pichon, *The Mirror The Mirror: Photographs and Reflections on Life with M. R. Bawa Muhaiyaddeen* (Philadelphia: Published Privately by the Author, 2010) 9.

15. The incorporation document (Law No. 41 of 1974) is most telling. In it, Bawa is now being referred to as Sheikh, a noticeably Muslim title derived from a sixteenth-century Arab compound for "old man," now used generally to refer to a leader of an organization or community, whether it be religious or secular. The document identifies his complete name and title as His Holiness Sheikh Muhammed Muhiyadeen Guru Bawa and states its purpose, among other things, as being "the promotion and the study and understanding of Sufism (mysticism) among *all* persons seeking knowledge" (italics added). We notice a shift here toward Islam, while still leaving open the possibility of perennialism. Indeed, one of the prominent founding members of the SSSC was the well-known journalist and social activist Theja Gunawardena, who, inspired by the second president of the Theosophical Society Annie Besant, authored a book called *Theosophy and Islam* (Colombo: Felix Printers, 1983) in which the universal tenets of spirituality are expounded within the framework of comparative religion. More shall be said about this below.

lifestyles, which involved not only the use of mind-altering drugs but also a significant turn to the East in a quest for new forms of spirituality radically different from mainstream Judaism and Christianity.[16] It only seems appropriate that Bawa should make his appearance on the international stage here, in a city that was founded on religious tolerance and pluralism.

The Tree That Fell to the West

Halfway around the world from the pear-shaped land mass known as Sarandib to the medieval Arab seafaring traders who brought Islam to the Buddhist island, an American female with uncontrollable mystical inclinations met a Muslim man in 1968 who was a graduate student at the University of Pennsylvania. He told her numerous awe-inspiring tales about his encounters with a holy man named Bawa, as his intimates called him in his native island home.[17] The sage and his perennial teachings instantly enchanted the young mystic because she desired answers to her questions concerning not only the nature of her own deeply personal experiences but also those concerning the larger meaning of humankind's spiritual quest. She began corresponding with Bawa shortly thereafter, who had by then hired a personal scribe and translator to whom he would dictate responses that were sent at regular intervals to this New Age seeker in Philadelphia. In an era prior to cell

---

16. The famous phrase "turning East" is borrowed from Harvey Cox, *Turning East: Promise and Peril of the New Orientalism* (New York: Viking, 1979). Although the majority of those on alternative quests searched within Hinduism, Buddhism, and, to a lesser extent, Taoism, Sufism quietly made strides into the Western spiritual marketplace as well. See Amira El-Zein, "Spiritual Consumption in the United States: The Rumi Phenomenon," *Islam and Christian-Muslim Relations* 11 (2000) 71–85; Celia Genn, "The Development of a Modern Western Sufism," in *Sufism and the Modern in Islam*, ed. Martin van Bruinessen and John Howell (London: Taurus, 2007) 257–78; Marcia Hermansen, "In the Garden of American Sufi Movements: Hybrids and Perennials," in *New Trends and Developments in the World of Islam*, ed. Peter B. Clarke (London: Luzac Oriental,1998) 155–78; Marcia Hermansen, "Hybrid Formations in Muslim America: The Case of American Sufi Movements," *Muslim World* 90 (2000) 158–97; Marcia Hermansen, "What's American about American Sufi Movements?" in *Sufism in Europe and North America*, ed. David Westerlund (London: RoutledgeCurzon, 2004) 36–63.

17. Alternatively, he is referred to with the honorific form of Bawangal, consisting of the term *bawa* (father) plus the Tamil plural suffix, making it honorific; that is, "revered father."

phones, Skype, and e-mail, Bawa was conducting spiritual counseling using aerograms, those thin sheets of paper that folded in upon themselves to create a lightweight, self-sealing envelope to transport written words from one end of the earth to the other, albeit ever so slowly. Answers to questions therefore took several weeks, sometimes months, at a time to arrive.

During this lengthy period of back and forth correspondence, she desired to join him at his *ashram* in Jaffna but realized that she was too poor to do so, as she was divorced and had a child to support.[18] Instead, she made preparations to sponsor a visit by Bawa to Philadelphia. She slowly gathered other seekers around her who could help her foot the bill to accomplish this onerous task. Hence, in early 1971, she and her nascent "fellowship" made final preparations to bring the *guru* to Philadelphia. To officially secure him a visa, she and a small core of his first devotees informally founded the Bawa Muhaiyaddeen Fellowship shortly before his arrival on October 11, 1971.[19] Thus, the humble *guru* or *swami* who spoke no English nor wrote or read any language came to the United States as Guru Bawa Muhaiyaddeen, the founder of what would then have been termed a cult by sociologists, despite the group's choice of the nonsectarian term *fellowship*.[20] By what means Bawa ob-

18. These correspondences comprised the data for my paper titled "Modern Anxieties and Sufi Solutions," presented in 2009 at a talk to the members of the Boston University Center for the Study of Asia. I am indebted to the attendees for their comments, especially my colleagues Augustus Richard Norton and Corky White, whose queries have been incorporated into this chapter.

19. The Commonwealth of Pennsylvania, Department of State Corporation Bureau approved non-profit corporation status to the "Guru Bawa Fellowship of Philadelphia" on June 19, 1972, but allowed the document to be amended on March 5, 1977, to change the name to the "Bawa Muhaiyaddeen Fellowship of Philadelphia," thereby dropping the title *guru* officially from the organization's name. The mission statement in the original 1972 document states that its purpose is to pursue wisdom regarding the reason for the creation of the human species and its future destiny.

20. It is difficult to use the term *cult* neutrally today, but it was in common use, especially among sociologists and journalists, at the time when Bawa first arrived in the United States via London. For a useful attempt to create a model for defining cults within their historical and cultural context, see Allan W. Eisner, "An Outline of a Structural Theory of Cults," *Journal for the Scientific Study of Religion* 11 (1972) 319–33. Martin Marty, "Sects and Cults," *Annals of the American Academy of Political and Social Science* 332 (1960) 125–32, views them as positively oriented around a charismatic leader, while James T. Richardson, "From Cult to Sect: Creative Eclecticism in New Religious Movements," *Pacific Sociological Review* 22 (1979) 139–66, focuses on the transition from "cult" to "sect," which is relevant to understanding how the Fellowship eventually becomes an established denomination, as discussed below.

tained the necessary documents to be issued a passport and visa are still unclear, as there are many unanswered questions concerning to which country he actually belonged.[21]

Establishing Roots in the New World

The twenty-one people who met Bawa and his party of three Sri Lankan translators at the airport collectively moved into the aforementioned row home located at 254 South 46th Street in West Philadelphia, where Bawa gave discourses every evening to anyone who wished to listen, after which he regularly fed the entire gathering with food cooked in the home's kitchen. There were no exorcisms here, but the process of healing continued uninterrupted in the sense that the motley crew that came to hear him speak a strange Dravidian language were instructed to give up drugs and meat, shave their beards, cut their hair, wash their clothes, and get jobs. In other words, Bawa wanted them to give up the counterculture and become productive members of society. He also demanded complete submission and dedication only to him. In giving oneself up completely to Bawa, he taught, the highly difficult to achieve mystical union with God could be sought, but with no guarantee of success. In more than one instance, members of his inner circle told me that Bawa "saved" them.[22] By the Fall of 1972 the group had gathered momentum and drawn up a final charter for the organization, in which Bawa mandated three presidents, three secretaries, and three treasurers.

Before that, however, the organization was referred to as a cult by outsiders, especially the largely Baptist population that lived in the area surrounding the farm that would be founded by Bawa and his followers during his American ministry.

21. When I inquired about this, in Colombo, an American woman belonging to the inner circle told me that when he applied for his Ceylonese passport, he simply asked someone in his entourage what her birthday was, then used it as his own. Still, what other documentation was provided to the authorities to demonstrate residency or prove citizenship remains unclear, and merely asking about it from the Sri Lankan cadre simply produces spontaneous eruptions of laughter. Clearly, the historical Bawa is subordinate to the liturgical one.

22. Two memoirs written by a couple of Bawa's "children" are available, both of which provide poignant and intimate perspectives on those who were drawn to him. See Mitchell Gilbert, *One Light: An Owner's Guide for the Human Being* (Merion Station, PA: One Light, 2005); and Sharon Marcus, *My Years with the Qutb: A Walk in Paradise* (Toronto: Sufi Press, 2005). Although very different personalities, these two authors provide a good sense of the diversity within the ranks of Bawa's North American fellowship.

These individuals, with the exception of those departed, are still among the sixteen members of the executive committee that assumed control of the Fellowship after the death of the founder.

Known for his regular participation in interfaith dialogues with ministers of other faiths, his infectious charisma drew in more and more people until the house could no longer accommodate the entire group. The Fellowship grew large and prosperous enough to purchase a Jewish community center on the outskirts of the city in 1973 that was converted then into a Fellowship house where Bawa's "American family" could reside comfortably with his Sri Lankan entourage. Now that the Fellowship was officially registered as a not-for-profit organization, a significant stage of the movement's institutionalization had been achieved: it was now on the path to becoming a sectarian community that needed to define itself vis-à-vis other denominations. Two earlier stages of development in Jaffna and Colombo now culminated in the establishment of a truly transnational movement that loosely linked the northern commune and farm in Jaffna, the SSSC in Colombo, and the Fellowship in Philadelphia.[23]

During these early years of his American ministry, there was not a strong emphasis on any one particular religious tradition. Instead, as one member of Bawa's "inner circle" told me, he taught Hinduism to Hindus, Christianity to Christians, Buddhism to Buddhists, and Judaism to Jews. But gradually, Bawa told his inner circle to give up such practices as yoga and meditation and solely adopt the recitation of Sufi *zikr* instead. The evolution of his teaching thus moved from universalistic generalizations that suggested organized religion to be the greatest obstacle to achieving a mystical state of awareness to a more specific Islamic path grounded firmly in Sufi mysticism, which became evident a few years later when Bawa and his "children" began building a mosque on the Fellowship grounds that was completed and dedicated in May of 1984. It now serves as a multiethnic center of prayer and worship for immigrant Muslims as well as Bawa's American convert family.[24] From

23. Other semi-autonomous branches would emerge primarily in North America, most significantly in Toronto, with smaller ones throughout the United States. There are two others in Sri Lanka as well, dominated by Malay Muslims, one located in Matale, the other in Wattala.

24. The mosque also contains a *madrasah*, where immigrant children study Arabic side by side with Euro-American children on Sunday mornings, much in the manner of Christian Sunday school, while the parents attend the Sunday morning meetings

the time he arrived in Philadelphia until his death on December 8, 1986, Guru Bawa, who later became Sheikh Bawa, then finally Qutb, led a transnational existence, moving back and forth between his homeland in South Asia and his newly constructed Fellowship in Philadelphia.

While the next fifteen years saw the growth of the organization in North America, Bawa did return intermittently to Sri Lanka for a total of four visits, always bringing along a retinue of his American "family" members with him.[25] It was during the second trip back that he and forty-one of his American children built a nondenominational structure in Muslim architectural style in Mankumban, located on the coast of a tiny island connected to the mainland by a causeway within walking distance of the Jaffna *ashram*. Bawa named it God House, and it was formally dedicated on February 17, 1975.[26] This serene site, surrounded by palm trees, only meters from the ocean, is still in use today, having

---

held in the Fellowship house's meeting room where Bawa used to give discourses. Nowadays, they listen to taped sermons previously given by Bawa, which are then discussed. Similar Sunday sessions are held weekly in Colombo as well.

25. These return trips occurred on the following dates: May 1972–February 1973; February 1974–July 1975; November 1976–August 1978; and December 1980–November 1982, composing roughly one-third of his ministry from the time of his arrival in the United States until his death. Discussions with a variety of American and Sri Lankan disciples about these visits suggest that there were often ambiguous tensions between the two ethnic groups concerning different expectations, which apparently annoyed Bawa. By 1976 the Fellowship had already established ten national and international centers and recruited seven thousand members, according to Fellowship officials. The number may, however, be exaggerated, as suggested below.

26. The site is dedicated to Mary, the mother of Jesus, whom Bawa said came to southern India with St. Thomas after Jesus's ascension into heaven. She died and was buried on the Indian coastline near the straights that separate India and Sri Lanka, according to Bawa. The original shrine was inundated, so he promised Mary that he would build her a new one on dry land. After seeing the site in a vision during the 1940s, he actively began searching for it and identified the place 150 meters from the beachhead at Mankumban (heap of sand). He began work on it in 1954, but lacked the funds to continue after the foundation was laid. Despite offers from Sri Lankan patrons to cover the cost of completion, Bawa refused until he came back in October of 1974 with his American children to complete the job the following year. See Le Pichon, *The Mirror: Photographs and Reflections on Life with M. R. Bawa Muhaiyaddeen* (Philadelphia: Published Privately by the Author, 2010) 50. Services followed by a communal meal are held there on Fridays, mostly attended by local Tamil Hindus. A Singaporean Muslim follower of Bawa told me after one such Friday service in 2010 how surprised she was that the rites were so "Hindu" in nature. Interestingly, she did not fully participate in the rites on that day, but observed from the sidelines.

miraculously survived the brutal civil war that drastically affected the Tamil portions of the island in recent decades.[27]

Bawa's last trip was decisive, in that he fell into a coma. His entire entourage, American and Sri Lankan, felt that his chances of surviving and returning the United States were slim, so preparations for his funerary rites were being made when according to an American eyewitness, he suddenly awoke and proclaimed that the angel of death had come to whisk him away, but he requested more time to complete his mission on earth, which he was apparently granted.[28] He then returned to Philadelphia with his American retinue for the last time to spend the remainder of his days preparing for his ultimate departure. During those last four years, Bawa's health was in constant decline, and he rarely left his bedroom, where he was hooked up to a respirator to help him breathe, which was necessary after many decades of heavy smoking.[29] One female of the inner circle stated that when he was dying he asked her in confidence if she really wanted him to remain on earth in his present condition. She had to respond no. Bawa passed peacefully on December 8, 1986, on his bed in the Fellowship house surrounded by his inner circle of children.

His corpse was ritually cleansed and prepared for burial in Philadelphia, then transported in a hearse to East Fallowfield, a rural location in Pennsylvania, located approximately forty miles outside of Philadelphia, where the Fellowship had earlier purchased fifty-eight acres of land in 1980 to serve as both a Muslim cemetery and communal farm. The saint now rests in a *mazar* (shrine) built for him by his followers,

27. Indeed, it was Bawa's miraculous power, according to locals, that protected the site, even though other structures all around it were bombed out. When I visited in 2010, other buildings, including a nearby Catholic church, were being repaired while God House "shone like a jewel," according to the caretaker of the shrine at that time.

28. Back in Philadelphia, Bawa later told his children that during the period of his coma he was helping four people go through the pain of death, which physically exhausted him, and from which he never completely recovered. See Le Pichon, *The Mirror: Photographs and Reflections on Life with M. R. Bawa Muhaiyaddeen* (Philadelphia: Published Privately by the Author, 2010) 204.

29. Bawa had earlier claimed in his initial correspondences with the founder of the Fellowship that he had the power to absorb into himself the illnesses and pains of others, which often left him weak and fragile as a result. Some very pious individuals even say that it was not his incessant chain smoking that gave him pulmonary problems but rather his compassion for suffering beings, which led one Buddhist admirer in Sri Lanka to tell me that Bawa was a *bodhisattva*, a compassionate being.

which was dedicated on November 28, 1987.[30] Consequently, a number of his inner circle, mostly married couples starting families of their own, settled in a cluster around the site, within walking distance from their beloved spiritual father.[31] Since Bawa's entombment, the location has become an international pilgrimage site and place of contemplation for visitors from North America, Europe, the Middle East, and South Asia. Annual remembrances are held for the saint on his death anniversary, the twenty-fifth of which was marked in March of 2011.

Rough estimates provided by the Fellowship suggest that Bawa has approximately 10,000 children worldwide today, with many more non-paying sympathizers. Most of the Americans are now convert Muslims, although virtually all in Jaffna remain Hindu, with some Tamil Christian admirers as well. Buddhists are less in number, but not completely unknown. The weekly and monthly gatherings in Colombo, Matale, and Wattala, on the other hand, are predominantly attended by Muslims, except for one artist originally from the hill country around Kandy, who told me that he attends Christian, Muslim, Hindu, and Buddhist services regularly, since all benefit him spiritually. He is one of the few remaining perennialists frequenting the Sufi recitations sponsored by the SSSC in Colombo.[32] All of this suggests that there is a trend both in

30. One female attendant at the burial recalled with a smile that Bawa, who was a master trickster adept at using humor as a teaching tool, pulled a final joke on his Fellowship family. She reminisced that when the hearse was taking Bawa's corpse to the cemetery, the driver had to stop for gas, which she found funny, since Bawa always said that one should always prepare ahead for a journey. See Le Pichon, *The Mirror: Photographs and Reflections on Life with M. R. Bawa Muhaiyaddeen* (Philadelphia: Published Privately by the Author, 2010) 206.

31. This is true of the Fellowship house as well, since most members live within walking distance or a short drive from the site, which they visit frequently, often at odd hours, to pray and perform *zikr*.

32. Numbers are difficult to ascertain because it is virtually impossible to know who is a member and who is a sympathizer, or who simply attends for the free food distributed in abundance on a regular basis. In all likelihood, the number quoted above seems slightly exaggerated, but it does appear to be the case that the number of active participants in the Fellowship has not dwindled. Indeed, it seems as if the younger generation that grew up only vaguely remembering Bawa or born after his death are taking the Fellowship in new directions by drawing on their media savvy, something the inner circle generation had not been able fully to exploit. On the youth of the movement, see Benjamin H. Snyder, "Heartspace: The Bawa Muhaiyaddeen Fellowship and the Culture of Unity" (BA thesis, Bryn Mawr College, 2003). The web-meister of the SSSC's Internet site based in Colombo, for example, told me that they receive hundreds of thousands of hits from all over the world, the most coming from the United States, but others also from unexpected locations, such as Saudi Arabia.

Colombo and in Philadelphia to deemphasize the multidenominational quality of such meetings, while in Jaffna and Matale the Muslim character of the group and its rites are more eclectic, thereby also problematic for the leadership which seeks to purify the community.[33] Given this background of evolving strategies and practices, let us turn now to the vexing issue of identity before concluding.

Liturgical versus Historical Bawa

Mohamed Mauroof, who has written the only ethnographic account of Bawa's Fellowship, provides us with a well-documented study based on participant observation. The text does stray off course at times, but provides a number of insights into the movement, even acknowledged by the stringent standards of the Fellowship itself. In particular, he distinguishes between the "liturgical Bawa" and the "historical Bawa."[34] The former refers to his *ruh*, the transcendental figure that links the latter in an initiatory chain to all of the preceding prophets and saints that goes back to the beginning of time to the creation itself. The latter refers to his *nafs*, or physical manifestation in the world of appearances (*duniya*). Although members of the Fellowship insist that Bawa was timeless and unchanging, it is my contention that we must separate out the liturgical Bawa from the historical one, without losing sight of their intimate connection on the level of religious ideology. Hagiography is, after all, as much fact as fiction for those who truly believe in Bawa's vocation. In this sense, the two have to be seen in a dialectical fashion that oscillates between what is factually known about the historical Bawa and the mythic dimensions of his superhuman career in the past, present, and

---

33. One prominent member of the Jaffna group told me emphatically that Bawa taught everyone not to convert; hence, most remain Hindus. In Matale, there is another problem. The late founder of that branch was also dedicated to Satya Sai Baba, the non-denominational holy man from south India who attracted a worldwide following before his death in 2011. There is some evidence that reformist Muslims are pressuring such groups to cleanse their practices and beliefs or be considered transgressors. On this tension between reformist Muslims and Sufis in Sri Lanka, see Victor de Munck, "Islamic Orthodoxy and Sufism in Sri Lanka," *Anthropos* 100 (2005) 401–14. For an interesting study of Sai Baba, which implies parallels and begs for comparison with Bawa Muhaiyaddeen, see Deborah A. Swallow, "Ashes and Power: Myth, Rite and Miracle in an Indian God-Man's Cult," *Modern Asian Studies* 16 (1982) 123–58.

34. See Mohamed Mauroof, "The Culture and Experience of Luminous and Liminal Komunesam" (PhD diss., University of Pennsylvania, 1976).

future. The dilemma of reconciling the two images of Bawa has led to what Max Weber referred to as rationalization, an attempt to explain the mystical or the enchanted in empirical ways suitable for mass consumption by other groups and individuals with whom the Fellowship is in contact, and from whom it seeks validation as a legitimate denomination.[35] Legitimization naturally leads to the necessity of dialogue with other religious traditions, something of which Bawa was acutely aware.

Based on oral histories and ethnographic data compiled on his ministry, I wish to suggest therefore that this humble but charismatic Sufi preacher from Sri Lanka had to make a conscious transition from the generic *guru* to the distinctive *shaykh* to separate himself from the "guru invasion" mentioned above that took place in the United States during the latter 1960s and early 1970s. According to the current imam of the Philadelphia mosque, he dropped the title of *guru* in 1973 after witnessing Guru Maharaj Ji being paraded around the Houston Astrodome as part of his Millennium 73 extravaganza on television, during which he declared himself Lord of the World (*jagannath*).[36]

In his attempt to establish himself as a legitimate Muslim wise man, distinct from the variegated Hindu and Buddhist teachers that stormed the United States, Bawa gradually abandoned the eclectic Theosophical system of thought that he utilized in Sri Lanka and adopted one based on Islamic *shariah* (orthodoxy) and *zikr* (recitation), which ultimately would lead his followers to mystical gnosis. At the same time, however, he continued to preach in a universal idiom that transcended religious boundaries and reflected a perennial attitude that suggested there is only one God, regardless of what He is called. In the end, though, it is

35. For a discussion see, Max Weber, "The Social Psychology of the World's Religions," in *From Max Weber: Essays in Sociology*, ed. H. H. Gerth and C. W. Mills (New York: Oxford University Press, 1946) 267–301. For Weber, rationalization leads to disenchantment, which some in the movement cite as the reason for why they feel alienated from the administration of the Fellowship. Disenchantment results from the imposition of intermediaries who divert direct experience and re-channel it through figures of authority on the executive committee that are responsible for the bureaucratic dimension of the group's infrastructure. In other words, it is the priests and scribes that create the barrier between the student and the teacher, a point reiterated below. On the importance of hagiography in studying Bawa, see Korom, "Charisma and Community: A Brief History of the Bawa Muhaiyaddeen Fellowship," *Sri Lankan Journal of the Humanities*, 2012.

36. This is a few years earlier than the dates mentioned above, which suggests to me that the process was not one that happened instantaneously but was discussed over a period of time that eventually led to the dropping of the title once and for all.

apparent that Bawa Muhaiyaddeen was operating within a very distinct pattern of Sufi proselytism, a time-honored one that eschewed syncretism in favor of traditionally self-perceived axioms about the superior nature of Islam.[37]

From this perspective, we have to situate the three staged "comings" of the historical Bawa during his earthly career in an historical and intellectual context, which correspond exactly with the stages of institutionalization adumbrated above. The first is his northern Sri Lankan phase, where he presented himself, and was perceived by others, as a typical Hindu *guru* or Sufi *zinda pir* (living saint), characterized primarily by pragmatism (i.e., farming, healing, settling disputes, and the like). The second phase sets in when he begins to minister to the elite of Colombo. This phase is more philosophical, tapping into the theosophical movement that was well established in Sri Lanka by the 1970s.[38] The third phase coincides with his arrival in the United States. Here he is first understood as the typical perennial mystic, so popular in the newly emerging New Age movement of that period, which perpetuates freethinking, universalism, and antidogmatism.[39] It is during this phase that Bawa had to Americanize the movement, which involved democratization and the creation of a distinct identity within a mosaic

37. This position has been argued most cogently by Richard M. Eaton, *The Rise of Islam and the Bengal Frontier, 1204–1760*, Comparative Studies on Muslim Societies (Berkeley: University of California Press, 1993), who makes the convincing case that Sufis in deltaic Bengal only used preexisting idioms, such as poetry, symbolic imagery, religious titles, etc., to rhetorically persuade people that Islam is the true religion, superior to all others, in his particular case, Hinduism. See also Richard M. Eaton, "Sufi Folk Literature and the Expansion of Indian Islam," *History of Religions* 14 (1974) 117–27, where he first formulated his ideas about conversion in the context of the medieval Deccan.

38. See, for example, George Bond, "The Contemporary Lay Meditation Movement and Lay Gurus in Sri Lanka," *Religion* 33 (2003) 23–55. This partly explains the appeal that he had for people such as the aforementioned Theja Gunawardena, who, although a Buddhist by birth, was drawn towards the universalism that Bawa preached at the outset of his mission, ultimately leading her to write a small book on Islam and theosophical teachings, much in the same vein as Besant's papmphlet earlier published by the Theosophical Society of India. See Annie Besant, *Islam in the Light of Theosophy: A Lecture* (London: Theosophical Publishing Society, 1912).

39. For a succinct statement on the particulars of New Age thinking, see Wouter Hanegraaf, "New Age Spiritualities as Secular Religion: A Historian's Perspective," *Social Compass* 46 (1999) 288–312. On Sufism and the New Age specifically, see Peter Wilson, "The Strange Fate of Sufism in the New Age," in *New Trends and Developments in the World of Islam*, ed. Peter B. Clarke (London: Luzac Oriental, 1997) 179–209.

of new religious movements. This entailed weeding out eclecticism by weaning away spiritual shoppers from other mystical paths available in the American marketplace of religion in order to pledge allegiance solely to him and to Islam.

Bawa thus comes to emphasize, ultimately, a distinct Islamic message that focuses on a fourfold spiritual developmental pattern, firmly ground in Muslim orthodoxy. The progression moves from *sharia* (revealed law), which involves discerning right from wrong and permissible behavior to phase two, known as *tariqa* (path), the strengthening of determination, to *haqiqa* (truth), the beginning of communication and union with God, leading finally to *marifa* (gnosis), a more perfected state of union with God that results in *sufiya*, a state of constant remembrance (*zikr*) and contemplation (*fikr*) that transcends the "four religions," which Bawa defined in ascending order as Hinduism, Zoroastrianism, Christianity, Islam.[40] Notice how Islam is now conspicuously placed at the zenith of the vertical hierarchy in this scheme, in which there is no trace whatsoever of the cliché of all religions being one and the same.

In making the strategic move described above, Bawa successfully sowed the seeds of Islam, which then took root and sprouted in the current phase of development. As I understand it, we are now in the fourth stage of institutionalization, during which what Weber would call the "routinization of charisma" occurs. It is precisely after Bawa's death that what Weber terms the "charisma of office" is established, when Bawa's selected acolytes now become figures of authority responsible for maintaining and employing the saint's charisma through his *Amt* (office). Utilizing the privileges of the founder's office involves, not always to everyone's liking, the creation of a hierarchical bureaucracy that is responsible for the economic and ideological maintenance of the group, which involves, among other things, creating stricter rules of belief and behavior, strengthening institutional infrastructure, and expanding membership by disseminating the founder's teachings through various forms of media, such as an aggressive publications program and the

---

40. In this scheme, Buddhism is understood as an aspect of Hinduism and Judaism as one of Islam. See Gisela Webb, "Tradition and Innovation in Contemporary American Spirituality: The Bawa Muhaiyaddeen Fellowship," in *Muslim Communities in North America*, ed. Yvonne Y. Haddad and Jane I. Smith, SUNY Series in Middle Eastern Studies (Albany: SUNY Press, 1994) 75–108.

launching of an official internet site.[41] In the process, the Fellowship has become more Islamic in the fourth phase than it ever was in the past, which is not always seen as a positive development by the laity.[42] Even though not everyone is pleased with the developments that have taken place since the death of the charismatic founder, one could argue, as do members of the executive committee, that such steps are absolutely necessary for the survival and continued growth of the group.

The main questions I sought to ask and provide answers to above are: how does an unknown recluse from an obscure suburb of a town located on an island in the Indian Ocean rise to fame and establish himself as a global authority on matters of the soul in a seemingly accidental or coincidental manner?[43] Moreover, what strategies did Bawa and his "handlers" employ to manage his image as he moved from Sri Lanka to the United States and gradually transitioned from an eclectic *guru* to a disciplined and normative Sufi *shaykh* who emphasized Islamic orthodoxy as a foundational platform for ultimately achieving a mystical state of gnosis? In asking such questions, one must carefully move away from the emic, or insider point of view, to analyze objectively how a

41. See online: http://www.bmfstore.com/Scripts/default.asp/, where one can find a variety of books, CDs, and DVDs distilled and edited from Bawa's oral teachings by the Fellowship Press, from where they are published and disseminated.

42. A number of the members feel that "Islamizing" the Fellowship goes against Bawa's original teachings, and some ex-members go so far as to say that building the mosque was a mistake. There is therefore a division in the movement today between those who wish to be five-times-a-day pray-ers and those referred to as "loosey-goosey" Sufis, who do not think of themselves as Muslims and only want to perform *zikr*, the Sufi practice of recitation advocated by Bawa. One could argue that the latter adhere to the perennial notion of Sufism as something unattached from Islam, such as one finds in early Orientalist writings as well as in those of pop Sufi figures who author best selling books. Idries Shah (1924–1996), for example, an Indian-born Afghan who was educated in England, where he spent the bulk of his adult life, is the most widely read Sufi in the world. His books, despite academic condemnation, continue selling in huge quantities around the world, espousing a universal philosophy that pre-dates Islam. For an overview of the "Orientalist 'Discovery' of Sufism," see Carl Ernst, *Shambhala Guide to Sufism* (Boston: Shambhala,1997) 8–18.

43. This is another etic, outsider point of view that would not be acceptable to most Fellowship members, since they would claim that nothing happens by chance. Indeed, some, both in the United States and Sri Lanka, have stated to me that I did not choose to study Bawa but Bawa chose me to study him. To do it correctly, from their perspective, however, I would have to become one of them and present an emic, insider point of view. My attempt here and elsewhere continues to be to find a middle ground between the two categories that fairly assesses the data from both perspectives, thereby satisfying the expectations of my field consultants as well as my academic cohorts.

marginal "cult" evolves into a "sect," then ultimately a "denomination" as it temporally ages and doctrinally matures. This is what I see happening within the Fellowship at our current moment in time. It is precisely in this movement, which is both temporal and reflective, that the role of dialogue with other traditions comes into play. Given this developmental process that requires rationalization on the one hand and reification of an unchanging tradition skillfully taught by Bawa to his children on the other, it is useful to reconsider the questions raised at the outset. In the following conclusion, then, I want to go back to the possibility and scope of interreligious dialogue.

Speaking Sufi

South Asia has been the stomping grounds for religious encounter and dialogue since the first Aryans crossed the Hindu Kush into the Indus Valley. Hindus debated Buddhists, Greeks debated Hindus and Buddhists, Muslims debated Hindus, Christians debated all of them. Somewhere on the margins of this mix, Jews and Zoroastrians also lent their more silent voices to the multivocalic mix that earned India the rather dubious title of the land of tolerance.[44] However, it is by no means clear how transparently tolerant the majority religion, Hinduism, really was in terms of accepting the truth claims of all other religions. Tolerance, after all, always involves its opposite, intolerance.[45] The stereotypical assumption of Hindu tolerance, based mostly on pithy statements in the Vedas, led generations of Orientalists to attempt to locate where this philosophical flexibility resided, and it was finally found to be embedded in so-called neo-Hinduism, which was largely a response to

44. Still the best source for understanding the encounter of religions in the Indian subcontinent is Wilhelm Halbfass, *India and Europe: An Essay in Understanding* (Albany: SUNY Press, 1988). See also Halbfass, "India and the Comparative Method," *Philosophy East and West* 35 (1985) 3–15, for the use (or lack) of the comparative method in India.

45. Paul Hacker, "Religiöse Toleranz und Intoleranz im Hinduismus," *Saeculum* 8 (1957) 167–79, reminded us of this point long ago. Toleranz, Hacker argues elsewhere, is nothing more than what he terms "inclusivism" (*Inklusivismus*), which he defines as claiming for one's own religion what really belongs to an "alien sect." See Paul Hacker, "Aspects of neo-Hinduism as Contrasted with Surviving Traditional Hinduism," in *Paul Hacker, Kleine Schriften*, ed. Ludwig Schmithausen (Weisbaden: Steiner, 1978) 580–608.

Christian missionary activity and modernity.[46] Analyzing a broad range of evidence, Arvind Sharma concludes that the modern, or neo-Hindus, at least, hold, "not that all religions are equal or true or one or the same, but rather they are all valid. But that all religions are valid does not mean that all religions are of the same value for everyone, or at all times. Nor need a recognition of the validity of all religions necessarily imply their approval. The fact that one tolerates something does not automatically mean that one approves of it."[47] This statement could very well apply to the worldview of Bawa Muhaiyaddeen also. After all, although I cannot prove it definitively, I believe he was originally from south India, so he was heavily steeped in the longstanding tradition of Sufi adaptations to the Indian, and by extension Sri Lankan, religious climate.[48]

As we have seen, Bawa began his public career without emphasizing Islam at all, even though he expounded the esoteric concepts of Sufism within a terminological framework comprehensible to Hindus. Thus, *zikr* becomes *mantra* (recitation, often of nonsensical syllables). Adam becomes Ati Sivam (primordial Shiva), and so on. By drawing upon ideas already well established in the Hindu lexicon, he could espouse Muslim ideas without actually talking about Islam, such as when some people say he came to them in dreams and gave them the *kalimah* (Islamic statement of faith) to recite, without actually calling it *zikr* at

46. Tolerance itself, Hacker implied, was a product of modernity, but inclusivism goes back much further in time. Hacker was, of course, incorrect in asserting that inclusivism was solely a Hindu trait, as the contributors to Gerhard Oberhammer, ed., *Inklusivismus: Eine indische Denkform* (Vienna: Publications of the De Nobili Research Library, 1983) all point out decisively; but his insistence that inclusivism is not the same as tolerance is still a valid point of departure for discussing the conversation between religions.

47. Arvind Sharma, "All Religions Are: Equal? One? True? Same?: A Critical Examination of Some Formulations of the Neo-Hindu Position," *Philosophy East and West* 29 (1979) 67.

48. See Korom, "Charisma and Community: A Brief History of the Bawa Muhaiyaddeen Fellowship," *Sri Lankan Journal of the Humanities*, in press. Bawa once said to a Malay follower who related it to me in August of 2010 that God had only endowed him with the ability to speak one language: Tamil. Given that Tamil is spoken only in south India and Sri Lanka (and by members of the Tamil diaspora), it makes perfectly good sense to assume that he came from Tamil Nadu, even though the claim has been made within the Sri Lankan Bawa circle that he was in the Indus Valley in present-day Sind prior to the arrival of the Aryans. From this point of view, the original inhabitants of the Indus Valley civilization were Semites who spoke a form of proto-Tamil, which has been cited by his followers as the reason the two brothers who discovered Bawa in the jungle did not understand his speech at first.

first.[49] To a person not knowing anything about Islam, the alien sounding phrases in Arabic that proclaim "there is no god but God" could just as easily be understood as a Hindu *mantra* used for yogic meditation by a practitioner of *tantra*. In fact, in his earliest publication, Bawa refers to the *kalimah* as the *guru mantra*.[50] With his later literate Muslim audiences in the cities of Sri Lanka, however, he could assume some prior knowledge of basic Quranic concepts and esoteric Arabic terminology, which allowed him to be more specific in presenting details pertaining to Islam, yet still incorporating the vocabulary of Hinduism, such as when he calls the true teacher a *jnana guru* (wise teacher), rather than an *asal shaykh* (true teacher).[51]

Having elaborated on the ambiguous in-between nature of Bawa's teachings when seen in historical and comparative perspective, let me explore the two questions raised at the outset. First, is interreligious dialogue really possible from the perspective of Bawa Muhaiyaddeen? Bawa often stated that his own identity and past were irrelevant. As an inner circle member told me in conversation at the 2011 death anniversary gathering, "he could out-humble the humblest." His own, recorded response about who he was or how others perceived him is worth quoting at length here: "My appearance to the people who see me depends on how the various groups of them choose to view me . . . The Muslims say that I am a Tamil [= Hindu] swami. The Tamils say that I am a Muslim swami . . . The Christians say that I am a Tamil swami . . . In this manner each such group to whom I go, keep on ascribing names to me . . . If there are any more such names, I am happy to have them."[52] In other

49. Quite a number of people told me that Bawa had come to them in dreams before they met him, and many say he continues to do so even after his death. I have recorded this experience from such diverse people as an American college professor in the United States to a Sri Lankan practitioner of *reiki* in Russia. On the significance of dreams in Islam, see Nile Green, "The Religious and Cultural Roles of Dreams and Visions in Islam," *Journal of the Royal Asiatic Society* 13 (2003) 287–313.

50. Muhaiyaddeen, *The Pearl of Wisdom*, 84, where he says that it contains *guru shakti* (teacher power) that takes one home to the Father.

51. Bawa regularly used such terms as *dharma* (charity), *jiva* (life), *jnana* (wisdom), *karma* (action), *kundalini* (serpent power), *maya* (illusion), *moksha* (bliss), *prana* (vital breath), *shakti* (spiritual force), *upaya* (trick), etc. in his discourses, even after his Islamic message was made quite clearly and openly in the later stages of his career. But he sometimes used them in a distinct way that differs from their widely accepted meanings within Hinduism and Buddhism, as with *dharma* and *upaya*, for example.

52. M. R. Bawa Muhaiyaddeen, *Wisdom of the Divine*, vol. 4 (Colombo: The

words, names and designations are a distraction, but most people need to classify the world into orderly units, so for *their* sake, he is a guru or sheikh, not for *his own* sake. Later in the same discourse from which the above quote is taken, he says that he takes whatever form is necessary to bring comfort to people.[53] Bawa claimed it was easy for him to change bodies, but one form he never took was Muhammad's, for nobody can take that form, except the Prophet himself. Bawa is here employing what is known as *hila*, a device similar to the Buddhist *bodhisattva*'s use of skillful means (*upaya*) as a method to help others. In the end, such skillful means are nothing more than instruments of healing and awakening, having no significance in and of themselves, just as the categories of religion are in and of themselves vacuous, from his perspective.

Members of the Fellowship are always quick to point out how Bawa regularly attended inter- and intrafaith meetings, during which he would debate Jewish rabbis, Catholic priest, Protestant ministers, Buddhist monks, Hindu gurus, Muslim imams, and New Age entrepreneurs. In virtually all of the accounts, Bawa emerges from the verbal proceedings victorious in the eyes of his children.[54] At the same time, the more philosophically inclined within the Fellowship are very cautious about the use of terminology, and they would not condone many of the terms I have employed above. Words such as *movement, follower, disciple, convert,* and many others, for example, are frowned upon by this class of thinkers, as I was repeatedly told in the early days of my research. Why? Because they are of the opinion that Islam is a universal principle, the culmination of the natural history of religion on earth. Therefore, there is no movement because it was always there, since the

---

Serendib Sufi Study Circle, 1988) i. When a Muslim sweetshop owner from the east coast of Sri Lanka asked me what I was doing in Jaffna one sultry day in late July 2010, I asked him if he knew who Bawa was. He responded that he didn't know *who* he was, but all he could say was that he knew *what* he was; namely, a powerful "friend of God" (*wali*).

53. In one poignant reminiscence, a member of his inner circle said that Bawa once whispered to her in confidence that he was Jesus. See Le Pichon, *The Mirror: Photographs and Reflections on Life with M. R. Bawa Muhaiyaddeen* (Philadelphia: published privately by the author, 2010) 34. There is also an apocryphal story I heard more than once about a terminally ill man who came to a Buddhist monk seeking comfort, and the monk told him to go to Colombo, where there was a holy man who had taught the Buddha himself!

54. On the role of competition narratives, see Nile Green, "Oral Competition Narratives of Muslim and Hindu Saints in the Deccan," *Asian Folklore Studies* 63 (2004) 221–42.

beginning of time when it was implanted in the center of Adam's fore-head. According to this line of thought, then, there is no conversion because we are all Muslims within, whether we know it or not. What, then, I was asked, are we converting *from* and converting *to*? Second, because Bawa constantly spoke of himself in demeaning terms as the "ant man," who was not in the business of building a financial empire or perpetuating a cult of personality, his inner circle insists that members are not followers or disciples, since the only thing that we are follow-ing is already there within us, residing in the heart (*qalb*), which Bawa equates with a *kovil* (temple).

Because the eternal Bawa is not a corporeal entity, *per se*, there is nothing to follow nor any discipline to which one would adhere.[55] This *via negativa* perspective, although somewhat platitudinous, does, how-ever, raise issues about the second question; namely, with whom and about what are we speaking? If everyone is already a Muslim and all re-ligions are already a level, albeit a lower one, of *din*, which I would here equate with Islam, as Wilfred Cantwell Smith did in a much discussed book,[56] then we are not talking about interreligious dialogue at all but rather intrareligious dialogue; or, to take it one step further, if there is only one true path, then there can be no sectarian divisions within it, hence, no initiatic chain nor lineages, which would explain why Bawa discouraged inquiries about his own *silsila* (lineage). Is it then the case that we are dealing with monologue rather than dialogue? Are we, in the end, simply speaking to the monistic God within? Some contemporary mystics, such as Meher Baba, would say so, which is why they stopped speaking altogether.[57]

55. Some, although a small minority, believe wholeheartedly that the corporeal Bawa did not exist in human form, was not born of a mother, and had no human fam-ily. In other words, his human body was an illusion. One Malay follower in Sri Lanka told me that once when he was massaging Bawa's body, he was shocked to notice that he had no bones. In other words, his body was like a sponge or water balloon, a sheath full of liquid, but no solid matter. According to this person, Bawa was the *awwal qutb*, the primordial axis, consisting of pure light (*nur*), of which the historical Bawa was a mere reflection.

56. See Wilfred Cantwell Smith, *The Meaning and End of Religion* (New York: Mac-millan, 1962; reprinted, Minneapolis: Fortress, 1990).

57. Bawa himself is said to have not spoken during his "hidden years," which is why many believe he had such a high-pitched voice. Bawa had told them that due to his practice of silent *zikr*, his vocal cords dried up and shrank, affecting the timbre of his voice after he broke his silence.

Bawa was much like the Buddha in thinking that there are certain questions that "lend not to edification" because they are mere intellectual exercises.[58] Sufi lore is replete with stories about masters erasing one's entire lifetime of learning, with a simple touch of the hand to the chest, as Jilani was said to have done to Suhrawardi.[59] If it is anti-intellectual and based more on orthopraxy than on orthodoxy, then why even bother praying five times a day? Bawa would respond that it is because one cannot go to college if one has dropped out of kindergarten. In this sense, *sharia* is a foundational platform for higher practice. Perhaps it is the case that talking about religion is also a platform for graduating to higher levels of understanding based on the conviction that there is ultimately one truth, which is Islam. Everything else is merely an "exchange equivalence," as Tony Stewart has called it; that is, making one's point by utilizing the vocabulary of the other.[60] Bawa continued the practice of exchange equivalence after he came to the United States by borrowing Christian vocabulary and incorporating it into his already rich and eclectic lexicon. He also added imagery of various sorts drawn from the American vernacular landscape to facilitate the process of indigenization. But once a cult-transformed-into-sect has established its religious credentials by becoming "routinized" in doctrine and practice, the need for equivalence melts away into an ocean of well chiseled and hardened doctrine that emerges from the routinization process, which frees a now legitimate denomination from the need to be apologetic, allowing it to develop its own dogma. Dogma development involves purificatory acts to purge elements deemed unorthodox by the exegetes of the scriptural canon, in this case the members of the Fellowship's

---

58. It is in this regard, as well as in his discussions of the world as suffering from which we need relief, that Bawa's worldview may have been shaped partly by Buddhist principles to which he was exposed during the Sri Lankan phase of his career. On this, see Korom, "Charisma and Community: A Brief History of the Bawa Muhaiyaddeen Fellowship," *Sri Lankan Journal of the Humanities*, 2012. While not the subject of much scholarly attention, the interaction between Buddhism and Islam needs much more serious inquiry. For a suggestive indication of what could be done, see David Scott, "Buddhism and Islam: Past to Present Encounters and Interfaith Lessons," *Numen* 42 (1995) 141–55.

59. For example, Islam, *Sufism in South Asia*, 398–99, where he writes that Jilani had the power to bleach a page of writing white simply by touching it.

60. Tony Stewart, "In Search of Equivalence: Conceiving Muslim-Hindu Encounter through Translation Theory," *History of Religions* 40 (2001) 260–87.

bureaucratic machinery who are responsible for standardizing Bawa's message through editing and publishing his many discourses.

The Fellowship is still involved in multidenominational events on a fairly regular basis (especially since 9/11), but the rules have changed now. In the final analysis, we can conclude that the South Asian religious environment certainly had an influence on Bawa's teachings in their formative phase to create what some of his children refer to as "Dravidian Sufism."[61] But since it also had to adjust to the American climate, it has become an American denomination, now with heavy Arab accents, which sometimes overshadow the Dravidian roots of the movement, as some disgruntled "loosey-goosey" Sufis were quick to point out after the twenty-fifth death anniversary of their venerable teacher. At the event, the simple rituals of the past gave way to complicated recitations in Arabic performed by professional Pakistani cantors, much of which was unintelligible to most of the people in attendance at the saint's shrine on that calm spring day in March of 2011.

Those American children of his who wish to return to the charismatic days of Bawa's fifteen years among them, yearn for the simplicity of the practice as taught to them by him, which drew just as much on American culture as it did on Indian and Arab. The kindergarten/college example cited above is just one of many that indicates the Christianization of the Fellowship's development. Gombrich and Obeyesekere famously referred to the reformation of Sri Lankan Buddhism in modern times as "protestant Buddhism," drawing attention to the types of rethinking and restructuring that took place to make Buddhism more familiar to the Western world by drawing on concepts such as rationality and monotheism conceptually and Sunday meetings, scripture classes for the young, hymn singing, rowed seating, etc. on the structural level, while emphasizing democracy politically.[62]

61. Dravidian or Tamil Sufism has a very distinct history, which runs parallel to the development of vernacular Sufi traditions in other parts of South Asia. One example should suffice. Although Bawa was non-literate and preached in a style using parables and storytelling that his followers understand to be distinct, his language is by no means unique, for he is tapping into an old tradition in south India of using formulaic phrases and epithets in poetic and prose narrative, both of which are also apparent in the *meijnanam* genre, which Bawa sang frequently. See, for example, M. M. Uwise, *Muslim Epics in Tamil Literature* (Madras, India: Semmal, 1976); and his student Mohamed Sahabdeen, *The Sufi Doctrine in Tamil Literature* (Madras, India: Basharath, 1986) for the peculiarities of Tamil Sufi lyricism.

62. Richard Gombrich and Gananath Obeyesekere, *Buddhism Transformed*:

To conclude, Bawa was highly skilled at contextualizing and adapting his teachings to his immediate surroundings. To succeed in the United States, he created a form of what we might tentatively call "protestant Islam," which emphasized similarity in difference by borrowing Christian social structures and congregational practices while simultaneously developing a linguistic discourse of distinctness.[63] In the early days of his habitation in the United States, Bawa needed to speak comparatively to draw people into his fold; and he did so by utilizing whatever semiotic means were available to him, including what he gleaned from American television programming, of which he was an avid viewer. He would then incorporate whatever he watched into his sermons in a folksy way to relate his own worldview to the commonsensical experiences of the everyday American citizen. Dialogue with other religions for Bawa was thus less about acknowledging the legitimacy of other religious traditions or teachers, it seems to me, and more about rhetorically proving the superiority of his own teachings by persuading others of the absolute Truth inherent in his own embodied wisdom (*jnana*). After his death, however, as I implied above, the need to draw comparisons and analogies diminished as the Fellowship matured. A generous portion of its growth and ageing involved the process of Islamization, I have suggested, which by nature involves purification, but as Bruno Latour has reminded us, every attempt to purify paradoxically leads to more hybridity.[64] Hence, the Islamization of the Fellowship over the last quarter of a century has also resulted in the establishment of a distinctly American form of Islamic practice based on civility, democracy, and transparency.

Religious Change in Sri Lanka (Princeton: Princeton University Press, 1990).

63. As Hanks has pointed out, textual practices always work in tandem with other semiotic forms, many of which are paralinguistic in nature. See William F. Hanks, "Dialogic Conversations in the Field of Missionary Discourse in Colonial Yucatan," in *Les Rituels du Dialogue: Promenades Ethnolinguistiques en Terres Amérindiennes*, ed. Aurore M. Becquelinand and Phillippe Erikson (Nanterre, France: Société d'Ethnologie, 2000). In the case of the Fellowship, this would involve such dialogic acts as veiling, abstaining from alcohol at public functions, avoiding pork, and other visible ways of performing Islam in the public sphere.

64. Bruno Latour, *We Have Never Been Modern* (Cambridge: Harvard University Press, 1993).

12

Transmitting the Rudao 儒道

Concepts and Visions of Creativity in New Confucianism

John Berthrong

The teaching 述 而 不 作 "to transmit but not create [i.e., innovate]" (*Lunyu* 7.1) has bedeviled Confucian philosophers for generations. Master Kong's dictum [Kongzi 孔子 or Confucius] seemingly stifles any scholarly creative effort from within the Confucian Way[1] *rudao* 儒道 by trespassing beyond a verbatim transmission of the wisdom of the past. Of course, regardless of what Kongzi might have meant about the teaching of the wisdom of the former sages, the cumulative effect of his attempt to preserve the legacy of the early Zhou paragon sages engendered one of the most profoundly creative acts of any scholar, not just in China, but also for all humanity. The true story of the history of any tradition is that no transmission is simply a verbatim repetition of the past because the tradition is always transformed by changing times and circumstances.

---

1. I have written about the general history of the Confucian Way in a number of publications including John Berthrong, *All under Heaven: Transforming Paradigms in Confucian-Christian Dialogue*, SUNY Series in Chinese Philosophy and Culture (Albany: SUNY Press, 1994); Berthrong, *Transformations of the Confucian Way*, Explorations (Boulder: Westview, 1998); and Berthong and Evelyn Nagai Berthrong, *Confucianism: A Short Introduction* (Oxford: Oneworld, 2000); and these books in turn reference many other studies of the Confucian Way.

This juxtaposition of what Ru² scholars actually transmitted has been contested from the very beginning of the Chinese philosophical and spiritual discourse. By now the alert reader will have noticed that I have used a number of different terms in discussing "Confucianism." In fact the English terms Confucian and Confucianism, and their cognates in other European languages, were seventeenth-century creations of the early learned Jesuit missionary-scholars when they encountered what the Chinese literati of the Ming dynasty called the teaching or school of the Ru 儒家 (School of the Scholars), with individual 'Confucians' entitled *ruzhe* 儒者. What is in a name? A great deal actually. For instance, there has been an endless debate on what kinds of Western philosophical, social, political and religious typologies best fit Confucianism in comparative studies.

In a globalized twenty-first century my Chinese friends have no problem in understanding what I mean when I talk in English about Confucianism—or when I say *rujia* 儒家 in Chinese. In the world of traditional China, and certainly so from the Tang-Song period (906–1279), Chinese were aware that their intellectual world was roughly divided between what they called the *Ru, Lao* 老, and *Fo* 佛 schools, lineages and teachings. These approximately correspond to what we now call the Confucian, Daoist, and Buddhist traditions.

The most common way to describe these three traditions was to call them *jia* 家 School (a family) or *jiao* 教 Teaching. In modern usage the notion of *jiao* is often identified with both philosophical and

2. The term *ru* 儒 is the closest Chinese equivalent to the English term *Confucian*. The history of getting from *ru* in Zhou China to contemporary New Confucianism is a fascinating story in and of itself.

Other scholars, such as Liu Shu-hsien, *Understanding Confucian Philosophy: Classical and Sung-Ming* (Westport, CT: Praeger, 1998) and Gilbert Rozman, *The East Asian Region: Confucian Heritage and Its Modern Adaptation* (Princeton: Princeton University Press, 1991) have provided useful historical and sociological typologies of the range of the Confucian Way. For instance, Liu (*Understanding Confucian Philosophy: Classical and Sung-Ming* [Westport, CT: Praeger, 1998] 13–14) argues that there are three main stands of the tradition: 1) Spiritual Confucianism, 2) Politicized Confucianism, and 3) Popular Confucianism. Rozman, *The East Asian Region: Confucian Heritage and Its Modern Adaptation* (Princeton: Princeton University Press, 1991) 161, has an even more intricate typology. There are 1) Imperial Confucianism, 2) Reform Confucianism, 3) Elite Confucianism, 4) Merchant Confucianism, and 5) Mass Confucianism. While there is a great deal of overlap, I am partial to Rozman's general line of argument because it distinguished nicely between various social forms of Confucian thought and practice, and also registers Merchant Confucianism, a particularly relevant type when we consider the impact of Ruist/Confucian teachings in Japan.

also religious teachings. Each one could also be called a Dao 道, a Way. So, for instance, the great Zhu Xi (1130–1200) 朱喜 of the Southern Song, called his teaching *daoxue* 道學 the Teaching of the Way. By this choice of terminology Master Zhu was making the audacious claim that *his* form of the Confucian Way was the only core teaching that truly merited the esteem of being deemed authentic Ru tradition as the true Dao or proper way of life and moral personal and social conduct. Zhu's master narrative was that the *daoxue* school transmitted the orthodox mainstream of the Confucian Way recovered by Zhu's revered Northern Song masters after its occultation following the death of Mengzi 孟子 (Mencius) in Warring States China more than a thousand years before. It was Zhu's *daoxue*, along with later developments within neo-Confucianism, which was transmitted to Korea, Japan and Vietnam and now shows signs of a vigorous if ill-defined contemporary renewal called New Confucianism. Mao's cultural revolution notwithstanding, the Confucian Way is again a major topic of public and scholarly discussion and debate in East Asia.

The question comes into better focus if we compare Confucianism with the three great West Asian religions. Can traditional or contemporary New Confucianism be considered a religion? Frederick Streng provides a definition of religion that is broad enough to include the religious dimensions of the Confucian Way. Streng writes "The definition of religion . . . focuses on the role of *processes of change* through which people bring into their lives what they consider life's highest values. In this analysis of religious life, our formal definition is as follows: Religion is a *means to ultimate transformation* [italics in original]."[3]

Since the nineteenth century no great philosophical, social, or spiritual tradition has been more buffeted by aggressive Western colonial expansion and the acid bath of modernity than Confucianism.

---

3. Frederick, Streng, *Understanding Religious Life*, 3rd ed., Religious Life of Man Series (Belmont, CA: Wadsworth, 1985) 2. Streng was an accomplished buddhologist and because of this he was sensitive to the need to provide a working definition of religion that would include Buddhism, Daoism, and Confucianism. It is a definition that actually works quite well for the Confucian tradition in any of its major phases. Confucians believe the cosmos is processive in nature and that it is a relational matrix of interconnection things and events. Moreover, the Confucian sense of spirituality always implies a process of self-transformation aimed at the goal of becoming a sage *shengren* 聖人. There is an immense literature about whether or not even a broad definition of religion such as Streng's can capture the full range of the vision of the Confucian Way.

Confucians, we need to remember, were considered to be in charge of Chinese and Korean (and to a lesser extent Japanese and Vietnamese) traditional cultures during the catastrophic encounter with the belligerent imperial Western powers. With the fall of the Qing dynasty in 1911, Chinese revolutionary movements marginalized almost all aspects of traditional roles of the Confucian elite in Chinese culture. The reasoning was simple: if the Confucians were on the bridge of the Titanic when it hit the iceberg that sank the ship, it was time to get rid of the captain once and for all. By the 1920s only a very few scholars continued to make the case that a reformed Confucianism might have something to contribute to modern Chinese culture. Confucianism dramatically and abruptly lost its leading role in structuring families through hallowed ritual, the elite educational system, and its role as the official ideology of the Chinese state. Nonetheless, Confucianism refused to die and has made a comeback though it is far too early to say what form New Confucianism, as contemporary Confucianism is now called, will take in the future.

The current revival is not really surprising. Confucianism, as C. K. Yang wrote decades ago, was really a diffuse religious, philosophical, ethical, and social teaching.[4] For instance, there was never a formal Confucian priesthood or ecclesial organization. Of course, there was the support of the imperial state for Confucianism as the teaching necessary for membership in the governing elite. There were, of course, both official and private Confucian academies and temples for various ceremonies to honor the First Sage, but these also fell into rapid decline by the early part of the twentieth century.[5] I could go on at some length about the shape and scope of the New Confucian revival in China, but a number of recent works provide a great deal of information of what is happening in terms of the revival of New Confucianism.[6]

4. C. K. Yang, *Religion in Chinese Society* (Berkeley: University of California Press, 1961).

5. Interestingly enough, some New Confucians are attempting to re-found traditional style academies as part of the agenda of restoring the Confucian way to its former glory. Some go as far as dress in traditional late literati clothes as well.

6. See, for example the writing of Stephen C. Angle in *Human Rights and Chinese Thought: A Cross-Cultural Inquiry*, Cambridge Modern China Series (Cambridge: Cambridge University Press, 2002); or Angle, *Sagehood: The Contemporary Significance of Neo-Confucian Philosophy* (Oxford: Oxford University Press, 2009); Peter K. Bol, *Neo-Confucianism in History*, Harvard East Asian Monographs 307 (Cambridge: Harvard University Asia Center, 2008); Umberto Bresciani, *Reinventing Confucianism:*

The more pressing question is, what sort of Confucianism is migrating to and welcomed by a growing public in the North Atlantic World? What is being received? How is it understood in a completely new cultural world? Unfortunately any set of answers to these questions is likely to be very murky at present.

The first answer to the question of transmission is that the new immigrants from China, Taiwan, Korea, Japan and Vietnam to North America are transmitting the memory of their ancestral Confucianism. In some cases this memory is complex and well informed about the history of the Confucian Way. However, my completely random sample of East Asian immigrants suggests that, save for a growing list of scholars who now teach in North American universities, most immigrants do not have a critical memory or understanding of the broad sweep of Confucian history in all of its variegated glories. Rather it is like what Tu Weiming has called a form of cultural DNA.[7] In another personal caveat, I cannot count how many times I have had first and second or now even third generation Asian American students tell me in about the fifth to sixth week of an Introduction to Chinese Philosophy how they now suddenly see the intellectual lineage of conversations they have with their parents and grandparents about matters of life orientation, philosophy or religion. Of course this communication breakthrough is not limited to Confucianism but also includes Daoism and Buddhism as well.[8] Nonetheless, habits of the mind-heart *xin* 心 die hard and college encounters with family traditions certainly make my undergraduates much more self-aware of Confucianism as part of global and globalizing philosophy and spirituality. As the East Asian Diaspora continues to

---

The New Confucian Movement, Variétés Sinologiques 90, new ser. (Taipei: Taipei Ricci Institute for Chinese Culture, 2001); Yuli Liu, *The Unity of Rule and Virtue: A Critique of a Supposed Parallel between Confucian Ethics and Virtue Ethics* (Singapore: Eastern Universities Press, 2004); John Makeham, ed., *New Confucianism: A Critical Examination* (New York: Palgrave Macmillan, 2003); or Makeham, *Lost Soul: "Confucianism" in Contemporary Chinese Academic Discourse*, Harvard-Yenching Institute Monographs 64 (Cambridge: Harvard University Asia Center, distributed by Harvard University Press, 2008); Bo Mou, ed., *History of Chinese Philosophy*, Routledge History of World Philosophies 3 (London: Routledge, 2009); or Mou, *Chinese Philosophy A–Z*, Philosophy A–Z series (Edinburgh: Edinburgh University Press, 2009).

7. Wei-ming Tu, *Centrality and Commonality: An Essay on Confucian Religiousness*, SUNY Series in Chinese Philosophy and Culture (Albany: SUNY Press, 1989).

8. I confess that I have never yet had any of my students mention Legalism or Mozi as part of their intellectual or spiritual patrimony. In terms of the Chinese tradition, they all think in terms of Confucianism, Daoism, or Buddhism.

grow in North America I do not want to discount the role of the cultural DNA in the transmission and reception of Confucianism in the future.

The Reception of Confucian Spirituality

If we take the West Asian religions, Judaism, Christianity, and Islam, as the common paradigm for what constitutes religion, then it is often hard to make the case for Confucianism as a religious or spiritual tradition. However, if we track Streng's essentially functional and comparative approach to religion as ultimate transformation, we observe that whereas Confucianism definitely does not resemble West Asian religions, it does have distinct religious dimensions. Moreover, some Confucians embrace more of the religious dimensions of the tradition than others and there is a diverse spectrum of being religious in a Confucian fashion. Rather like in Judaism, one can be a Confucian without having much of an interest in any of the religious dimensions of the tradition and it would never occur to other, more spiritually oriented Confucians, to question your commitment to the Confucian Way because of a lack in the religious dimensions of the tradition. So how would a person in traditional China understand that she or he was a Confucian and not a Buddhist or Daoist? The simple answer is that she or he would be guided by an abiding commitment to the Confucian classics and not the scriptures of Buddhism or Daoism. Of course this is a grand overgeneralization but it works well enough to distinguish who would be considered a Confucian, Buddhist, or Daoist. Many of these questions are discussed in much greater detail in the two-volume study of the Confucian spiritual tradition edited by Tu Weiming and Mary Evelyn Tucker.[9]

One more caveat is in order. One of the tricky things about identifying who is or is not a Confucian is that traditionally you would not say that you are a Confucian. That would be considered a form of hubris. You became a Confucian, as it were, when other Confucians and the larger community of Confucian scholars recognized you as such. Again in very broad strokes, this communal recognition indicated that you demonstrated an adequate knowledge and understanding of the canonical and commentarial texts of the tradition such that others recognized

9. Tu Weiming and Mary Evelyn Tucker, eds., *Confucian Spirituality*, 2 vols., World Spirituality 11A–11B (New York: Crossroad, 2003–2004).

you as a scholar within the Confucian Way.[10] However, this is a traditional habit that appears to be changing because many New Confucians today self-identify as Confucians. The New Confucians continue to self-identify as Confucians, as far as I can tell, by using roughly the same criteria of the classical literati: you are a Confucian because you affirm your commitment to the canonical texts[11] and the traditions that flow from them—even when the tradition is radically revised and transformed to appeal to modern taste.

While it is difficult to track the arrival of Confucianism parallel to the emergence of Buddhism or Daoism in North America, there actually are some institutional forms of Confucianism that are of note. One of the most interesting is the new Confucian Institutes now dotting the American academic landscape. Supported by the Chinese government and linked to a host of Chinese and North American universities, these institutes have set about promoting the study of Chinese language and culture. While not dedicated to the promotion of any particular form of traditional or New Confucianism, the institutes are eager to encourage the scholarly study of Confucianism as an integral part of past and present Chinese social, intellectual, economic and even religious history.

But we are still left with the question about what appeal Confucianism will possibly have in the chaotic postmodern landscape of the North American academic world, and in fact the world beyond the republic of letters in the wider American religious world. This is an impossible question to answer for at least two main reasons.

First, as I have noted above, it is impossible to say what forms New Confucianism will take. Will there be many competing schools? Will

10. So when people sometimes ask me if I am a Confucian, I make a little speech along the lines of what I have written above. When asked if other Confucian scholars recognize me as a Confucian, I say that, yes, it appears that I am. My Chinese friends tell me that they find it intriguing to listen to me talk about Confucianism because (1) I do seem to know a lot about it but (2) I will often have insights or interpretations that are novel from an East Asian perspective. That does not mean that my friends always agree with me, but it does mean that I am included in the discussion as a fellow scholar. In fact, from the time of the great early Jesuit mission-scholars there is even a term for people like me: *xiru* 西儒 or Western Confucians.

11. The most robust list is, of course, the thirteen Classics. It was a list that grew over the centuries as classical texts deemed Confucian were added to the list until it reached its zenith in the Song dynasty (960–1279). What is fascinating is that just as the canon reached its maximum number, Zhu Xi also created the Four Books, all taken from the longer list, to be the epitome of the authentic teachings of the ancient sagely rulers.

the Confucian fever, as it has often been called in China, have a life beyond colleges and universities both in China and the West? Will it become politicized between conservatives who want to use Confucianism in support of robust Chinese nationalist self-identity to contest Western influences that are flooding into China from Europe and North America? Or will it become a liberal beacon for a New Confucian worldview that embraces cosmopolitan democracy and a recognition and positive import of cultural diversity? Even now it is easy to find voices on both ends of this spectrum and all kinds of stopping points in between. So it is frankly impossible to say now what kind of Confucianism will become the main export to the Western world over the next few decades. Yet surely it is the case that Confucianism will also tag along with the vast flow of goods and information that is now flowing between Europe, the Americas, South and Southeast Asia, Africa and the Middle East. China has a global reach and ambition and at least for some Chinese, this includes the positive presentation of the Confucian Way.

Second, how will Western audiences receive New Confucianism in its various modes? Here again we are entering the realm of prophecy. Frankly who would have thought even thirty or twenty years ago that China would have become the second largest economy in the world, an economy that will surpass the American economy as the largest within a decade or two, depending on which economist you believe. So we need to ask, what can New Confucianism export from East Asia to the rest of the world?

As an example, I have come to the conclusion that the five classical Confucian virtues, *ren* 仁 humanness or co-humanity, *yi* 義 appropriateness or justice, *li* 禮 civility or ritual, *zhi* 知 discernment/wisdom, and *xin* 信 faithfulness,[12] are actually a very respectable and viable contemporary version of a sophisticated form of virtue, role, or conduct ethics. I truly believe that anyone interested in contemporary global philosophy ought to engage with the five Confucian cardinal virtues. While they clearly, in terms of Western ethical typologies, represent a form of virtue ethics, they also have a twist that has caused scholars such as Roger Ames and Henry Rosemont to label them role ethics, implying

12. This is my favorite translation; but there are a host of other fine possible renderings of each of these terms depending on the text in question. As with so many Chinese philosophical terms, there has been an incredible sedimentation of shades of meanings over the centuries of their use in Confucian discourse, both in common speech and in philosophical elaboration.

that these virtues only make sense as models for the roles we play in any social order.[13] Further, Bo Mou has added the notion of conduct ethics that combines attributes of both virtue and role ethics.[14] As Kongzi wrote, "Virtue is never solitary; it always has neighbors."[15] Confucian ethics were and are always social, always relational. I have discovered that this style of relational, role, and conduct oriented ethical system makes a great deal of sense to my students and colleagues.

The Question of Boston Confucianism[16]

The question of reception of Confucianism is further complicated by how information about the Confucian tradition is being mediated to Western audiences. Actually there have been a number of phases in the introduction of reliable information and fine critical scholarship about the Confucian tradition especially over the last six decades. While excellent work was certainly done prior to 1950, this date represents the beginning of the teaching career of Provost and Professor Wm. Theodore de Bary at Columbia University. Everyone in Chinese studies is intimately aware of the series of great resources books and individual monographs that have flowed from the Columbia University Press about all aspects of Asian culture and historical development since 1950. De Bary also trained a corpus of students who have continued the Columbia tradition in Confucian studies.[17] Moreover de Bary himself was very

13. Henry Rosemount Jr. and Roger T. Ames, *The Chinese Classic of Family Reverence: A Philosophical Translation of the Xiaojing* (Honolulu: University of Hawai'i Press, 2009); Roger T. Ames and David L. Hall, *Focusing on the Familiar: A Translation and Philosophical Interpretation of the Zhongyong*, (Honolulu: University of Hawai'i Press, 2001).

14. Bo Mou, *Chinese Philosophy A–Z* (Edinburgh: Edinburgh University Press, 2009) 29–30.

15. Edward Slingerland, trans., *Confucius Analects: With Selections from Traditional Commentaries* (Indianapolis: Hackett, 2003) 37, provides for an excellent modern translation along with very useful selections from the best traditional commentaries that puts the various sayings that constitute the *Analects* into a context that allows the reader to better understand what Confucian scholars made of these sometimes very emigmatic sayings.

16. In many ways it would be more accurate to call this Columbia and Boston Confucianism because of the work of scholars such as Wing-tsit Chan and William Theodore de Bary at Columbia University.

17. One could also add the names of great scholars from Berkeley, Chicago, Harvard, Yale, and Princeton, and so forth, to this list as well. I mention de Bary to honor

interested in and published widely about neo-Confucian thought. So from the 1960s on neo-Confucian studies have been well represented in the scholarly world. However, I think it is more than fair to say that the current trend in Confucian studies is an emphasis on the classical War- ring States period. This now also includes brilliant studies of the Confu- cian tradition before Kongzi, which would have made complete sense to Kongzi because he strongly believed that he was actually transmitting the wisdom of the sages of the Zhou and semilegendary early history of China to his disciples.

In the current period, the best-known proponent of Boston Con- fucianism is Professor Robert C. Neville of Boston University. A very special part of Neville's concern for comparative philosophy for the last four decades has been the study of Confucian thought. After hav- ing written the original article about 'Boston Confucianism,' a title that Neville clearly meant to be both serious and ironic at the same time, he has continued to publish on the topic of the role of a revived Confucian- ism in the modern world. His most sustained treatment of the Con- fucian Way is found in the collection of reworked essays he published in 2000 as *Boston Confucianism: Portable Tradition in the Late-Modern World* and the later 2008 study, *Ritual and Deference: Extending Chinese Philosophy in a Comparative Context.*[18]

Neville's point about the portable nature of Confucian discourse is a highly charged and contested issue among East Asian intellectuals, especially when it concerns non-Asian scholars. Just how Confucianism might be exported beyond its East Asian home is unclear when attempt- ing to judge the probability of portability from excellent to slim or even nonexistent. Those who hold that Confucianism is basically not for ex- port know as well as anyone else that the *rudao* has moved successfully in the past from China to Korea, Japan and Vietnam. The point is that Confucianism was always part of the entire package of cultural signi- fication and cannot be detached or delivered separately from a much deeper reception of the Chinese cultural project, including mastery

---

his role as the doyen of Confucian studies.

18. Robert C. Neville, *Boston Confucianism: Portable Tradition in the Late-Modern World*, SUNY Series in Chinese Philosophy and Culture (Albany: SUNY Press, 2000); and Neville, *Ritual and Deference: Extending Chinese Philosophy in a Comparative Context*, SUNY Series in Chinese Philosophy and Culture (Albany: SUNY Press 2008). These two works, in many ways, are perfect examples in rich detail of a long-lasting Confucian-Christian dialogue.

of literary Chinese as the medium of instruction and reflection. These scholars contend that Confucianism has never taken root anywhere without the concomitant appropriation of classical or literary Chinese[19] as the medium of its study and propagation. These colleagues hold that any flourishing of Confucianism beyond its East Asian home is severely restricted and that it is at best superficial without a profound command of the original texts in their tradition Chinese versions.

Other scholars hold that the mastery of classical or literary Chinese may not be the *sine qua non* for the creation of alternative cultural settings of Confucianism in the modern world. Not all East Asians were or are fully literate in literary Chinese and yet they participated and are contributing, in various degrees, to traditional and New Confucian cultural discourse. But the linguistic mastery of literary Chinese is not really at the heart of the debate. Contemporary New Confucians, the revivers of the tradition in the Chinese cultural world, these days no longer write in literary Chinese because much of their audience does not read these older forms of Chinese.[20]

The truly interesting question is who is considered competent to talk seriously about the renewal, transformation and transmission of the tradition now. As with all living philosophical or religious traditions, those who consider themselves members or are considered members by others are those who can speak for the tradition. We are seeing the emergence of a modern version of New Confucianism in the works of diaspora Chinese intellectuals writing in the English language such as Wing Tsit-chan, Tu Weiming, Liu Shuxian, Julia Ching, A. S. Cua, Zheng Chongying (Cheng Chung-ying), Roger T. Ames, Wm. Theodore de Bary, Robert Neville, Billioud, S. Chan, John Makeham, and Stephen Angle et al. (the list could be extended if we also review the work of other scholars writing in French and German). If these thinkers and

---

19. This distinction is this: classical Chinese is early Chinese writing up to the Han dynasty whereas literary Chinese, for the most part, is a style promoted from the Tang-Song period until its demise as a universal educational requirement in the early twentieth century.

20. However it is fair to note that in their academic writings New Confucians do quote extensively from the traditional *rudao* texts and assume that their readers can follow classical and literary Chinese even if is no longer a common form of written exchange. The situation is rather like that of the Catholic Church until very recently when almost every academic priest could reliably read Latin.

their colleagues back in China take Neville, Angle, and de Bary[21] seriously, then don't Neville, Angle, and de Bary fit in among those who have cherished and promoted the Confucian Way over the last two and a half millennia?

Perhaps the first thing to note is that the creation of something as transculturally exotic as Neville's 'Boston Confucianism' expresses two crucial traits: (1) an aspect of the general revival of Confucianism; and (2) the spread of interest in Confucianism outside traditional East Asian cultural world/s. These two traits are actually inextricably interrelated. I would wager that if there had not been an actual revival movement such as New Confucianism in East Asia, there would never have been anything like Boston Confucianism. Of course, Western scholars of traditional Chinese philosophy and religion would have continued to write about the history of Confucianism in East Asia. But more than likely they would have done so as if it were a 'dead' tradition, one that was no longer a viable concern even if it demanded attention as part of the vast storage vault of Chinese intellectual history. This is not what happened. The Confucian Way has been revived—though there are immense differences in opinion about just what we mean by the revival of Confucianism in the twentieth and twenty-first centuries. As a rekindled tradition it has become an object of interest not just as a historic relic, however important in global history, but also as an object of concern for scholar practitioners of the Confucian Way. Moreover, Western intellectuals such as Neville, Ames,[22] Angle, and de Bary have now found the historical and the revived New Confucianism objects of historical and contemporary philosophical and theological interest. In short, New Confucianism along with Boston Confucianism, have entered, for good or ill, the intellectual world of Late-Modern North Atlantic philosophy and religion.

---

21. Of course de Bary and Angle are skilled in the study of classical and literary Chinese.

22. For instance, Roger T. Ames, *Confucian Role Ethics: A Vocabulary*, Chi'en Mu Lecture Series (Honolulu: University of Hawai'i Press, 2011), does not deal, for the most part, with New Confucianism but dwells on the classical period with some comments about Neo-Confucianism. Nonetheless it is a completely modern re-visioning of the Confucian Way and in this regard could well be considered a Western New Confucian text. Ames points out that nothing could better represent the Confucian Way than a meditation on its origins in terms of the challenges the contemporary world poses to the typical holistic view Confucians take of the world and their history in it.

Moreover, Neville's explanation and articulation of Boston Confucianism is an excellent example of comparative Christian theology growing out of and informed by a longstanding interfaith dialogue in which Confucianism has had a lasting and profound impact on his work as a comparative theologian and philosopher of religion. It is actually in his second book devoted to reflections on Confucianism, *Ritual and Deference* (2008), that Neville fleshes out complex elaborations of aspects of Confucianism into his larger theological and philosophical project. The main focus of Neville's reflections on Confucianism in much of this work is the notion of *li* 裡 as rite, ritual, deference, or civility, which he highlights as the comportment of deference in the various roles, actions and virtues that constitute individual and communal human life. This is actually a very interesting example of how the comparative study of philosophy, in this case the contribution of the great classical Confucian Xunzi 荀子 on ritual theory, becomes an integral aspect of Neville's own philosophical and theological reflection.

This long engagement in Confucian-Christian dialogue leads Neville to a comparative theological stance that is both speculative and practical. Neville is justly famous for his dedication to speculative philosophy on a comprehensive scale. But what is fascinating here is that his exploration of Confucian ritual theory as it is embedded in the complex moral anthropology of Master Xun allows him to conjoin his speculative philosophy with a comparative practical theology. Writing as a Christian comparative theologian, Neville argues for the incorporation of the wonderful complex Confucian notion of ritual as model for civility and deference as a way of life for modern North Americans in order to discover the practice or comportment, as he would say, of an ethicoreligious virtue translated from the Confucian Way to the Christian movement. Hence interfaith dialogue as comparative theology becomes a means for the transmission of an important element of Confucian thought and praxis from East Asia to modern Boston.

The next question, of course, is how can English-speaking Confucianism such as Neville's Boston Confucianism be adjudicated? The simple answer is that it will be up to the global Confucian community of scholars to give a reasoned answer to the question of the necessity of linguistic competence for membership as an authentic twenty-first-century Ruist scholarly republic of letters. But even this simple question is hard to answer because Confucianism has never been an organized religion or philosophic school. There is no Bishop of Rome to rule on who or who is not a good Confucian—even though the Pope did once make such a ruling when debating about the nature of the Confucian rites and their relationship to the Christian faith. Ultimately, one of the best rules developed out of modern interreligious dialogue is that every tradition has the right to define who is and who is not a member of that tradition. It is the general consensus of the community that counts the most in terms of the recognition of membership. My guess is that the issue of who is or is not a true Confucian is going to be another empirical and historical question for future study. It will all depend on the future of these two 'movements.' Will Boston and Columbia Confucianism flourish in the sense that North Americans will begin to know a great deal about the Confucian tradition or will something more be needed for their inclusion in any future history of the Confucian Dao?

But merely having knowledge of the Confucian Way does not a Confucian make. There is a point where knowledge blends into commending the tradition as having something worthwhile to say to every human being. As I wrote above, I have come to believe strongly that the five cardinal Confucian virtues are as fine a set of ethical goals and ideals as the human race has yet developed. I have no problem whatsoever in commending them to my students including those who are devotedly Christian in orientation. In this limited sense, the Confucian Dao qua Boston and Columbia Confucianism has come to the West, to paraphrase the title of J. J. Clarke's fine study of Daoism's, to impact the cultural world of the Euro-American West.[23]

Before East Asian Confucians recognize that Boston and Columbia Confucians are truly members of the genealogical transmission of the Confucian Way, there will have to be many more Western scholar-practitioners of Confucianism than there are now. Again, only the future will reveal whether this will happen or not. And in the end, it will be the community of Confucian scholars, as has always been the case, which will ultimately recognize Western scholars as fellow Ruist intellectuals. Only then will we all know whether the history of Boston and Columbia Confucianism is merely ironic or anticipatory of yet a new chapter in the history of the development of the Confucian Way.

23. J. J. Clarke, *Oriental Enlightenment: The Encounter between Asian and Western Thought* (London: Routledge, 1997).

What Appeals in New Confucian Spirituality?

Along with the fact that Confucianism is going to become more and more a part of the patrimony of global philosophy in the twenty-first century, there is also the fact that China will simply have more and more of a religious and intellectual impact on North American culture as the century goes along.[24] So what is appealing about the Confucian, neo-Confucian and New Confucian worldviews in terms of its diverse religious or spiritual dimensions? Along with its contributions to debates about virtue, role and conduct ethics for instance, is there something else that is appealing about the Confucian Way to modern North American religious sensibilities?

There is one aspect of the Confucian Way's religious dimension that seems to resonate strongly with North Americans. This is what various scholars have called the proclivity of Confucians to express a fondness for an immanent transcendence or transcendent immanence.[25] Within the Four Books, the basic curriculum of Confucianism since the Song dynasty, the last of the collection is the *Zhongyong* 中庸, often translated as the *Doctrine of the Mean* or more recently as *Focusing on the Familiar* by Roger Ames and David Hall. Zhu Xi, who organized a set of classical texts as the Four Books, believed that the *Zhongyong* should be read last because it most profoundly expressed the spiritual depth and dimensions of the Confucian Way.

In elaborating the notion of *cheng* 誠 sincerity, integrity, or self-realization,[26] as the ability for a person to achieve full self-actualization in the midst of the myriad things of the cosmos, Ames and Hall make the following points: the *Zhongyong* states "Creativity (*cheng*) is the way of *tian* (天之道); creating is the proper way of becoming human (人之道).[27]" Then the text states, "only if one is able to make the most of the natural tendencies of processes and events can one assist in the transforming and nourishing activities of heaven and earth; and only if we can assist in the transforming and nourishing activities of heaven and

---

24. Jay L. Garfield and William Edelglass, eds., *The Oxford Handbook of World Philosophy*, Oxford Handbooks in Philosophy (Oxford: Oxford University Press, 2011).

25. For examples of this see Tu and Tucker, *Confucian Spirituality*, 2 vols.; Tu, *Centrality and Commonality*.

26. Ames and Hall translate it as "creativity"; *Focusing on the Familiar*, 104.

27. Ibid.

earth can human beings take their place as members of this triad."[28] Or as some other translations put it, human beings form a triad with heaven and earth in order to complete the true natural dispositions of heaven, earth, and humanity. In theological language this process is certainly some kind of trinity, although almost everyone points out that this is definitely not a foreshadowing any Christian doctrine of the Holy Trinity.

Be this as it may, the great Victorian translator James Legge, in a lengthy footnote to his translation of the *Zhongyong* text, called this unity *can* 參 of heaven, earth and humanity a vain and idle babbling. As much as Legge genuinely came to respect the Confucian tradition, the religious dimension of this particular chapter was a bridge too far for him. It implied a very robust immanent transcendence that was distant from Legge's nineteenth-century Reformed Protestant theology. But it is not distant to my twenty-first-century undergraduates and other theological colleagues. When I tell the students about this little episode in the history of the transmission of Confucian texts to the North Atlantic world, they are perplexed, and not by the *Zhongyong* but rather, for the most part, by Legge's inability to appreciate this profoundly relational and expansively humanistic Confucian spirituality.

The philosophical aspect of the transmission is comparatively simple to explain, even if it is open to endless debate. It is the relational quality of much of early Chinese classical thought. Things are simply related one to the other (*gantong* 感統) and the co-creativity and co-humanity of things, events and persons is quite a common teaching. As Kongzi said, virtue loves company and the *Yijing* chimes in with teaching that the natural human ethical disposition, when transposed onto and from the cosmos, manifests the ceaseless relational generativity of the Dao as *shengsheng bu xi* 生生 不 息.

As manifesting spiritual harmony this sense of profound relationality or connectivity is understood in the *Zhongyong* as expressing, as the modern New Confucians such as Mou Zongsan, Tu [Du] Weiming, and Liu Shuxian would put it, immanent transcendence. Perhaps the favorite proof text for this immanent transcendent sensibility is found in Zhang Zai's [1020–1077] famous Western Inscription. "Heaven is my father and Earth is my mother, and even such a small creature as I finds an intimate place in their midst. Therefore that which extends throughout

---

28. Ibid., 105.

the universe I regard as my body and that directs the universe I consider my nature . . . In life I follow and serve [Heaven and Earth]. In death I will be at peace." [29] At least for some North Americans a part of the Confucian Way has already been transmitted and understood as affirming a theological or spiritual vision of the intimate and profound relationship of the transcendent and the secular, the majesty of *tian* 天 [heaven], the fecund power of *di* 地 [earth], and the humaneness *ren* and *cheng* as the self-actualization of co-humanity. What will North American students and scholars make of the Confucian Way? No one really knows.

Moreover, in the modern and globalizing world, cultural transmission is a two way street. Frankly speaking the East Asian side is already much better prepared to make this an exciting case of cross-cultural transmission. The simple reason for this is that the Chinese, unlike most Western intellectuals, have already become very bi-cultural. That is to say, because of the impact of the imperial West on East Asia the Chinese, Koreans, Japanese, and Vietnamese had no choice but to learn about all the various facets of Western culture, including philosophy and religion. That this knowledge came at the barrel of a gun did not dissuade the Chinese, for instance, from considering Western classical music and the symphony orchestra as grand and wonderful imports. When I visit with my friends at Shandong University's departments of philosophy and religious studies we talk with passion about Plato, Aristotle, Aquinas, Whitehead, Barth, Rorty, Kripke, Davidson, Heidegger, Sartre, Rosemary Reuther, and a host of other European and American thinkers. And then we turn to Kongzi, Mengzi, Laozi, Xunzi, Zhuangzi, Zongmi, the Sixth Patriarch, Zhou Dunyi, the Cheng Brothers, Zhu Xi, Wang Yangming, Dai Zhen, the New Confucians, and a host of other Daoist, Buddhist, and Confucian scholars. It would be nice to find more and more philosophy departments in North America where similar conversations could go on. In all fairness, this is beginning to happen and more philosophy departments are hiring experts in various forms of Asian philosophy. Religious Studies is ahead of the game if for no other reason than undergraduates will flock to courses on Asian religion in large numbers and hence this interest warrants the hiring of experts in traditional and contemporary Asian religious studies.

29. William Theodore De Bary, Irene Bloom, and Richard Lufrano, eds., *Sources of Chinese Tradition*, 2 vols., 2nd ed., Introduction to Asian Civilizations (New York: Columbia University Press. 1999) 1:682–84.

Nonetheless, chance and fate happens to one and all, philosophers and theologians included. We cannot foresee how powerful political, economic and ecological patterns will affect the transmission of information from one part of the world to another. At present the Chinese educational world is growing as rapidly as its economic power and it is clear that the current government is more than willing to invest in what it sees as the essential infrastructure of education as a way to ensure the continued growth of the Chinese successful quest for wealth and power. But we all know how fragile the Chinese economic miracle is in terms of the imbalance between the rich and poor and the massive ecological harm being done across China by the fervid industrialization of this vast country. Though less noticed by the Western media, much the same can be said about India and Brazil's rapid rise as an emerging major economic and political powers.

Be this as it may, it seems unlikely that the genie of globalization and diversity will go back into a bottle of mutual isolation. As the sociologist of knowledge Peter Berger has said over and over again, the one thing we can now say with confidence about globalization and modernization is that it brings cultural diversity into global mix for everyone.[30] How people chose to deal with the diversity, including experimenting with new philosophies and forms of spiritualities, gives rise, again as Berger notes, to not one but many modernities.

---

30. Peter Berger and Anton Zijedrveld, *In Praise of Doubt: How to Have Convictions without Becoming a Fanatic* (New York: HarperOne, 2009).

Contributors

John Berthrong is Associate Professor of Comparative Theology at the Boston University School of Theology. His teaching and research interests are in the areas of interreligious dialogue, Chinese religions and philosophy, and comparative philosophy and theology. His publications include *All under Heaven: Transforming Paradigms in Confucian-Christian Dialogue* (SUNY Press [Chinese Translation from Renmin Chupanshe 2006]), and *The Divine Deli* (1999). He is coeditor, with Professor Mary Evelyn Tucker, of *Confucianism and Ecology: The Interrelation of Heaven, Earth, and Humans* (1998). He also collaborated with Evelyn Nagai Berthrong on *Confucianism: A Short Introduction* (2000). He coedited, with Liu Shu-hsien and Leonard Swidler, *Confucianism in Dialogue Today: West, Christianity & Judaism* (2004), and most recently published *Expanding Process: Exploring Philosophical and Theological Transformations in China and West* (2008).

James W. Heisig is a permanent research fellow at the Nanzan Institute for Religion and Culture in Nagoya, Japan, where he has worked since 1978. He is coeditor of *Japanese Philosophy: A Sourcebook* (2011). His other books include *El cuento detrás del cuento: Un ensayo sobre psique y mito* (1976); *Imago Dei: A Study of C. G. Jung's Psychology of Religion* (1979); *Philosophers of Nothingness: An Essay on the Kyoto School* (2001); *Dialogues at One Inch above the Ground: Reclamations of Belief in an Interreligious Age* (2003); *El gemelo de Jesús: Un alumbramiento al budismo* (2007); and the recently completed *Nothingness and Desire: A Philosophical Antiphony*. He is also coeditor of Tetsugaku, a collection of books on Japanese Philosophy (in Italian) and the Nanzan Library of Religion and Culture.

Marcia Hermansen is Director of the Islamic World Studies program at Loyola University Chicago, where she teaches courses in Islamic studies and Religious studies in the Theology Department. Her books include *Shah Wali Allah's Treatises on Islamic Law* (2010) and *The Conclusive Argument from God: A Study and Translation* (from Arabic) of Shah Wali Allah of Delhi's, *Hujjat Allah al-Baligha* (1996). She was an associate editor of the Macmillan *Encyclopedia of Islam and the Muslim World* (2003) and is coeditor of the forthcoming volume *Muslima Theology: The Voice of Muslim Women Theologians*. Dr. Hermansen has contributed numerous academic articles in the fields of Islamic thought, Sufism, Islam and Muslims in South Asia, Muslims in America, and women and gender in Islam. Her studies of the American Muslim community have included articles on conversion, Muslim youth and girls, and American Sufi movements.

Thomas P. Kasulis is Professor of Comparative Studies at Ohio State University, where he teaches religious studies, philosophy, and East Asian studies. He is a former president of the Society for Asian and Comparative Philosophy and the American Society for the Study of Religion. His most recent books are *Intimacy or Integrity: Philosophy and Cultural Difference* (2002); *Shintō: The Way Home* (2004); and the coedited volume with James W. Heisig and John C. Maraldo, *Japanese Philosophy: A Sourcebook* (2011). He is currently completing a history of Japanese philosophy.

Frank J. Korom is Professor of Religion and Anthropology at Boston University. He is the author and editor of a number of books, including *Village of Painters* (2006) and *Hosay Trinidad* (2003). His most recent research has been on Tamil Sufism and its transnational linkages. Currently he is the coeditor of the journal *Asian Ethnology* and a member of the academic advisory board for the Kolkata Museum of Modern Art.

David L. McMahan is Professor of Religious Studies at Franklin & Marshall College in Pennsylvania. He received his PhD in religious studies from the University of California at Santa Barbara. He is the editor of *Buddhism in the Modern World* (2012), and author of *The Making of Buddhist Modernism* (2008); *Empty Vision: Metaphor and Visionary*

Imagery in Mahāyāna Buddhism (2002); and articles on Mahāyāna Buddhism in South Asia and Buddhism in the modern world.

James W. Morris is Professor of Islamic Studies and Comparative Theology at Boston College. He has taught Islamic and religious studies at the University of Exeter, Princeton University, Oberlin College, and the Sorbonne. He lectures and leads workshops in many countries on Islamic philosophy and theology, Sufism, the Islamic humanities, the Qur'an, and Shiite thought. Recent books include a translation of Ostad Elahi's *Knowing the Spirit* (2007); *The Reflective Heart: Discovering Spiritual Intelligence in Ibn 'Arabi's "Meccan Illuminations"* (2005); and *Orientations: Islamic Thought in a World Civilisation* (2004); together with the forthcoming *Openings: From the Qur'an to the Islamic Humanities* (2013).

Peter C. Phan holds the Ignacio Ellacuría, SJ, Chair of Catholic Social Thought at Georgetown University. His publications include *Culture and Eschatology: The Iconographical Vision of Paul Evdokimov* (1984), *Eternity in Time: A Study of Rahner's Eschatology* (1988), *Mission and Catechesis: Alexandre de Rhodes and Inculturation in Seventeenth-Century Vietnam* (2006), *Christianity with an Asian Frace* (2003) and *Being Religious Interreligiously* (2004); Phan is editor of a multivolume series titled Theology in Global Perspective, and of a multivolume series titled Ethnic American Pastoral Spirituality.

Deepak Sarma is Associate Professor of South Asian Religions and Philosophy at Case Western Reserve University. He is the author of *Classical Indian Philosophy: A Reader* (2011); *Hinduism: A Reader* (2008); *Epistemologies and the Limitations of Philosophical Inquiry: Doctrine in Madhva Vedanta* (2005); and *An Introduction to Madhva Vedanta* (2003). He was a guest curator of Indian Alight Paintings, an exhibition at the Cleveland Museum of Art. After earning a BA in religion from Reed College, Sarma attended the University of Chicago Divinity School, where he received a PhD in the philosophy of religions.

Jonathan D. Sarna is the Joseph H. & Belle R. Braun Professor of American Jewish History at Brandeis University, and chairs its Hornstein Jewish Professional Leadership Program. He also chairs the Academic Advisory and Editorial Board of the Jacob Rader Marcus Center of the

American Jewish Archives in Cincinnati, serves as Chief Historian of the National Museum of American Jewish History in Philadelphia, and writes the "Now and Then" column for the Jewish *Forward* in New York. Sarna is the author or editor of more than thirty books on American Jewish history and life. His *American Judaism: A History* won six awards including the 2004 Everett Jewish Book of the Year Award from the Jewish Book Council. Sarna is a fellow of the American Academy of Arts and Sciences and of the American Academy of Jewish Research. His *When General Grant Expelled the Jews* (2012) has just appeared from Schocken/Nextbook.

Robert J. Schreiter, CPPS, is Vatican Council II Professor of Theology at the Catholic Theological Union in Chicago, where he has taught since 1974. He has also held visiting professorships in Germany and in the Netherlands. He has published eighteen books, among them *Constructing Local Theologies* (1985); *The New Catholicity: Theology between the Global and the Local* (1997); and *Reconciliation: Mission and Ministry in a Changing Social Order* (1998). He is a coeditor of Studies in Interreligious Dialogue and editor of the Faith and Cultures series for Orbis Books. Schreiter is past president of the American Society of Missiology and of the Catholic Theological Society of America.

Swami Tyagananda is Hindu chaplain at Harvard University and MIT, and spiritual head of the Ramakrishna Vedanta Society in Boston. A graduate of Bombay University in India, he has been a monk of the Ramakrishna Order since 1976. His publications include *Monasticism: Ideals and Traditions* (1991); *Values: The Key to a Meaningful Life* (1996); *The Essence of the Gita* (2000); and *Interpreting Ramakrishna: Kali's Child Revisited* (2010).